Who's in My Classroom?

Who's in My Classroom?

Building Developmentally and Culturally Responsive School Communities

Gess LeBlanc, Ph.D.
with Tim Fredrick, Ph.D., and
Youth Communication Writers

Keith Hefner and Maria Luisa Tucker, co-editors

JOSSEY-BASS™
A Wiley Brand

Jossey-Bass
A Wiley Imprint
111 River St, Hoboken, NJ 07030
www.josseybass.com

Jossey-Bass books and products are available through most bookstores. To contact Jossey-Bass directly, call our Customer Care Department within the U.S. at 800–956–7739, outside the U.S. at +1 317 572 3986, or fax +1 317 572 4002.

Wiley also publishes its books in a variety of electronic formats and by print-on-demand. Some material included with standard print versions of this book may not be included in e-books or in print-on-demand. If this book refers to media such as a CD or DVD that is not included in the version you purchased, you may download this material at http://booksupport.wiley.com. For more information about Wiley products, visit www.wiley.com.

Library of Congress Cataloging-in-Publication Data is available. LCCN: 2021027851

ISBN 9781119824138 (paperback), 9781119824145 (ebook), 9781119824152 (ebook)

Cover image: Notepad Paper © Hudiemm/Getty Images
Cover design: Paul McCarthy

FIRST EDITION

SKY10028399_072221

Contents

Introduction

Ms. Lombardo took the time to get to know me. She would talk to me about the books I was reading to connect with me. I gradually began to feel safe around her. I still don't know how she was able to see the loneliness that so many before her had failed to notice, but I do know that she was determined to make it right. She was committed to being that one person in my life who I could rely on and confide in.

—Anonymous Youth Communication teen writer,
from the story "My Teacher Saved Me from Solitude"

THERE'S AN adage that says that you can't teach what you don't know. While the origins of the quote appear to be unknown, the idea is that effective teachers must know their subject matter.

But knowing your subject matter is just one element of good teaching. I wrote this book because I believe you also can't teach WHO you don't know.

Over the past few decades, researchers in education and psychology have found convincing evidence that learning is also strongly influenced by students' sense of who they are and their beliefs in their ability to learn. It is also influenced by their experiences at home and their level of cognitive and emotional development. This research has important implications for how we prepare teachers to enter the field and how we support them during their careers. It helps us rethink our notions of what it means to be an effective teacher. Yes, we need to know our subject matter. But getting to know students is also crucial to our effectiveness as educators.

I'm a developmental psychologist. Over the past 20 years, I've worked as a faculty member in the School of Education at Hunter College of the City University of New York where I support the preparation of teachers, school leaders, and counselors. During that time, I've become increasingly interested in how children's experiences inside and outside the classroom influence their learning and engagement in school. As a Black man and father of two Black sons, I've focused especially on how those experiences influence the school engagement of BIPOC (Black, Indigenous, and people of color) youth and other young people who may feel "unseen" in school, including LGBTQ+ students and youth who live in poverty.

As an expert in the field of child and adolescent development, I've worked as an educational consultant at the state level, and with urban, suburban, and rural school districts. My focus has been helping teachers design lessons that address students' cognitive, physical, social, and emotional needs in ways that also demonstrate an understanding of their students' lives and cultures.

One of the most rewarding features of my work with teachers and schools is talking with students about how they're experiencing school. We talk about what helps them learn and obstacles that make learning more difficult. We also discuss what makes a good teacher. I've had the opportunity to ask these questions of more than 1,000 children ranging from age 8 to 18. I've never had a child tell me that their teacher was a good teacher because they knew a lot about a subject area like math or English. What they tell me is that good teachers get to know them. They make them feel like they're cared for. They make lessons interesting and engaging by connecting them to students' lives.

It's a good sign that students expect teachers to know their subject matter. But for students, that's not enough. Good teachers do two things at once: We work to understand our students while simultaneously helping them to understand the content that we are charged with teaching.

But with the increasing ethnic, racial, and linguistic diversity in schools throughout the United States, the challenge of "knowing" our students is ever growing: It's virtually certain that we will have students in our classroom whose life experiences are very different from our own. These differences can present challenges to getting to know them. But they also present opportunities to learn about others, and ourselves, in ways that make us more effective teachers and make teaching more interesting. But what does it mean to "know" students and why is knowing students so important?

Once upon a time, many teachers and students shared similar racial, religious, and socio-economic backgrounds, which made it easier for teachers to "know" their students. That's important because academic research suggests that teachers are more effective when they have knowledge of their students' cultural backgrounds and how they develop cognitively, physically, socially, and emotionally. As the evidence base has grown, the field of teacher education and professional development has increasingly emphasized the importance of developmentally appropriate and culturally responsive teaching.

For example, through its Developmentally Appropriate Practice (DAP) framework, the National Association for the Education of Young Children (NAEYC) emphasizes that knowing how children develop and learn, knowing the individual needs of children, and knowing their cultural backgrounds are critical to supporting learning. Similarly, the field of Culturally Responsive Teaching has emphasized the importance of understanding students' cultural backgrounds and understanding how culture shapes their experiences in school. This research has raised awareness of the importance of designing lessons that reflect an understanding of who children are—both developmentally and culturally.

This book is grounded in the understanding that development is shaped by culture. Conversely, to teach in ways that are responsive to children's cultural backgrounds, we need to understand how they develop. Thus, we introduce the concept of Developmentally and Culturally Responsive Teaching (DCRT). That's a mouthful, but the concept is simple: DCRT applies the principles of culturally responsive teaching in ways that are responsive to the developmental needs of students. It is grounded in four tenets:

1. Our beliefs and expectations about children from backgrounds different from our own influence how we teach.
2. Enhancing our knowledge of child and adolescent development makes us more effective teachers.
3. Understanding the relationship between culture and development makes our teaching more effective.
4. Lack of awareness of how schools shape children's perceptions of themselves and their abilities makes our teaching less effective.

Developmentally and Culturally Responsive Teaching is important because when teachers have knowledge of their students they're more effective educators. That knowledge can come from many sources, including colleagues, parents, and school records, and even social science research. But the most important source is students themselves.

That's why students' voices are centered in this book. In each chapter, I summarize key social science research about youth development and culture, and I pair the research findings with true stories by young people that bring the research to life. The young people reflect on personal, developmental, and cultural experiences that influenced their learning and behavior in school. Their stories have an immediate emotional and intellectual effect. They may remind you of students you have taught. And you will learn about the feelings and experiences behind student behavior that we seldom have access to.

The diversity of experiences in the students' stories and their reflections on those experiences are vivid examples of why it's important not to assume that we understand what our students are going through. Together, the academic findings and the student testimonials make a powerful case for the value of developmentally and culturally responsive teaching.

This book will help teachers, counselors, and youth workers who want to better understand their students so they can enhance their practice. It will help administrators and policymakers create school settings that are more likely to advance student achievement. However, this is not a workbook or manual. It does not provide you with a script of everything that you need to know about teaching children from diverse cultural and racial backgrounds. Instead, it is a guide for how to develop a curious, nonjudgmental mindset that will help you: (1) break through superficial assumptions to really get to know your students; (2) see students' strengths more clearly and help them to reveal their strengths; and (3) go beyond the idea that demographic characteristics define your students' possibilities.

The book is divided into eight chapters that are designed to raise awareness, foster knowledge, and enhance teaching skills. Each chapter includes excerpts from stories by several students, plus a discussion of connections between students' experiences and educational and psychological research. And each chapter ends with ideas and resources that teachers and administrators can use to take action, called, respectively, "What Teachers Can Do," and "What Schools Can Do."

In Chapter 1, we provide an overview of Developmentally and Culturally Responsive Teaching (DCRT), explain why it's so important, and discuss resources that teachers and schools can use to enhance their knowledge of child and adolescent development.

Chapter 2 focuses on how our beliefs and assumptions about our students shape our interactions with them. It also explores ways to change negative beliefs and undo bias.

Chapter 3 examines how identity development occurs within the context of school and discusses culturally responsive ways in which teachers and schools can help support positive identity development.

In Chapter 4, we focus on race and gender, and look at how teachers and schools can foster positive racial and gender identity development.

Chapter 5 looks at how students' experiences outside of school influence their experiences within school. Specifically, we focus on the impact of stress and trauma, and discuss ways in which family dynamics, housing and income insecurity, foster care, and other stressors shape how young people learn and behave in school.

In Chapter 6, we shift our focus to helping students heal from stress and trauma, and how teachers and schools can implement trauma-sensitive practices in ways that benefit all students.

In Chapter 7, we discuss the role that DCRT can play in improving school climate and culture, and how DCRT can serve as a tool for advancing broader goals related to educational equity.

Finally, in Chapter 8, we show how the stories by teens at Youth Communication can be put at the center of teaching and professional development.

Other Things to Know about This Book

Student Stories: All student examples in the book are from stories written by teens in the Youth Communication writing program. We describe a bit more about that work in Chapters 1 and 8. We give the age of the student at the time he or she wrote the story. All of these stories originally appeared in Youth Communication's print and digital magazines. As you will see, some of the students choose to be anonymous and others chose to have their names on their stories.

Language: Who are *I*, *We*, and *You*? When you see *I* in the text, it mostly refers to me (Gess LeBlanc) and my experiences. At times, it also references the experience of Tim Fredrick and other Youth Communication staff. Tim and I are both teachers who have experienced many of the challenges that all teachers face, so we often switch to *we* when writing about common issues that we all face in teaching.

You, of course, are the reader. The primary audience for this book is educators, including teachers and out-of-school staff, students who are studying to be teachers, and school and district administrators. Regardless of your race, gender, sexual orientation, religion, or other demographic or cultural descriptor that is important to you, if you are a teacher in today's increasingly diverse America, you are going to have students whose backgrounds are very different from your own. Thus, this book is for all educators.

Pronouns: In recent years, in our work with students and colleagues, we have learned not to presume someone's preferred pronoun or that a person fits into the male/female gender binary. Though it is stylistically inconsistent, in this book, we go back and forth between *he*, *she*, and *they*.

Resources: We refer to many resources that you can use to implement ideas in the book in your own classrooms, your school, and your district. If you are reading an electronic version of this book, you can just follow the link. Otherwise, we've given enough information to search for the resource. You will note that our references to the resources are suggestive; we don't describe the resources in detail. We encourage you to access the ones that fit the needs of your school and community.

However, we do offer professional development, which can include exploring and practicing many of the ideas in the "What Teachers Can Do" and "What Schools and Districts Can Do" sections of this book. (See the following chart for contact information for Gess LeBlanc and Youth Communication.)

Academic Research: We also refer to many academic studies and briefly summarize the key points that are relevant to DCRT. You are, of course, welcome to follow the footnotes to learn more about the findings and the nuances of the studies.

We hope this book will spur you to think about your teaching and to make changes in your classes, your school, and your district. We know that identifying practices that improve classroom teaching and district policies so students are more likely to achieve the best possible outcomes is a never-ending process. Our teaching and professional development work is part of that process, and we are always eager to improve it. We invite suggestions about the ideas in this book and welcome opportunities to work with school districts.

Gess LeBlanc

Hunter College

School of Education

gleblanc@hunter.cuny.edu

Tim Fredrick

Youth Communication

training@youthcomm.org

References

Bredekamp, S. and Copple, C. (1997). *Developmentally Appropriate Practice in Early Childhood Programs (Revised Edition)*. National Association for the Education of Young Children, 1509 16th Street, NW, Washington, DC 20036-1426.

Gay, G. (2000). *Culturally Responsive Teaching*. New York: Teachers College Press.

Ladson-Billings, G. (1994). *The Dreamkeepers: Successful Teachers of African American Students*. San Francisco: Jossey-Bass.

Nieto, S. (ed.). (2005). *Why We Teach*. New York: Teachers College Press.

Rogoff, B. (1990). *Apprenticeship in Thinking: Cognitive Development in Social Context*. New York: Oxford.

Venables, D. R. (2011). *The Practice of Authentic PLCs: A Guide to Effective Teacher Teams*. Thousand Oaks, CA: Corwin Press.

An Introduction to Developmentally and Culturally Responsive Teaching (DCRT)

I may not be the smartest in the class, but I am generally ambitious and hard-working. For a long time, though, math and science classes were an exception. I was content to get by with lower grades in them. That mindset changed thanks to my sophomore year physics teacher, Mr. Stevens (not his real name).

Taking physics seemed like some type of punishment. I brought a poor attitude with me to class each day, just wanting it to be over.

I ended up failing the first marking period. I convinced myself that it wasn't a big deal and continued with my sour outlook throughout the second marking period. I guessed that my teacher could see I didn't care and would be happy to keep failing me. But one day at the end of the second marking period, something unusual happened.

When the bell rang, I hopped out of my desk and started gathering my things. Just then, Mr. Stevens called my name.

I looked up. He said, "I'd like to speak to you once you're ready." I nodded. Great! He was going to give me a boring lecture on how I should take advantage of the free education I had been given or start asking why I didn't care about school. Blah, blah. He didn't know me; he just knew my performance in this one class, so I wouldn't let his aggression affect me. What could he do? Threaten to call my parents? So with my head up high I walked over to his desk, ready for anything he was going to throw at me.

Right away, he gave me a welcoming smile and asked how my day was going. Surprised at his friendly manner, I told him I was actually a little stressed about a geometry exam, but other than that, I was all right. I assumed it was small talk before he landed the big speech, but what he had to say next surprised me even more.

"I just wanted to let you know that I know you're not doing as well as you could be in your class. I'm positive you are capable of way more, Neha. I picked up your transcript from the guidance counselor's office today and I see you have good grades in your other classes. Physics is a little difficult for you, huh?"

I couldn't answer. I was trying to digest the fact that he actually went and reviewed my transcript. I wondered if it could be that he was actually curious about me as an individual.

But part of me was just defiant. He said I was struggling in "my" class—Hello? Physics was his class. Not mine. I was just forced to take it.

He continued, "I want to invite you to tutoring. I tutor Tuesdays and Thursdays and plenty of students come in. It does get crowded sometimes, so I can't always guarantee I'll be able to help you on the particular topic you're struggling with. But I'll try."

I tried to read his face, wondering what the catch was. The tutoring sessions weren't news to me, but I never expected him to reach out and invite me. Most teachers only pay attention to the students who look like they care. My geometry teacher always told us, "I'm not even going to bother with kids who do not want to help themselves." This teacher obviously had a different approach.

—Youth Communication writer Neha Basnet, from
"How I Conquered Physics, with Unexpected Help"

My First Lesson in Listening to Students

In the fall of 1992, I was a 24-year-old doctoral student in New York City. Like many of my classmates, I struggled to balance the demands of my courses with the need to support myself. Rather than look for work as an adjunct professor or a researcher, I took a job with a nonprofit organization helping to run an after-school program at a junior high school in East Harlem. Since I was pursuing my degree in developmental psychology, I figured, "What better way to learn about development than by working directly with developing youth?"

I had grown up in the northeast section of the Bronx, so it wasn't as though I was raised in a wealthy suburb of the city. But East Harlem seemed like a completely different world to me. We were in the midst of the crack and heroin epidemic of the early

1990s that hit East Harlem extremely hard. Unfortunately, the neighborhood became synonymous to some people with drugs and crime.

When I told friends about my new job, I could see the concern on their faces. "Are you *sure* you want to work there?" they asked. "You know that's not a safe neighborhood, right? It's like a war zone over there."

As I prepared for my first day of work, I tried to mentally prepare for the "war zone" that would soon be my new place of work. Since I was working with an after-school program, I arrived right before the students were dismissed. Before I even entered the school building, I noticed several adults with orange buckets. They were walking around the schoolyard picking up things. I was curious, so I moved a bit closer and asked what they were doing. They said that they were removing needles before the students could be dismissed into the yard.

I was stunned. I tried not to react, but I felt defeated even before I met my students. If that's what these children had to deal with every day, I thought, how could I possibly relate to them? As I walked to what would become my classroom, I felt sad for the students. While they were entering the room, I was thinking about their schoolyard and the challenges they faced each day just to get to school.

With a combination of anxiety mixed with ignorance and arrogance, I introduced myself, sat down with my students and asked them what they thought about their school and their neighborhood. I thought I knew how they would answer and expected their answers to lead perfectly into the motivational speech that I already rehearsed in my head. I was going to tell them the one about if they did well in school, they could go to a good college, get a job, "escape" their neighborhood, and have a better life.

But that's not how the conversation went. One student answered by saying that her neighborhood was loud. Almost without fully listening to the rest of her sentence, I was already hearing her say that being loud was bad and that she didn't like where she lived. As I began to feel sorry for her and what she had to endure, she continued, "But it's not a bad thing. They play music from my country and it reminds me of home. It helps me to sleep at night. I really love it here."

"I love it here too," another student shared. "This is my home. It's my favorite place in the city."

I have no idea what my face revealed at the time, but inside I was stunned. How could a place that people described as a "war zone" bring such comfort to my students? How could they love a place that I thought they would want to escape from?

I often think about that time because it reminds me of how my beliefs and expectations about students can influence how I teach them, what I think they're capable of, and how much I engage them intellectually. Most importantly, it reminds me of the value of getting to know my students.

At the same time I was beginning my work in East Harlem, the staff of Youth Communication was refining an award-winning journalism program in which public high school students learn to write powerful personal essays about the challenges in their lives. The teen writers commit to a rigorous process in which they write more than a dozen drafts under the tutelage of full-time professional editors before their stories get published. The writers come from a wide range of backgrounds, including youth living in foster care or homeless shelters. And the writers attend a wide range of schools, from the most struggling neighborhood schools to elite public and private schools. All of the student examples in this book are from their stories.

The stories show aspects of their lives unseen by all but their most trusted teachers. But like my East Harlem students, when the teens write about tough circumstances they don't dwell on the negative. Rather, as you will see, they focus on how they manage those challenges and even overcome them. Sometimes, of course, what we mistakenly see as a sad challenge, the writers see as an important part of who they are. Like the occasional conversations when students really open up in our classrooms, the stories are a valuable window into their lives. They show the stressors that we may not be aware of; they show what is valuable and important to them; and they show how teens use resourcefulness, creativity, and resilience to overcome challenges and achieve their goals. In short, they offer the kind of information that would help all teachers be more effective, but that too few of us have access to.

One goal of this book is to help equip teachers and school leaders with skills and strategies that will enable them to hear students' voices and to integrate their experiences into instruction. Fortunately, on that first day in East Harlem, I heard those voices. I asked my students to tell me about how they experience their neighborhood before I started imposing my stereotypes on them. Had I read some of the stories by teens at Youth Communication before that first day, I would have had a more nuanced and accurate understanding of the complexity of my students' thoughts and feelings.

For example, Roberta Nin Feliz, 16, describes her rough Bronx neighborhood very differently than I would have imagined it before my experience in East Harlem:

> At the entrance of my building, there are a few things you might smell: weed, urine, or food. But once you are inside, smelling the various scents of everyone's cooking is as pleasant as discovering an extra dollar in your pocket. Their cooking always smells *bien sazonao* (well-seasoned.) When you walk past apartment doors, you can usually hear the women of the building *bochinchando* (gossiping). The women usually gossip about the neighbor's daughter who got pregnant or the neighbor's son who sells drugs on the second floor. They can point things out better than even the most detailed forensic scientist.

Of course, Roberta is not oblivious to the problems in her neighborhood. But for her they exist in a larger context. In another part of her story, she writes:

> If you travel two blocks east from my block, you will come across a parking lot where men come to pee. As soon as it gets a little dark, the alcoholics and crackheads scatter to the gate and relieve themselves. It is bad enough that I have to avoid dog poop, I also have to avoid disgusting men's urine.

> But the most distinctive trait about my neighborhood is the smiles. Everywhere you look there is always someone smiling. On the same block where a 19-year-old kid died, you can find children playing hopscotch. The single mothers smile, the crackheads smile, the unemployed men smile, the dealers smile, the addicts smile, everyone smiles. Every corner you turn, you are guaranteed to always come across a smile.

The complexities and contradictions of her neighborhood have also helped Roberta to become a sophisticated observer who has learned to avoid the kinds of stereotypes that are often applied to her:

> I'd like to help one of my close friends. We've known each other since 6th grade. He has dyslexia so it's hard for him to do schoolwork. I remember him asking me to help him read. I tried, but he got frustrated and said, "I don't get this sh-t." Today, he's in a gang.
>
> Still, he's one of the most caring people I know. I can count on him to listen and give me sound advice. When I've gone through bad breakups he's there to remind me of my worth and help me stay positive. I tell him that he should stop fighting and be focused in school. He has six younger siblings that he has to be a role model for. There are periods of time when he stays out of trouble, but eventually it seems to find him.
>
> This friend is just one example of how being raised in the hood has made me more understanding and compassionate. Before I judge, I get to know a person because I know how it feels when people make assumptions about you based on where you live or your appearance. When I'm on the train I often feel that people are caught by surprise when they see me pull out a book by Shakespeare.

But other than showing respect, or just not making fools of ourselves, why is knowing students so important? Research within the fields of education and psychology shows that when we have knowledge of our students' cultural backgrounds and knowledge of how they develop cognitively, physically, socially, emotionally, and linguistically, it makes us more effective teachers.[1] The problem is that we often don't ask students the types of questions that help us to understand how they develop and what they need to feel supported.

Over the last five years, I've had the pleasure of conducting focus groups with children and adolescents from urban, suburban, and rural schools to better understand how they experience school. One of the most consistent findings of this work is that students often feel as though adults in their schools make decisions *for* them but without sufficient knowledge *of* them and without hearing *from* them. Many of the stories by teens in the Youth Communication writing program confirm these findings.

If you put yourself in their shoes, it's easy to understand how frustrating that could be. Imagine walking into your doctor's office. The doctor takes a quick look at you and then, before asking a single question about your symptoms or concerns, tells you what is wrong with you, prescribes medication and a lifestyle change, and says that if you didn't comply, you'll be in trouble. Even if they were right, I suspect that it would be the last time you visited that doctor.

Desmin Braxton, 17, looks back on that feeling of being judged and not listened to in his story "Labeled Troublesome":

> Walking through the front door of my middle school, it feels like someone's turned the temperature up. I start sweating as if I had a fever. It seems like everything just stops and all the attention is focused on me. Today feels like a trouble day.
>
> My music teacher stands at the corner of the hallway, looking at me like I've got something on my face. As I walk through the hall I see kids playing, fighting, ripping posters off the wall, and just chillin' in the hallway. The noise level is high.
>
> I spot my math teacher. He does not look happy to see me. He stares at me rudely with his arms folded and his jaw clenched, like I've already done something wrong.
>
> "Hello, Mr. Davis, how you today?"
>
> He continues to stare, so I continue walking through the hall to the auditorium. Before I get there, my social studies teacher from last year stops me.
>
> "Desmin."
>
> "What?"
>
> "Where are you going?"
>
> "To the auditorium, with my class."
>
> "Go there right now."

I start getting mad. It's crazy how he stops me even though he knows where I'm headed, but he walks past the other kids and doesn't say anything. It's like I have on a bright red shirt that says, "Stop me."

I admit I do things that get me in trouble at school. I like to talk in class, argue with the teacher and make people laugh. But I feel like the teachers and principals are always waiting for me to do something stupid so they can jump on my case. It's like we're in a war. The only question is who's going to strike first.

A lot of times it's me who makes the first strike. I do these little tests to see if a teacher is going to be respectful. If the teacher is cool, I'm not going to cross the line. But if he gets me mad, it's going to be a battle.

When I get a negative response from my teachers, I react with a rude comment, to let them know I do not like what they say. It makes me mad that they feel they can speak to me any way they want and try to make me afraid of them.

But the arguments with my teachers are cutting into my time for doing my work. It's making me fall behind in class so my grades are dropping. I end up focusing on the teacher and not learning the lesson. Then I'm stuck looking silly, without a clue on how to do the work.

Desmin wants to succeed. But he needs support that he's not getting. When I started working in schools, I was surprised by how many times I took part in meetings in which plans were made to "meet students' needs" and to "support their learning" without ever involving students. We were essentially telling them what was wrong with them and prescribing a plan to "help" them without fully understanding their needs, what wasn't working for them, or how they felt we could best support them.

Why It's Crucial to Know Your Students

Having developmentally and culturally responsive teachers is important for all students, but it's particularly important for students from underrepresented groups and those who have been historically marginalized. These are the students that many of us are least likely to know well. However, DCRT is not simply about helping White teachers to teach Black and Brown children better. Through my work in schools, I've witnessed first-hand White teachers teaching White students in ways that were not culturally responsive. I've also observed Black and Latinx educators teach Black and Latinx students in ways that were not culturally responsive.

More importantly, I've witnessed teachers of different races and ethnicities teach children very different from themselves in ways that demonstrated knowledge and deep respect and curiosity about their students' cultural backgrounds and showed that they believed they would succeed academically. For example, in the quote that begins this chapter, the teacher and student do not share a racial or ethnic background. Neha's teacher bridged whatever gap might have existed by showing genuine interest in Neha and her schoolwork.

So the focus of DCRT is to use our knowledge of who our students are, both developmentally and culturally, to shape classroom environments and schools that better support their needs. But it isn't that simple. What we *believe* about our students and what we actually *know* about them can be dramatically different. For example, I believed my East Harlem students wanted to escape from what I perceived as a war zone, but I didn't actually know that. It took a while—and many conversations with them—for me to acquire meaningful knowledge about their lives. I learned about their interest in going to college so that they could make a better life for themselves and their families. I also learned they worried about their families not being able to pay for college. Most importantly, I learned about the things that interested them and how school often felt disconnected from their lives.

As a parent, I remember having "conversations" with my teenage sons at the end of their middle school day that followed a frustrating pattern.

"How was your day?"

"Good."

"What did you learn today in school?"

"Nothing."

"You spent seven hours in school and you didn't learn anything?"

"Nothing that I was interested in."

"Well, do you understand everything? Do you need help?"

"I'm fine."

I was spending lots of time and mental energy trying to get a sense of what my sons learned in school, but I didn't spend enough time focusing on how being in school made them feel. Once I shifted from asking them about what they learned in school to what they *wished* they could learn in school or what would make school more interesting and enjoyable for them, our "conversations" shifted from interrogations to dialogues.

As I mentioned in the introduction, in recent years I've conducted focus groups with hundreds of elementary, middle, and high school students from urban, suburban, and rural public schools and urban private schools. I use four simple questions to learn more about their experience of school: (1) What are some of your favorite things about school? (2) If you were in charge, what things would you change about your school? (3) What are some things that your teachers do that help you to learn? And (4) What are some things that make it harder for you to learn in school?

Meanwhile, the teens at Youth Communication have written hundreds of stories about what works and doesn't work for them in school. They echo many of the answers that I have heard in those focus groups. Here are a few excerpts:

Ebony Coleman, 18, notes that caring teachers find creative ways to learn about students' lives and personalities:

> Even kids you think are a lost cause get engaged with the right method. If you
> know how their life is, you can use something that relates to them. Say the student's
> a hustler, and you know this because when they're in the lunchroom you hear them
> all the time. If you have a math lesson, you can apply the lesson to their life. I see
> that a lot and it works.

Margarita Martinez, 18, describes several methods that show caring:

> Mr. Hatchett not only teaches well, he believes in all his students and doesn't give
> up on us. Let's say one student complains that the work is hard. He will go up to
> the board and let the student tell him which part of the problem they don't under-
> stand. He'll explain it, do another problem, and let the student try it. Later, he'll

call on that student so they start getting motivated. And during independent study, he's constantly asking the class if anyone needs help. No one is left behind.

Renea Williams, 18, says don't overdo it:

> Teachers shouldn't act like students. You can be their friend, help them with school-work, and let them come to you and talk about their lives. But I hate it when you act your students' age and use the slang students use. It's unprofessional.

Evin Cruz, 19, says don't give up on a student:

> Sometimes you just truly don't get it, and then you need a teacher to be patient and explain it over and over, maybe a different way, to make sure you understand. The teacher shouldn't just give up and think, "He doesn't get it, but he'll learn eventually"—he probably won't! With school, it's a snowball effect: If you don't know one thing, it's harder for you to learn other things.

There's a consistent message from the teens in my focus groups and the teen writers at Youth Communication: It is important for students to feel like their teachers care about them, and when teachers get to know about their lives outside of school it can have a big impact on their learning. Students also report that they often struggle to manage the demands of school and life, and when teachers adapt how they teach in a way that's responsive to their reality, it makes students more eager to learn.

Why Understanding Child and Adolescent Development Is Crucial for Teachers

As important as it is to listen to individual students, there are other things teachers need to know about youth, in general. As a developmental psychologist, I believe that one important way to "know" students is to have knowledge of how they develop physically, cognitively, linguistically, socially, and emotionally.

For more than two decades, I've worked as a professor in Hunter College's School of Education where I teach courses in the developmental sciences to undergraduate and graduate students preparing to become teachers. I've learned that understanding how children and adolescents develop makes us better prepared to support their needs. By their needs, I don't exclusively mean their academic needs. Rather, I focus on developmental needs—needs that are typical of all students within a particular age range, such as during adolescence.

For example, all students need to be intellectually engaged, to feel competent, and to feel a sense of accomplishment. But for adolescents, there's also a critical need for self-understanding and the need to reflect on what makes them who they are. They need to better understand how their race and gender shape their sense of identity and the identity of groups in which they claim membership. And they need to better understand their personal beliefs and their values. All students also need the opportunity to express themselves creatively. For adolescents, this creative expression helps them to discover their talents and their voice and agency and it helps them to explore their thoughts and feelings in ways that enable them to exert control over their lives.

All students also need to engage with others in a supportive and nurturing environment. With adolescents, positive relationships with peers are especially critical to helping them to recognize their own emotions, how to recognize the emotions of others, and how to respond to others with empathy and care.

I remember looking back at one of my old elementary school class photos. What stood out to me was the range of heights. I was one of the taller students, so I was in the back row, but I wasn't the oldest student. In fact, I remember clearly that a few classmates on the shorter side were actually the oldest ones in the class. It seems perfectly reasonable for us to accept and even expect a wide range of physical development across students in the same grade, and to know that those physical characteristics are not fixed. But why is it less likely for us to expect the same variability regarding cognitive, social, or emotional development? Why is it that we often associate physical development with social and emotional development? I remember once being frustrated by the "lack of maturity" demonstrated by one of my middle school students, who happened to be the tallest student in my class, until I found out that he was my youngest student.

Scholars and policymakers within the fields of education and psychology have highlighted the need for educators to be knowledgeable about how children and adolescents develop.[2] For example, through their Developmentally Appropriate Practice framework, the National Association for the Education of Young Children suggests that knowing how children develop and learn, knowing the individual needs of children, and knowing their cultural backgrounds are critical to supporting their learning.[3] A comprehensive report by the National Institute of Child Health and Human Development published in 2007 states that "aspects of development—neural, cognitive, social, psychological, physical and ethical—have far-reaching effects on children's ability to learn."[4]

Similarly, a 2010 report published by the National Council for Accreditation of Teacher Education notes that "teacher knowledge of the social, emotional, and cognitive domains, coupled with the ability to effectively apply strategies based on developmental principles, translates to increased student engagement and improved learning outcomes."[5]

Several studies have also found that teachers with knowledge of child and adolescent development are more likely to design and implement lessons that address not only the academic, but also the social and emotional needs of their students.[6] As a result of these findings, two common teacher performance assessments—the Danielson Framework for Teaching (which is used to assess the performance of teachers) and the edTPA (which is used to assess the performance of students preparing to become teachers)—emphasize the need for teachers to demonstrate knowledge of their students' strengths and learning needs.

While development is variable, it is not necessarily linear. For example, during childhood and adolescence, increases in age are associated with enhanced motor skills and more complex thinking. But during adolescence, we also see behaviors that might easily be interpreted as a reduction in complex thinking. Through his research, psychologist Dr. David Elkin found that while adolescents generally advance in cognitive complexity as they age, in certain instances, they may think in ways that are more typical of younger children than burgeoning adults.[7] Think back to your own adolescence. Do you remember ever thinking that your life was terrible and that no one in the world could possibly understand what you were going through? Do you remember feeling like you couldn't leave your house because you had a pimple on your nose or because your hair wasn't just right and you thought everyone in the world would notice it? Dr. Elkin found that this type of thinking is typical for adolescents and reflects limitations in their cognitive development that constrain how they make sense of the world around them.

We can see these developmental stages in the writing of Youth Communication teens. Amber Perez, 18, faced a problem that would be very tough for anyone her age: living in a shelter. But as a teen, she still overestimated how other kids would respond. Though she acknowledged that "The shelter wasn't as bad as I thought it would be" because at least her family had a private room. Then she added, "Living in a shelter made me feel even more shy and withdrawn since I was ashamed of living there. Even if I did make friends, how could I tell them where I lived?"

When she started high school, she longed for friends. She writes:

> The night before, I sat in my room with my mom and we talked for a while. "Maybe you should come out of your shell and talk to people. I know they'll like you. What's not to like about you?" my mom said. "What is there to like about me?" I thought to myself. "I'm not that pretty, I don't dress like everyone else, I don't have a lot of money, and I'm living in a shelter."
>
> I knew it would upset my mom to say these things out loud so I just said, "Yeah, you're right." Even though my mom and I have a bond, I don't like telling her what's going on in my head. She gets too worried. It's already hard for me to open up, and her reactions only make things worse.

Amber did make a few friends, but she was ashamed to disclose that she lived in a shelter. Fortunately, she was assigned a school counselor who was sensitive to the fact that adolescents often feel like they are "the only one" and that life will never get better. Here, Amber describes how a skilled counselor helped her see her life in a larger frame:

> After meeting with a few different counselors, I was assigned to Ms. Millie. She always has a smile on her face and every time she sees me she asks if I'm OK, and even when I say I'm fine she knows when I'm not telling the truth. We have a connection.

But even with Ms. Millie's counseling, I started feeling depressed. Besides living in a shelter and feeling ashamed about it, I was stressed by my constantly fighting siblings. I was messing up in school, disrespecting my teachers, and missing class. I told her I never knew life could be so complicated.

Ms. Millie helped me deal with it all. She'd often say: "I know you may feel alone right now but trust me, Amber, you're not. There are a lot of kids in this school who've been through what you're going through." It felt good not being the only one. I felt a little less embarrassed. But I still refused to tell anyone where I was living.

She'd also say: "You want to be strong, Amber, for your family, but mostly for yourself. You deserve that. Create a distraction; get more involved. Sooner or later you'll be out of there."

I took her advice and joined an all-girls club, called, "Her Story," as well as youth court and youth service. I also figured the more clubs I was in, the more colleges would want me. And they did distract me, like she said.

In the beginning of my sophomore year I was still a little on the edge. But I kept my head up. "One day you're going to look back at all this and smile because you survived it," my counselor told me. "Everything is going to work out, just keep holding on."

I repeated those words to myself every day.

Ms. Millie helped me realize that living in a shelter is nothing to be ashamed of. I can now talk to my friends about my experience, and they don't judge me.

Ms. Millie helped me appreciate my strength. Sometimes I remind myself: Wow, I did this. I can get through anything. I brought my grades back up and made the honor roll, fought my shyness, made good friends, participated in a lot of clubs, and soon I'll be off to college. Three years ago, I never thought I'd have accomplished so much.

Amber's counselor supported her in a way that was developmentally and culturally responsive. She began by addressing her developmental need to feel emotionally supported by building a connection with her. She then provided Amber with specific support that addressed two aspects of her cognitive development: her belief that she was the only student living in a shelter and her fear that no one would be able to understand what that experience was like for her.

The Adolescent Brain Is Still Developing

In addition to being a physical and psychological process, development is also neurological. When educators like Millie help students like Amber change their thinking and their behavior, it can have a positive impact on their brain development.

Each domain of development is influenced by our brain, so the study of developmental psychology has benefited from improvements in neuroscience over the last few decades. Functional and structural MRIs have enabled researchers to better understand how the brain works, how it's shaped by certain experiences, and how it adapts under certain conditions.

One well-accepted concept related to the study of the brain is the idea of plasticity. Similar to the way in which plastic's flexibility allows it to be shaped in response to pressure, the brain is also flexible in terms of how it responds to life conditions and our experiences. For teachers, the concept of plasticity is critical because it helps us to understand that our students' prior histories are not their destinies. While negative experiences can shape the brain in harmful ways, positive experiences can shape the brain in beneficial ways.

Research also reveals that neural connections that are used regularly become stronger and more complex. Conversely, the brain treats seldom used connections as nonessential and eventually prunes them away to enhance functioning. Much like pruning a tree to strengthen its remaining branches, this process—referred to as synaptic pruning—strengthens neural connections and makes cognitive processing more efficient.

We also know that the development of these synapses is influenced by our experiences. For example, learning things through different modalities or making connections between what we learn in one context and what we learn in another promotes synapse formation.[8] This helps to explain why when our teachers connected something that we learned in our math class with something that we learned in our social studies class it helped us to learn it better. It also helps to explain why when teachers connect what students are learning in school to their lives outside of school it's so impactful for students. Those explicit connections between what they're learning in school and their lives outside of school strengthen neural connections that deepen their conceptual understanding.[9]

Amber learned to think differently and act differently, which made her a better student and happier person. But it's also likely that the changes in her thinking and behavior affected her brain development in positive ways, which further reinforced her ability to succeed. Conversely, had Amber not gotten support, both her behavior and her brain development might have suffered. The activities she began to participate in didn't just "distract" her; they helped to build new neural pathways.

Development Is Shaped by Multiple Settings

Another important way to think about how adolescents develop is to think about the different settings that influence development. My research is informed by the work of the late developmental psychologist Urie Bronfenbrenner. His well-regarded theory is that development is influenced by our individual characteristics (such as our age, gender, race, or ethnicity) and our experiences within multiple settings that influence us all at the same time.[10] He describes these experiences as "proximal" or up-close influences (such as our experiences within our families or our experiences in school) and "distal" or more distant influences (such as the type of jobs our parents had). He argues that we are influenced by the interplay between them (such as when parents' work schedules make them unavailable to assist their children with homework).

Drawing on Bronfenbrenner's work, I believe that supporting our students' developmental needs means paying close attention to how these simultaneous influences shape their development. In the following excerpt, Hoa Vu reflects on how her father's abandonment and her mother's poverty impacted her social development and her relationships with her peers:

> One night four years ago, while other children were enjoying the end of a lazy summer day, I was sitting on the sidewalk outside my apartment building with all my stuff. My mother often told me not to sit on the sidewalk, but tonight she didn't say anything. My brother sat on one of our suitcases with his head down. It was late. The city streets were quiet. We had been evicted.
>
> It was a good thing no one was around because I hated the look people gave me when they felt sorry for me. The landlord gave me that look when he saw my brother and me packing up our childhood toys. The cops who told us that we were evicted gave us that look when they saw us place our suitcases on the sidewalk.
>
> Every time we moved we got the look that became known to me as the look of pity. And we moved a lot. The first time was when I was around 7. That's about when my father left us. Until then, I had grown up in an apartment in Ridgewood, Queens, with both parents and my brother.
>
> My mom used to work in telemarketing, but she stopped when my brother was born. After my father left, she didn't seem able to support us. My mother would convince a landlord to let us move in, but after we couldn't pay the rent for a few months, we would have to move to another place. This was a pattern that I considered normal. We moved so many times I didn't think it was strange.
>
> For the next four years, I moved in and out of four shelters. My mother didn't do what the caseworkers told her to so we could get housing or even public assistance, which is one of the requirements to continue living in a shelter. Every time we moved, I had to start over with a new caseworker and try to explain my mother's refusal to talk to them, which I didn't understand myself. Eventually, they all gave up on us.

> Living in shelters changed me. Almost from the first night, I started acting differently. I used to be the conversation starter, but not anymore. I grew quiet. I didn't want to make ties to people that I would have to cut when I moved again. Because I carried this logic with me I didn't make many friends.

As Bronfenbrenner suggests, the simultaneous influences of living with a single parent, living in poverty, and experiencing housing insecurity collectively shaped Hoa's view that having close relationships with her peers would be a liability. Instead, she believed that she could better protect herself and her emotions by not making friends. In school, she might appear as a "loner" or an "outsider" who might even seem to be socially withdrawn, socially awkward, and unable to make friends. In fact, it wasn't that she lacked the skill or desire to make friends. Rather, she "logically" decided that the cost of trying to make new friends, and the pain of losing them, would outweigh the benefits of those friendships.

Why Cultural Responsiveness Is Crucial for Teachers

Of course, there's more to knowing students than brain development and the settings our students inhabit. Recent research within the field of developmental psychology is revealing important information about the role that culture plays in the psychological developmental of children.[11] Culture is the shared values, norms, and beliefs that we hold because of our group membership,[12] plus the quality of life that we experience as a function of our income.

According to psychologist Jonathan Tudge, it's through their interactions with people within their cultural group that children "learn what is expected of them, the types of activities considered appropriate or inappropriate for them, how they are expected to engage in these activities, the ways other people will deal with them, and the ways in which they are expected to deal with others."[13] In this way, culture shapes our development by influencing how we adapt to our social and physical environment.

Culture also shapes how we adapt (and sometimes have difficulty adapting) to school. Over four decades ago, Ronald Gallimore and his colleague Roland Tharp provided a well-documented record of this through their study of the Kamehameha Elementary Education Project (KEEP). KEEP was founded to address the lag in literacy development that was observed among Native Hawaiian children when they entered Honolulu public schools.[14] To address this, the project developed a reading program for kindergarten through 3rd grade students that was designed to be responsive to the culture and language of Native Hawaiian students.

This research found that classroom teaching is more effective if it is "culturally compatible." They noted that culturally compatible teaching reflected a concern for three types of educational experiences students were engaged in outside of their classroom (what they referred to as "cognition"):

- the manner in which students interacted in social settings (social organization);
- the conversational patterns that students typically demonstrated (sociolinguistics); and
- the factors that influenced their feelings of self-efficacy (motivation).[15]

When the pedagogical practices of teachers were responsive to the culture and language of the students (such as by including more peer-to-peer activities and providing students with more opportunities to learn at their own pace), they reported greater levels of self-efficacy and motivation. These increases were directly linked to increases in student achievement. As a result, research in this area finds that the most effective teachers transform their pedagogy to make it responsive to the cultural experiences of their students.[16]

Some researchers suggest that one way in which teachers can respond to the cultural experiences of students is by actively soliciting their voice.[17] In light of this, several studies have highlighted the importance of learning students' perspectives on what they feel makes teachers effective. For example, almost 30 years ago, a study by education scholar Etta Ruth Hollins and her colleague Kathleen Spencer regarding students' views on their experiences in school found that positive relationships between teachers and students increased academic achievement. They also found that teachers' responsiveness to students' personal lives generated positive feelings that led to greater student effort. Additionally, they found that students preferred teachers who enabled them to use experiences from their personal lives in completing assignments and this led to increased engagement in class discussions.[18]

Similarly, when Tyrone Howard, a noted scholar in the field of culturally responsive teaching, asked African American students to discuss what made their teachers effective, they reported that the most effective teachers established a sense of family and community within their classrooms, displayed a genuine level of caring for their students, and consistently reaffirmed their belief that all students were capable of achieving success.[19]

Several more recent studies confirm that students consistently judge a teacher's effectiveness based on how much they perceive the teacher to know about them and how much the teacher creates a classroom environment that responds to them as individuals.[20] Effective teachers are viewed as being able to develop a rapport with students that makes them feel connected to their teachers.

David Etienne, 16, attended extremely strict schools in Haiti. He shared a cultural background (though not a social class background) with his teachers, followed the rules, and learned to repeat what he had been taught. It was only when he immigrated to the United States and he experienced more responsive styles of teaching that he realized what he was missing. He writes:

> [In Haiti] our fear of punishment pushed us to learn whatever we were assigned, so in a way, the teachers were effective. We did what we had to do, whether it was memorizing a passage, solving a math problem, or learning vocabulary words.
>
> But looking back, I see that I never grew mentally in that school. They didn't teach us to think broadly or to be creative. Instead, I was always either doing what I was directed to do, or sitting back waiting for more directions. My classmates and I were taught what we needed to know to survive inside a classroom—things like dates and events in history—but not a lot that would help me survive in the world.
>
> When I came to the United States I didn't know what to expect. On my first day of school in New York, I met my new teacher, Mr. Jean Pierre, who also was Haitian. He greeted me with "*Sa kap fèt la*, Boss?" which means "How are you doing, Boss?" in Creole.

> That short sentence alone told me a lot. Normally in Haiti, teachers only speak French to students, because those who speak French are looked upon as superior. But Mr. Jean Pierre spoke pure Creole with me, and that made me feel that the person I was going to spend my days with at this new school would be able to understand me.

Of course, some teachers mistake "developing rapport" with lowering their standards or spending inordinate amounts of time socializing with students. But students do want to learn, and while they will go along with a teacher who skimps on standards, most students want a teacher who has both high expectations and finds ways to make them feel seen. Here's how Mohammed Hussain describes that balance:

> Mr. Seltzer, my 8th grade teacher, was the embodiment of high standards. Tests were difficult. Pop quizzes could be given at any time He gave us lots of home-work and expected us to do it. Throughout the year, we wrote frequently— outlines, research papers, book reports—and Mr. Seltzer expected us to produce quality work.
>
> When I saw my low grades at the start of the year—in the 70s, when I was used to 90s—I realized that I could easily fail the class.

If you believe the stereotypes, Mr. Seltzer sounds like the kind of teacher that students would loathe. But Mohammed describes why that wasn't the case:

> [Though] Mr. Seltzer held us to extremely high standards . . . still he was never boorish or a jerk to us. We could see his affection and regard for us despite his sternness. He once commented to me that he had many children, and it was not until later that I realized he was talking about his students. To Mr. Seltzer, we were his children and he expected us to be amazing and not disappoint him; just what he would expect of his own children. In turn, all of his students—those who loved to learn and even those who were not particularly motivated to do so—tried their best to live up to his standards.
>
> [In the end] I got an 80 average. Though this was lower than I was used to, it meant more to me than a 90 from another teacher. An 80 from Mr. Seltzer was a real accomplishment.

Another important challenge in understanding how students develop is that people in the fields of education and psychology have relied (and often continue to rely) too much on theories of psychological development that are based on White European cultural norms.[21] Over three decades ago, education scholar Martin Haberman offered a prescient caution that "teachers committed to a theory of development will hold expectations of what is normal and typical which they will inevitably transform into what is desirable. They will then develop and hold expectations for preferred behavior which supports their particular theory and makes them insensitive to other explanations and understandings."[22]

Because of this tendency to define White cultural development as normative and desirable, the development of BIPOC students may be judged using an inappropriate standard. *Differences* in their development may be viewed as *deficiencies* that are attributed to race, culture, or ethnicity. Therefore, to be more effective in supporting the learning needs of all students, we need to be cautious in how those theories are applied so that we use them to inform but not constrain our teaching.

Connections between Home and School Help Students Meet High Expectations

Several scholars have discussed the importance of making connections between home culture and school as a hallmark of culturally responsive teaching.[23] For example, Geneva Gay defines *culturally responsive teaching* as using the cultural knowledge, prior experiences, and performance styles of diverse students to make learning more appropriate and effective for them.[24]

More recent studies, however, have revealed that many students experience disconnects between home and school. Students experience these disconnects when their cultural beliefs and practices outside of school clash with those found in school.[25] Such disconnects have been described as home-school dissonance. *Dissonance* is defined as the perceived differences between the values and practices present in students' homes or out-of-school environments and those prominent throughout their formal schooling experiences.[26]

For example, in a study examining how such perceived dissonance influenced the emotional and academic well-being of adolescents, the researchers reported that, "Students from cultures outside the mainstream may experience a sense of dissonance when they encounter a devaluing of their beliefs and behaviors at schools that reflect the dominant White, middle-class ideology."[27] They also found that students reporting high levels of home-school dissonance also reported lower levels of academic efficacy, self-esteem, grade point average (GPA), and higher levels of anger and self-deprecation. Other researchers have also found that such dissonance is associated with lowered academic motivation and increased disruptive behavior in school.

In her book *The Dreamkeepers: Successful Teachers of African American Children*, Gloria Ladson-Billings describes culturally responsive teaching as a pedagogical approach that highlights the importance of making connections to students' cultural backgrounds throughout the teaching and learning process.[28] Some of the ways in which teachers demonstrate culturally responsive teaching include designing student-centered lessons, teaching in ways that make connections to students' experiences outside of school, and having and communicating high expectations for all students.

Of course, there are countless ways to make content seem more relevant and engaging to students that also align with traditional academic goals. Here are just a few examples from students at Youth Communication.

Annmarie Turnton's teacher used a connection to home culture in a way that made a classic social science concept come alive:

> For 12th grade economics we examined the current value of the Haitian dollar and calculated what we already knew—that most Haitians are living below the poverty line. Ms. Casey explained Maslow's "hierarchy of needs" principle—which holds that people will only worry about higher order concerns once their basic needs have been met—and we discussed how the inability to meet the first level in Maslow's hierarchy could affect everything else in Haitian society, like literacy rates and civil and political unrest. This lesson on interrelatedness made our subject matter seem more relevant and important.

> Although she demanded a lot of us, Ms. Casey was also compassionate. She told us
> that she was our second mother, the one who gave us life, not in the physical form,
> but in the mental form.

For Angelica Petela, 17, connections to her home culture and her teen culture were meaningful:

> My global history teacher used to read us ethnic folk tales and make us illustrate
> them as though things might look back then. He made us create a social media page
> for an ancient person, like Cleopatra.

Ebony Coleman's English teacher made a 1957 film feel relevant to today's students:

> We studied *12 Angry Men*, and we had to write essays on what we'd do if we were in
> the characters' shoes. It was almost as if we were in the story, and it actually led to a
> huge discussion.

Evin Cruz felt no connection to poetry. In fact, he "scoffed" at it, so his teacher had to scramble to find points of connection. But Evin was a New York teen who listened to rap and no doubt had elders in his extended family:

> [My poetry teacher] got a spoken word poet to come to class and perform, and
> listening to his poem, I could visualize what he was talking about—Manhattan
> collapsing in on itself. He also showed us a YouTube video of a reading of Dylan
> Thomas's poem, "Do Not Go Gentle Into That Good Night," about the poet's
> father dying—and it was like, whoa, that's dark, that's deep.

The Importance and Meaning of High Expectations

Over the past 20 years of supporting teachers, I've learned that having high expectations is very important—for the effect on the student and on the teacher. You can see it in the preceding examples where teachers were making connections while also maintaining high standards. When teachers believe that their students can achieve at high levels and tell them so, they tend to teach in ways that are more engaging, and their students are likely to work harder to meet those expectations.

Several years ago, I observed a middle school science class. The teacher projected a picture of a flower on the SmartBoard and then went on to discuss the different parts of the flower. While discussing one part of the flower, he mentioned the feel. "It's extremely soft and feels almost like suede," he said. He then discussed its smell by describing it as "sweet smelling" and "like perfume." As I watched the students, I noticed that they were having a hard time focusing on the lesson.

A solution was directly across the street: a park with flowers in full bloom. Yet, rather than have the students touch and feel actual flowers, he designed an abstract lesson about flowers that the students had a hard time understanding. Frustrated by what I observed, I asked him why he didn't simply take his class across the street to the park. "My students can't handle that. It'll be a huge behavioral issue if I take them."

"Oh, so they had a hard time the last time you tried to take them?" I asked.

"No, I mean, I've never taken them over there, but based on their behavior in here, I know what to expect."

"So do they get to go outside in their other classes?" I asked.

"I really don't know. I never asked them before."

Having low expectations about his students' abilities to behave led the teacher to limit how he taught and limit his students' opportunities to explore actual flowers. Of course, the teacher could have been right. They could have gone outside and behaved exactly as he had predicted. Or, he could have discovered that by making connections to things outside of his classroom and giving his students the opportunity to explore and be immersed in nature, they might have demonstrated a higher level of interest and engagement. The point is that by having low expectations of them, he ensured those were the only ones they had a chance to meet.

Sylinda Sinkfield, 17, struggled in a traditional high school and eventually transferred to an alternative school. She was the kind of student for whom many people would have had low expectations, especially in a semi-structured learning environment. Here she writes about how the high expectations in her new school's internship program—and the opportunity to meet them—increased her motivation and enhanced her learning in science:

> Last fall, I was looking for an internship that would give me some science credits, but I wanted something in the Bronx, which is where I live. The only internship was at the Botanical Garden, which is a place in the Bronx that has plants and flowers from all over the world that people can come look at.
>
> Now, you know if they tell you that you are going to work with plants, you probably think it's going to be boring. Well, this internship became one of the best experiences of my life.
>
> The Botanical Garden has "discover carts." These carts tell you about a certain type of plant in a particular area of the garden. For example, in the desert there is a desert cart that has cacti. (That's plural for cactus.)
>
> One day during training, Karl, my program director, told me I would be working at the orchid cart in the tropical rainforest and giving talks to visitors on orchids. My talks would involve telling visitors about the parts of an orchid, showing them the inside of the flower, and explaining how it is pollinated. (I learned all of this during training.)
>
> At first I thought to myself, I am not going to be able to handle this.
>
> My first day at the orchid cart was scary. My hands were wet from the fear of messing up. A man named Norman came over to my cart. He worked in the Botanical Garden and knew a lot more than I did. I gave my first talk to him. But he was a pain because he kept correcting me.
>
> After that experience with Norman, I decided I needed to do a lot of research on orchids so I wouldn't make those mistakes again. I went to the library in the Botanical Garden and looked up orchids. I found out that I had much to learn. As I began to learn more and more about orchids, I started to love them, and my program director couldn't get me away from them.

> Before I started working at the Botanical Garden, I couldn't understand why people
> would want to look at trees and plants. Now I realize that trees are not just trees.
> What I mean is that trees don't look the same to me anymore. I can walk up to a
> turkey oak tree and know what it is because of the nuts. I didn't even know there
> was such a tree called turkey oak before.

One of the core beliefs of DCRT is that schools shape how students feel about themselves and what's possible for their lives. In Sylinda's case, her internship provided her with the opportunity to see her Bronx neighborhood as a place where science actually happens and a place where people from around the world come to learn about plants. Her internship also provided her with the opportunity to help others learn as she taught them about orchids. Ultimately, these connections between the science she learned in her classroom and her application of her scientific knowledge in the real world increased her interest in science and helped her to see trees in new ways—as a scientist would.

Growing Recognition of Culturally Responsive Education

School districts increasingly recognize the connection between cultural responsiveness and academic achievement. For example, New York State recently adopted its Culturally Responsive and Sustaining Education Framework. The New York State Education Department (NYSED) states that, "The goal of the CR-S framework is to help educators design and implement a student-centered learning environment that affirms racial and cultural identities and fosters positive academic outcomes, develops students' abilities to connect across culture, empowers students as agents of social change, and contributes to their engagement, learning, growth, and achievement through the cultivation of critical thinking."[29]

A New America report published in 2019 noted that, "All 50 states embed some combination of culturally responsive teaching competencies into their standards."[30] But they found that many state standards are written in vague ways that do not provide teachers with sufficient guidance about how to meet the standards:

> Forty-seven states widely expect teachers to exhibit high expectations for all students, though no state explicitly addresses how low expectations are commonly associated with race, class, culture, language, gender and sexual orientation, or disability status.
>
> Similarly, New York asks teachers to be "responsive to the economic, social, cultural, linguistic, family, and community factors that influence their students' learning," yet the state does not provide an additional element that captures how teachers are supposed to be "responsive to" students' "cultural factors." Rhode Island likewise requires teachers to "design instruction that accommodates individual differences (e.g., stage of development, learning style, English language acquisition, cultural background, learning disability) in approaches to learning," but it provides no other elements to elaborate on this competency. Reasonably, a lack of specificity makes it difficult for educators to act upon the expectations.[31]

These findings make two things clear: States across the country are requiring teachers to demonstrate teaching competence in ways that are responsive to the developmental and cultural needs of students, and few states provide the rationale and support that make it possible for teachers to do so. That's why we wrote this book.

Becoming a Developmentally and Culturally Responsive Teacher

So what makes teachers developmentally and culturally responsive? In my work, I've found that developmentally and culturally responsive teaching is demonstrated when teachers design and implement lessons that engage students intellectually in a supportive and nurturing environment that values them as assets. You can see it in the learning experiences described by the students in this chapter, and you'll see more throughout this book.

Developmentally and culturally responsive teachers have a basic understanding of the developmental sciences, which we've briefly reviewed in this book. Study and experience help them also understand the characteristics of cognitive, physical, linguistic, social, and emotional development that are typical of students within the age ranges they teach.

Developmentally and culturally responsive teachers also model empathy and care and make connections with students by purposefully seeking to learn about them, their families, and how they've navigated life both inside and outside of school.

I've also found that developmentally and culturally responsive teachers have certain "habits of mind" that shape how they plan and implement lessons. For example, they acknowledge and question their beliefs and expectations about all children and particularly children from backgrounds different from their own. In developing their lessons, they also draw on their knowledge of children's cultural backgrounds and experiences outside of school. They view children's experiences outside of school as sources of strength that can positively contribute to school performance. They see their lessons as opportunities to foster their students' motivation and belief in their ability to succeed in school.

Ultimately, as Zaretta Hammond noted in her book *Culturally Responsive Teaching and the Brain*,[32] developmentally and culturally responsive teaching is "not a practice" but what "informs our practice" by enabling teachers to meet the developmental needs of children in culturally responsive ways.

Finally, here's a paradox. Having greater knowledge of the cultural backgrounds of your students isn't a prerequisite for being developmentally and culturally responsive. It's mostly a consequence of it. When we think of this knowledge as a prerequisite, it suggests that we can't teach in a developmentally and culturally responsive way until after we've acquired that knowledge. As we noted earlier, that can paralyze teachers. If you teach in a reasonably diverse school, just learning about the religions and home foods of your students could take months of study. Another problem is that teachers can treat getting to know their students as a one-off exercise in extracting information. I've seen teachers lead activities to quickly get to know their students at the beginning of the school year, but fail to sustain the discussion and curiosity throughout the year—or worse, use the information to form settled judgments about students. That can lead to surface-level and even stereotypical and biased perspectives of students. However, when we view this knowledge more as a consequence, then we focus on how we can employ developmentally and culturally responsive practices in an intentional and consistent way over time.

What Teachers Can Do

My work with teachers and school administrators has taught me that teachers who become more developmentally and culturally responsive become more self-aware of their current practices, deepen their knowledge of how their students develop and learn, and learn effective new teaching skills. Here are ways to do that.

1. Reflect on your current teaching and disciplinary practices.

In *"Why Race and Culture Matter in Schools,"* UCLA professor Dr. Tyrone Howard recommends that to become more culturally responsive we need to reflect on our responses to key questions, including:

- whether there are racial, ethnic, gender, or economic characteristics common to students who are referred for special needs services, gifted education, or AP courses;
- how frequently we differentiate instruction;
- whether we allow culturally based differences in language, speech, reading, and writing to shape our perceptions about students' cognitive ability; and
- how often we include nontraditional means of assessment (such as role-playing, skits, poetry, rap, self-evaluations, Socratic seminars, journaling, student-led conferences, or cooperative group projects) as part of our assessment practices.

Percy Lujan, 18, attended a school for recent immigrants from countries with widely varying political systems. An important goal for the school was to help students understand American democracy. Here's how one history teacher used creative approaches to deepen student understanding and assess learning:

When we studied the French Revolution, Ms. Sara helped us understand how history is still relevant by making us participate in the class as if we were history's protagonists. She first divided us into groups representing the three estates that existed in France at that time, and then she had members of each group research their assigned estate. We had to write and give a speech in front of the class, expressing the point of view of our estate. Ms. Sara and her assistant acted as Marie Antoinette and King Louis XVI, commenting on the ideas that they "liked" and acting offended about the ideas they didn't. That class discussion made me realize the beauty of democracy and why some people die to obtain it.

In addition to Dr. Howard's questions, I also ask the teachers I support to reflect on whether there are racial, ethnic, gender, or economic characteristics common to students who tend to receive discipline referrals.

Jeimmy Hurtado, 16, describes a classic case of gender-based disciplinary policies:

"You with the spandex, come here." My principal, who was lounging on the school security desk, motioned with her index finger for me to come forward. My legs stayed glued to the ground as I glanced around at the other students who rushed past me. It took me a moment to register that she was talking to me. I was the only one wearing spandex, but why was she calling me over? Every bad thing I had done immediately popped into my head—such as when I overused the school printer or accidentally took the school's art brushes home without writing my name on the list. I stepped forward.

"Go to the guidance counselor, and pick up a pair of gym shorts," she commanded.

She stood up and walked through the double doors into the guidance office. I followed her but my mind was elsewhere. I was getting in trouble for wearing leggings?

In my school, getting "gym-shorted" or "gym-shirted" is a punishment imposed on students who disobey the dress code, although I have only seen it imposed on girls.

The Department of Education dress code lists specific types of clothing that are prohibited, like extremely brief or see-through garments. But leggings or spandex are not on the list. I still had to pay $5 for a pair of shorts and experience a day of humiliation.

Although the dress code applies to both boys and girls, it seems to be mostly targeted to girls, which is sexist. Only a few rules actually impact boys, like the "no hats" rule, while the vast majority of rules are clearly intended to police girls' wardrobes only. How is it fair that boys are allowed to wear muscle tanks that reveal their broad shoulders, while women are restricted from wearing halter tops and tops with spaghetti straps?

Aniqa Tasmin, 17, attended another school in the same district and noticed the same discrepancies.

It seems like it is mostly girls who are called out. I've seen boys wearing offensive shirts that contain explicit sexual language that is demeaning to women and naked photos of women. They often wear muscle shirts to gym class that expose their chests. Yet I haven't known any boys to be "dress-coded." I have also observed that curvier women of color seem to be penalized for defying the dress code more often than skinny, White females are.

2. Enhance your knowledge of how your students develop and learn.

This chapter has focused on the importance of having a better understanding of our students so that we can better support them in school. One key component of understanding who they are is understanding how they develop. A wonderful resource for learning more about child development is Harvard University's Center on the Developing Child (https://www.developingchild.harvard.edu/). There, you'll find a resource library that includes current research in the field of child and adolescent development and specific tools and guides for supporting students' developmental needs. Another important and related resource is the Yale Child Study Center (https://www.medicine.yale.edu/childstudy/). Their Center on Social and Emotional Learning has been a leader in developing evidence-based practices to support the social and emotional needs of youth and adults.

To better understand how students learn and to better support the learning needs of atypical learners, I often rely on the work of Understood.org (www.understood.org). This site provides a detailed approach to identifying and supporting students' learning needs.

Special education teacher Ms. Ackert was able to provide high-quality support to Irving Torres, 18, in part because her school implemented a structure that helped teachers get to know students better. He writes:

> Ms. Ackert ended up being my teacher for three years, through 8th grade. I learned more in those three years than I thought possible. I attribute that to Ms. Ackert's skill as a teacher, but also the fact that I was fortunate to have a continuing relationship with one teacher who really knew me. This process of a teacher working with students for multiple years is called "looping."
>
> Looping is a great way to make students more interested in school. [In 7th grade], since Ms. Ackert and I had known each other for over a year, every time she spoke to me during class or asked me a question, she geared the question or assignment specifically to me, which made the work way more interesting.

To gain a better understanding of how students learn, I also ask them specific questions, including: (1) What are things that teachers do that help you to learn?; (2) What are some things that make it more difficult for you to learn in school?; and (3) What are the things that you would like to learn more about? Obviously, Irving would reply that a teacher who knew him enough to match schoolwork to his level and interests is an effective teacher. In another story, Irving described how valuable it was for him when Ms. Ackert stepped in to quickly squash stereotyping and bullying of special education students.

3. Enhance your skills in teaching in culturally responsive ways.

Developmentally and culturally responsive teaching is demonstrated through both instructional planning and instructional practice. I've relied on two helpful planning and practice resources in my work with teachers. The first is The Education Alliance at Brown University (https://www.brown.edu/academics/education-alliance/teaching-diverse-learners/strategies-0/culturally-responsive-teaching-0). On this site, you'll find practical and explicit strategies for teaching in culturally responsive ways. To see what developmentally and culturally responsive teaching looks like, I recommend The George Lucas Foundation's Edutopia website (https://www.edutopia.org/topic/culturally-responsive-teaching). The site includes a series of videos demonstrating culturally responsive teaching practices at the elementary, middle, and high school levels.

4. Listen to students' voices, and respond.

Throughout this chapter, we've demonstrated just how critical it is to value the voices of youth. But it isn't only important that we listen. It's important that we listen with intention and purpose and that we use what we hear to change our teaching practices. So, in addition to relying on the feedback that you might receive from a school administrator or a colleague regarding your teaching, you should also ask yourself questions such as, "What can I learn from my students about how I can better help them to learn?" "What can my students teach me about my current teaching practices?" and "What can I learn from my students that will help me to grow as a teacher?" The Youth Communication website, youthcomm.org, has scores of stories and story-based lessons with a diversity of youth voices.

What Schools Can Do

1. Assess how students' developmental needs are currently being met.

To measure growth in student learning, all schools gather baseline data about students at the beginning of the school year and compare it with end-of-year data to determine changes in skills and knowledge. In the same way that schools gather baseline data on students, I also recommend that they gather baseline data on the ways the school meets the developmental needs of their students.

As we discussed throughout this chapter, students have critical cognitive, physical, social, and emotional needs that, when supported, lead to better academic performance and other positive outcomes.

Hence, a key question that school personnel should explore and quantify is: "How well are we currently addressing those needs?" To address students' cognitive needs, schools can look at indicators that address students' needs to feel competent. For example, how does the school provide opportunities for students to demonstrate their competence beyond grades and test scores?

Irving describes a moment like that:

> One year, I found a writing program I wanted to join, but because I was in special ed I didn't meet the academic requirements. When Ms. Ackert found out, she was red with rage.
>
> She told me to make a poster board that displayed all my writing. She wanted me to present it to the principal, and to tell him I deserved to join the program. I did, and in the end he was impressed with my work and actually recommended me for an even better writing program.

To address students' physical needs, look at whether the school is providing opportunities for movement throughout the day. As you have probably noticed, most professional development workshops include activities where participants get up and move because long periods of sitting makes many adults antsy. Yet movement is seldom worked into lessons with adolescents, with predictable consequences. Schools should review school discipline statistics to determine if discipline referrals are triggered by students getting out of their seats or moving in their seats in ways that distract other students. This could indicate that their physical needs are not being met.

To support students' social and emotional needs, school administrators and school personnel should assess well how their curriculum currently includes lessons that build social and emotional skills in ways that align with state-level benchmarks such as the New York State Social and Emotional Learning Benchmarks (NYSED, 2018). For example, to support the development of social awareness and relationship skills they should also reflect on whether students have appropriate opportunities for peer-based activities in which students must work together to achieve a common goal. In classes like English and social studies, teachers can help students identify and name the social and emotional elements inherent in character development or political conflicts, for example.

Of course, having staff model social and emotional skills is even more powerful than teaching them. Successful schools also ensure that school personnel learn the language of SEL competencies and learn to recognize their own strengths and challenges in relation to those competencies. The Youth Communication website, https://www .youthcomm.org/curriculum-training/#curricula, has SEL resources and professional development that are designed to strengthen students' and staff members' SEL skills for grades 6 to 12.

2. Establish norms and expectations regarding the use of developmentally and culturally responsive teaching practices.

To foster a school community that aims to support students' developmental needs in culturally responsive ways, schools do better when they establish instructional norms and expectations that serve as the foundation for instructional planning and delivery. One way that I have been able to assist these efforts is through working with school administrators and teachers to create guiding questions documents that align with developmentally and culturally responsive teaching. The questions can help schools codify their expectations regarding instructional planning and make them transparent. For example, answering these questions can help teachers design more DCRT-responsive lessons:

- What real-world connections do you intend to develop during your lesson?
- How does your knowledge of your students inform your instructional planning?
- What opportunities for movement will you include in your lesson?
- What opportunities for interpersonal interactions will you provide to your students?
- What strategies will you use to ensure that all students are engaged in the lesson?
- How will you differentiate and diversify your assessments so that they are responsive to the needs of diverse learners?

3. Provide professional learning opportunities for teachers to support the use of developmentally and culturally responsive teaching skills.

It's also critical that schools provide opportunities for teachers to enhance their skills in teaching in a developmentally and culturally responsive way. For example, Youth Communication provides professional development based on stories like those by the teens featured in this book. The stories include students' out-of-school experiences that show their strengths and provide context for many student behaviors. In addition, when teachers talk among themselves about the stories and their reactions to them, they learn more about their colleagues and about themselves. Youth Communication's curricula also help them to recognize and strengthen SEL competencies in themselves and in their students.

Another often overlooked teacher-to-teacher professional support is intervisitation (when teachers visit a colleague's classroom and observe their teaching). Every school I support has created wonderful examples of impactful teaching practices that often go unnoticed. While formal professional development opportunities can be deeply effective, the opportunity for teachers to observe colleagues and sometimes even teach students they have in common can be far more effective. Drawing on the same guiding questions document, school administrators can focus the intervisitations so that teachers are addressing a specific aspect of developmentally and culturally responsive instruction such as observing how their colleagues provide students with opportunities for movement or the "real-world" connections that they make throughout the lesson.

Notes

1. Ladson-Billings 1994; Rogoff 1990; Nieto 2001.

2. Goffin 1996; Heisner and Lederberg 2011.

3. Bredekamp and Copple 1997.

4. National Institute of Child Health and Human Development, NIH, DHHS 2007, p. 33.

5. NCATE 2010, p. 2.

6. Bredekamp 1995; Comer and Maholmes 1999; Wilson, Floden, and Ferrini-Mundy 2002.

7. Elkind 1967.

8. Mayford, Siegelbaum, and Kandel 2012.

9. Hammond 2014.

10. Bronfenbrenner 1979.

11. Arnett, Chapin, and Brownlow 2018; Cole and Packer 2019.

12. Slaughter-Defoe, Nahagawa, Takianishi, and Johnson 1990; Keller 2017.

13. Tudge 2008, p. 147.

14. Tharp and Gallimore 1988.

15. Ibid.

16. Gay 2000; Ladson-Billings 1994.

17. Nieto 2005.

18. Hollins and Spencer 1990.

19. Howard 2010.

20. Brown 2007; Warren 2018.

21. Greenfield, Keller, Fuligni, and Maynard 2003; Nielsen, Haun, Kärtner, and Legare 2017.

22. Haberman 1988, p. 33.

23. Gay 2000; Howard 2010; Nieto 2001.

24. Gay 2000, p. 29.

25. Brown-Wright, Tyler, Graves, Thomas, Stevens-Watkins, and Mulder 2013; Kumar 2006.

26. Brown-Wright, Tyler, Graves, Thomas, Stevens-Watkins, and Mulder 2013.

27. Arunkumar, Midgley, and Urdan 1999, p. 442.

28. Ladson-Billings 1994.

29. New York State Education Department (2019). Culturally Responsive and Sustaining Framework, NYSED, p. 11.

30. Muñiz, J. (2019). Culturally Responsive Teaching: A 50-State Survey of Teaching Standards. newamerica .org/education-policy/reports/culturally-responsive-teaching/.

31. Ibid.

32. Hammond 2014.

References

Arnett, J., Chapin, L., and Brownlow, C. (2018). *Human Development: A Cultural Approach*. Australia: Pearson Australia.

Arunkumar, R., Midgley, C., and Urdan, T. (1999). Perceiving high or low home-school dissonance: Longitudinal effects on adolescent emotional and academic well-being. *Journal of Research on Adolescence* 9: 441–466.

Bredekamp, S. and Copple, C. (1997). *Developmentally Appropriate Practice in Early Childhood Programs (Revised Edition)*. National Association for the Education of Young Children, 1509 16th Street, NW, Washington, DC 20036-1426.

Bronfenbrenner, U. (1979). *The Ecology of Human Development: Experiments by Nature and Design*. Cambridge, MA: Harvard University Press.

Brown, M.R. (2007). Educating all students: Creating culturally responsive teachers, classrooms, and schools. *Intervention in School and Clinic* 43(1): 57–62.

Brown-Wright, L., Tyler, K.M., Graves, S.L., Thomas, D., Stevens-Watkins, D., and Mulder, S. (2013). Examining the associations among home–school dissonance, amotivation, and classroom disruptive behavior for urban high school students, *Education and Urban Society* 45(1): 142–162.

Cole, M. and Packer, M. (2019). Culture and cognition. *Cross-cultural Psychology: Contemporary Themes and Perspectives*, 243–270.

Comer, J. and Maholmes, J. (1999). Creating schools of child development and education in the USA: Teacher preparation for urban schools. *Journal of Education for Teaching*, 25: 3–5.

Dorado, J.S., Martinez, M., McArthur, L.E. et al. (2016). School Mental Health 8: 163. https://doi.org/10.1007/s12310-016-9177-0.

Elkind, D. (1967). Egocentrism in adolescence. *Child Development* 1025–1034.

Gay, G. (2000). *Culturally Responsive Teaching*. New York: Teachers College Press.

Goffin, S. (1996). Child development knowledge and early childhood teacher preparation: Assessing the relationship—A special collection. *Early Childhood Research Quarterly* 11: 117–133.

Goodman, J., Hurwitz, M., Park, J., and Smith, J. (2018). Heat and Learning. Working Paper 24639, National Bureau of Economic Research, http://www.nber.org/papers/w24639.

Greenfield, P.M., Keller, H., Fuligni, A., and Maynard, A. (2003). Cultural pathways through universal development. *Annual Review of Psychology* 54: 461–90.

Haberman, M. (1988). Proposals for recruiting minority Martin Haberman teachers: Promising practices and attractive detours. *Journal of Teacher Education* 39(4): 38–44.

Hammond, Z. (2014). *Culturally Responsive Teaching and the Brain: Promoting Authentic Engagement and Rigor Among Culturally and Linguistically Diverse Students*. Thousand Oaks, CA: Corwin Press.

Heisner, M.J. and Lederberg, A.R. (2011). The impact of child development associate training on the beliefs and practices of preschool teachers. *Early Childhood Research Quarterly*, 2nd Quarter, 26(2): 227–236.

Hollins, E.R. and Spencer, K. (1990). Restructuring schools for cultural inclusion: Changing the schooling process for African American youngsters. *Journal of Education* 172(2): 89–100.

Howard, T. (2010). *Why Race and Culture Matter in Schools: Closing the Achievement Gap in America's Classrooms*. New York: Teachers College Press.

Keller, H. (2017). Culture and development: A systematic relationship. *Perspectives on Psychological Science* 12(5): 833–840.

Kumar, R. (2006). Students' experiences of home–school dissonance: The role of school academic culture and perceptions of classroom goal structures. *Contemporary Educational Psychology* 31: 253–279.

Ladson-Billings, G. (1994). *The Dreamkeepers: Successful Teachers of African American Students*. San Francisco: Jossey-Bass.

Mayford, M., Siegelbaum, S.A., and Kandel, E.R. (2012). Synapses and memory storage. *Cold Spring Harbor Perspectives in Biology* 4(6): a005751.

Muñiz, J. (2019). Culturally Responsive Teaching: A 50-State Survey of Teaching Standards. newamerica.org/education-policy/reports/culturally-responsive-teaching/.

NCATE (2010). *The Road Less Traveled: How the Developmental Sciences Can Prepare Educators to Improve Student Achievement: Policy Recommendations*. National Council for Accreditation of Teacher Education, Inc.

National Institute of Child Health and Human Development, NIH, DHHS. (2007). *Child and adolescent development research and teacher education: Evidence-based pedagogy, policy, and practice*. Washington, DC: U.S. Government Printing Office.

New York State Education Department (2019). Culturally Responsive and Sustaining Framework, NYSED, p. 11.

Nielsen, M., Haun, D., Kärtner, J., and Legare, C.H. (2017). The persistent sampling bias in developmental psychology: A call to action. *Journal of Experimental Child Psychology* 162: 31–38.

Nieto, S. (ed.). (2005). *Why We Teach*. New York: Teachers College Press.

Rogoff, B. (1990). *Apprenticeship in Thinking: Cognitive Development in Social Context*. New York: Oxford.

Slaughter-Defoe, D.T., Nakagawa, K., Takanishi, R., and Johnson, D.J. (1990). Toward cultural/ecological perspectives on schooling and achievement in African-and Asian-American children. *Child Development* 61(2): 363–383.

Tharp, R. and Gallimore, R. (1988). *Rousing Minds to Life: Teaching, Learning, and Schooling in Social Context*. New York: Cambridge University Press.

Tudge, J.R.H. (2008). *The Everyday Lives of Young Children: Culture, Class, and Child Rearing in Diverse Societies*. New York: Cambridge University Press.

Venables, D.R. (2011) *The Practice of Authentic PLCs: A Guide to Effective Teacher Teams*. Thousand Oaks, CA: Corwin Press.

Warren, C.A. (2018). Empathy, teacher dispositions, and preparation for culturally responsive pedagogy. *Journal of Teacher Education* 69(2): 169–183.

Wilson, S., Floden, R.E., and Ferrini-Mundy, J. (2002). Teacher preparation research: An insider's view from the outside. *Journal of Teacher Education* 53(3): 190–204.

CHAPTER TWO

Recognizing and Undoing Bias—How Teachers' Beliefs Impact Students

In my experience, it is rare for majority-White institutions to explicitly make Blacks feel unwelcome or ostracized, but they often do this implicitly. For example, if a teacher overhears a student making inappropriate comments about race, I believe it is the teacher's responsibility to reprimand the student. This does not necessarily need to go as far as even detention but rather giving the student a stern warning to stop making comments like that. But I've seen teachers fail to do this, and their silence sends the message that racist comments are alright or only a joke, which makes students of color feel uncomfortable and unwelcome at the institution.

—Rainier Harris, 16, "Students of Color Protest an 'Unrecognized Culture of Bias'"

Helping Everyone Grow

Many years ago, I decided that it would be fun to teach my son, who was about 3 at the time, how to grow a small plant. We followed all the directions on the seed packet with scientific precision and waited excitedly for the new plant to grow. A week later, we realized that nothing was happening. No seedling and no indication that we had grown anything but a pot of soil. Frustrated, my son asked why it wasn't growing. I didn't have a clue, so I decided to walk my son through the process of what we did and talked with him about changes we could make. Did we add enough water? Did we have enough soil covering the seeds? Was it getting enough sunlight? After making a few adjustments to how much water we were giving it and moving it to another part of the house that received more sunlight, the seedling broke through the soil and a new plant emerged.

As I think back on that time, I realize the one thing that we didn't do was simply get a new seed. We never questioned whether the seed was bad—whether there was some inherent problem that made it incapable of growing. We focused our attention on trying to understand the conditions surrounding the seed (soil quality, water level, sunlight) and then modified our plan for supporting its growth.

This story is a helpful metaphor for working with students because it's important to acknowledge that sometimes they do things that we simply don't understand. Sometimes they seem like they don't want to learn or that they don't care about anyone or anything. It can be frustrating and disheartening to feel as though all our efforts to reach a child have failed. In those moments, we're likely to say that since it isn't us that's the problem, it must be them. It's also precisely in those moments that we need to break out of our preconceptions to see anew our students and the conditions that affect their learning.

Shateek Palmer, 15, looks back at a time when he was doing poorly and acting out in elementary school—fitting a stereotype of a Black boy who was frustrating school staff and ripe for being victimized by implicit bias. In this excerpt, he writes about the conditions in his life that were triggering his behavior, and then reflects back on that time:

> The first time I ever wrote about my feelings was when my grandmother was placed in the hospital. I was 9 years old. I knew I had to be strong for her, so I wrote about how much I loved her. I wrote in a notebook because I didn't want to show my feelings to other people.
>
> I felt good when I was writing about my grandmother because I was expressing my feelings without anybody knowing about it. Otherwise I just kept the bad feelings inside, until they came out as anger at someone else.
>
> A week after she went to the hospital, my grandmother died when her liver gave out. After that, all I did was go to school and come home and go to my room. Sometimes I wouldn't eat because I was so hurt. I knew it wasn't healthy how bad I felt.

I had so much anger in me, I started to take it out on people. I got into fights and I didn't respect anybody. I just didn't care about anything.

I was placed in a foster home a month later. I remember that night like it was today.

That whole night I couldn't sleep. I kept walking around the house. I was thinking about running away, but I didn't want to leave my siblings. So I began to write my feelings. I realized again that it's healthier to write your feelings down on a piece of paper than to let your emotions affect you in a negative way.

But my anger and sadness were so strong that I began to fight again, disobey my foster parents, and do badly in school. I just didn't want to listen to anybody because I felt alone in the world, like I was the only person going through problems.

[I was eventually] placed into my Great Aunt Stacey's home, where I still live. I was a little happier living with people I knew. Writing also continued to help make me less mad at the world. When I got mad at something or someone, I would walk away. The moment I got home, I would write about it. Like all teenage kids, I did get into a little trouble, but not as much trouble as I got into before.

To this day, I still write in a notebook, usually three pages every night before bed. It takes two to three weeks to fill up a notebook, and I have a stack of notebooks next to my dresser, starting from when I was 10.

I usually start by writing about the day, but often I go back in time to when I was 9 years old. I write about how my grandmother died, how I was taken away from my family, how I messed up in school, and how I got into a lot of fights. I describe the difference between what's going on in my life now and what I went through when I was 9. When I was 9 I wouldn't really talk directly about upsetting things like that.

Now I'm 15, and partly because of writing, I can control my emotions better. When I was 9, I didn't understand where all that anger was coming from and why I got in so much trouble. But when I look back at it now I'm like, "Wow, that kid went through a lot!" By writing, I forgive the 9-year-old Shateek.

Based only on the behavior they could see, it would have been easy for Shateek's teachers to see him as a "bad seed." Think how different the experience of school would be for a student like Shateek if the school community saw itself as part of the soil that was nurturing his significant but untapped talents. Meanwhile, how many 9-year-olds, or 15-year-olds, fall through the cracks because of conscious or unconscious biases we may have about them?

Whether we're working with children who seem similar to us—from the same neighborhoods, the same race and culture, the same socio-economic background—or with students who come from backgrounds different from our own, one thing remains: We have beliefs, expectations, and biases that influence how we interact with those particular children. Sometimes those beliefs and biases inform the expectations we have of our students. Our beliefs about what *kind* of child we perceive the student to be, rather than actual knowledge of the individual, can drive our actions in directions that make our teaching less effective.

The impact of our beliefs can be extremely subtle. Maybe we expect children with highly educated parents to be able to handle more challenging work. Maybe when a child has only one parent at home, we assume the child has less support and we give them less demanding work as a way of "helping" their parent. In either case, children's educational experiences are influenced not by their demonstrated abilities or desires, but by our beliefs about their abilities based on a presumption about their home life. It's only by recognizing these kinds of assumptions—our conscious and unconscious beliefs about the influence of socio-economic background, culture, family make-up, and so on—that we can start to see students more clearly and connect with them as individuals.

Of course, it's hard to question our unconscious beliefs. We don't even know we have them until they are made manifest by new experiences. Fortunately, experiences that challenge our unconscious assumptions and help to make them accessible to us are readily available in school: If we pay close attention to our students as individuals, we will learn all kinds of things about them. When they surprise us, as they often do, it helps us to recognize our unconscious beliefs.

Christina Oxley, 18, longs for teachers and peers who recognize her individuality and the individuality of all Black students rather than unconsciously lumping them together:

> Many people believe that all Black people share the same opinions and experiences regarding race. This plays out constantly in my life, like when a teacher has asked me to explain to my class how Black people feel about being called "Black," as if I am a representative of my entire race. Or when the whole class stares at me and waits for me to respond to a question the teacher poses about race. It is easier to isolate and discriminate against people when you don't recognize them as individuals with their own unique thoughts, opinions, and emotions.

> The idea that Black people are less than human, which is a legacy of slavery, can also be internalized within the Black community, and be detrimental to our own self-image. When the concept of blackness is flattened into a set of stereotypes, we aren't allowed to live up to our full potential as people. We need to be able to celebrate our Black identity and decide for ourselves how to live in it, rather than letting it decide how we live. Race is a social construct used to give and limit power to different groups of people, so I can reclaim power by defining my identity for myself.

I've had the privilege of observing first-hand many incredible teachers who've been able to overcome the implicit social pressure to flatten their students into a set of stereotypes. In my conversations with them over the years, I've noticed three behaviors that exemplify what it means to be a developmentally and culturally responsive teacher.

First, they acknowledge the biases they know they have, and the fact that they surely have biases they are not aware of yet. They reflect on how those biases have influenced or could influence their relationships with their students in both positive and negative ways.

Second, to head off potential bias, they work very hard to use aspirational language whenever they find themselves having a negative belief or lowered expectation about a student. As one teacher I've worked with for many years shared with me, "First, I remind myself that having a negative belief about a child doesn't make me a terrible teacher, it just makes me human. Then I tell myself that this child has the potential for greatness. Now I need to go help them to be great."

Third, they work extremely hard to hold all students to high expectations but in ways that are responsive to their individual needs. A middle school teacher I worked with once told me, "All of my students are equal but not the same. I might not hold all of them to the same expectation, but I can guarantee you that I hold all of them to high expectations."

What I've learned from these inspiring teachers is that interrogating our own assumptions, seeing students' strengths, and holding high expectations is a formula for minimizing bias and maximizing effective teaching.

Understanding Our Beliefs about Intelligence and Ability

Being able to focus on a student's strengths—even when that student's strengths confound our expectations—has a lot to do with our own fundamental beliefs about human intelligence and ability. In the following story, Angie Carty, 17, describes an experience of low expectations that is distressingly common among Black students, poor students, and others who don't "fit the profile" of an achiever:

> From a young age, I've been a smarty-pants. A family reunion is never complete without my dad bragging about how, at age 3, I figured out how to use our computer to get to his favorite chess website. I credit my big brain to my dad's focus on nurturing my intelligence.
>
> Sadly, the intelligence that was supposed to carry me through academics actually exposed me to discrimination. For a while, I thought it wasn't my place to flaunt my intelligence, due to what my teachers seemed to think a Black girl in a classroom should and shouldn't be.
>
> My first experience with discrimination happened in 4th grade. I was a quiet, shy 9-year-old who mostly kept to herself. One day, our homeroom teacher gave us

a quiz on 5th grade vocabulary. These were words we shouldn't have known, but I recognized some. Each night, my dad sat me on his lap and I'd read the newspaper with him, pointing out words that looked difficult. He encouraged me to sound things out, giving me definitions I could understand clearly, and then asking me to repeat them back. Some of those words were on the test.

As the kids around me scratched their heads and toyed with their colorful erasers, I stood up proudly from my desk and walked to the front, handing the teacher my paper and waiting to hear her praise me.

"Done already?" she said. But instead of delight, her voice was laced with skepticism. I nodded happily, peering at my paper to give my sloppily written answers a final once-over. I knew I'd aced it.

When I went back to my seat, I noticed she looked confused. Could she read my handwriting? When she finally said it was time for everyone to hand in their quizzes, I noted that many students hadn't finished.

As I was on my way out the door to lunch, she called my name.

I assumed she wanted to tell me how well I did on my quiz, so with a bright, semi-toothless smile, I bounded over to her in my light-up Skechers and stood by her desk dutifully. She rummaged through the papers, not looking up. She held out my test and said, blunt as the front end of a hammer, "There's no way you could have gotten all these right."

Not only was I surprised, I was confused. I took my test back, stared at it, and realized she was waiting for some kind of a response, maybe a defense. Was she expecting me to admit I had cheated? Why wasn't she praising me for getting my vocabulary right like she had reassured the other, lighter-skinned girls that not finishing was OK?

Would she have accused me if I was one of them; if my skin was whiter and my hair less kinky? Why was it so hard to believe that someone like me was capable of being smarter than the rest?

Unfortunately, all I did was nod and begin to cry—which she took as an admission of guilt. She called me a cheater. Then, she took my test and drew a big fat ZERO on it.

Our core beliefs about how children develop, how they learn, and even their capacity to learn, shape the way we teach and affect our students' outcomes. In her groundbreaking work, psychologist Carol Dweck proposed that we all hold beliefs or mindsets about ourselves and our abilities and that our mindsets influence our performance. As a result of her research, she learned that these mindsets fall into two distinct categories: a fixed mindset and a growth mindset. According to Dweck, "In a fixed mindset, people believe their basic qualities, like their intelligence or talent, are simply fixed traits. They spend their time documenting their intelligence or talent instead of developing them. They also believe that talent alone creates success—without effort."

Alternatively, "In a growth mindset, people believe that their most basic abilities can be developed through dedication and hard work—brains and talent are just the starting point. This view creates a love of learning and a resilience that is essential for great accomplishment."[1]

More recent studies have found that teachers also have different beliefs about whether intelligence is something that's fixed or something that can grow, and that those beliefs influence how teachers interact with their students. For example, Emily de Kraker-Pauw and her colleagues at the Universiteit Amsterdam investigated whether the type of feedback that teachers provided to their students differed based on their mindset. They found that teachers holding a fixed mindset provided feedback on what students had achieved, such as, "That's just not good"; "No, wrong"; "Yes, the right answer is 70%." In contrast, teachers holding a growth mindset provided feedback to support students in their process of solving problems, such as "Can you tell me how you discovered the solution?"; "That's an interesting idea . . . let's try"; "You don't have to do it immediately right."[2]

So which type of feedback did students respond to better? Dweck asked that question and found that when teachers praised their students for the process and strategies that they used to solve problems, the improvement in their performance, and their perseverance, it helped to build their resilience and increased their drive to learn. To illustrate this, she and her colleagues created an online math game that rewarded students for their effort, strategies, and process for solving problems rather than getting the right answer. They found that using this approach resulted in students being more engaged in the math tasks for a longer period than a comparison group of students using a math program that rewarded correctness.[3]

Developing a growth mindset is a two-part process: First teachers develop a growth mindset about their students; then they help students to develop a growth mindset about themselves.

One interesting way that Dweck and her colleagues have helped students to develop a growth mindset is to help them rethink what it means to exert effort and encounter difficulty when performing a task. They found that students with a fixed mindset believed that needing to work hard on something and experiencing difficulty were signs that they weren't smart. In their eyes, smart students didn't need to try hard in school. What Dweck and her colleagues did was to explain to students that research now shows that when they work harder to complete a task, it can stimulate new connections in their brains that help them to get smarter over time. These types of messages to students were associated with significant increases in their math scores compared to a group of students who did not get this "growth mindset" style of teaching.

This research demonstrates that our conscious and unconscious beliefs about our students—whether it's our beliefs about their interest in learning, how they learn, or even their capacity to learn—influence how we teach them. It influences the type and quality of feedback we provide. It influences the level of difficulty that we think they can handle. It even influences how engaging we make our lessons. Most importantly, research in this area demonstrates that a growth mindset enables teachers to transform how students feel about themselves.

Here's an example of a teacher who has a growth mindset about her students—including ones who are not yet showing their talent. Giselle John, 15, got off to a bad start in high school; she was nearly suspended for a fight in the second week. She writes:

I wasted time in class and failed almost all of my exams. I kept getting low grades because I was cutting and not doing the work. Sometimes I would just go home and sleep, or I wouldn't even go to school at all.

Giselle then got a job, which led to even more skipping. She was also moved out of an aunt's house to a foster care diagnostic center and then to a guardianship, and later, to a foster home. As Giselle entered 10th grade, it would have been easy to take a "fixed" mindset about her: just another girl who just didn't have the skills or the motivation to succeed in school. However, an English teacher who had a "growth mindset" about students had seen a glimmer of Giselle's language skills and was curious about why they weren't being manifested. Giselle continues her story:

When school began in September, I met my 10th grade English teacher, Ms. Stanford.

One day I was sitting in her classroom, falling asleep. Just before the period ended I awoke, only to see her looking at me.

"What's the matter with you?" she asked.

"Nothing," I answered softly.

I wanted to tell her what was on my mind. I needed someone to listen to me and I knew she would. I always noticed how the other kids related to her. She was friendly but stern. The other kids seemed to like her, even those she failed numerous times. I thought I could relate to her.

At the end of the class, I approached her table and asked if I could speak to her whenever she had time. She said yes and we made plans to see each other on her lunch time that same day, which happened to be mine also.

When I saw Ms. Stanford at lunch, I told her what was bothering me, and she listened.

> I had found someone who thought I was valuable. She took an interest in my life and I felt special. We developed a good relationship. I began to settle down and go to school more often.
>
> Ms. Stanford once told me that even before she knew me personally, she tried to get me out of regular English and into Honors English, because she knew regular English was no challenge for me. But it was difficult to change my classes because it would have changed my whole program for the semester. I felt good when she told me that because I never saw myself as a good student. It meant that I had potential.

Giselle had a lot of distractions and trauma in her life, which contributed to her own fixed mindset—seeing herself as a poor student with no potential. But over the next three years, as Ms. Stanford mentored her, Giselle's mindset evolved. She started taking honors courses, and by senior year, two AP classes. As she put it, "All that hard work paid off: I graduated from Prospect Heights High School ranked 17th in a senior class of 305 students."

I've learned that it's one thing to say that we should always have a growth mindset and it's another to maintain that mindset when things get tough. When we face challenging times as educators, the most important way that we can maintain our growth mindset is by pushing ourselves to teach in ways that match three core beliefs:

- that students may not be ready to learn, but are always capable of learning;
- that our feedback can shape our students' sense of not only what they've learned but also their belief in their ability to learn; and
- that our goal should always be to build from our students' strengths.

Most teachers start out with these beliefs. The real challenge is retaining them and putting them into action day after day, and year after year. Ms. Stanford worked in one of New York City's most challenging high schools. But her "growth mindset" led her to notice that even though Giselle was not quite ready to learn, she was capable. Then, her feedback helped change Giselle's conception of herself—from a poor student to one who could excel with hard work. Finally, perhaps because she was an English teacher, Ms. Stanford noticed that Giselle's academic strength was English and that if she created conditions where Giselle could succeed in that subject, it could spill over into others.

Recognizing—and Undoing—Bias in the Classroom

I've interviewed hundreds of prospective teachers for admission to our teacher preparation programs at Hunter College. We typically start with the standard question, "Why do you want to be a teacher?" While I've heard many compelling responses to that question, I've never heard someone say that they wanted to be a teacher because they didn't like children or because they wanted to provide them with a terrible educational experience. (If they did, we certainly wouldn't accept them!) Rather, they usually express a belief that all students can be successful in school and believe that they can positively shape the lives of their students.

Many teachers I know continue to hold on to those beliefs throughout their careers. Unfortunately, I know other teachers whose negative experiences over time caused them to be less positive and less aspirational. It's important to note that the change in their beliefs was spurred by negative experiences, not by something inherent to who they are. For some, it was the pressures and challenges of working in a school where they felt unsupported by administrators or colleagues. For others, it was the constant challenge of trying to deal with student discipline issues while also trying to teach content at a level that met standards that not all their students were prepared to meet. And for many, it was the frustration of trying to work within an inadequately funded educational system that increasingly devalued the role and expertise of teachers.

As we said earlier, unproductive beliefs—like that some students aren't capable of achieving much or adolescents are indifferent to schoolwork—don't simply appear. Like most dispositions or habits, fixed mindsets take time to develop and typically result from an accumulation of negative experiences and a feeling of powerlessness. Collectively, these experiences can result in teachers holding beliefs about their students that are less positive and less aspirational. Ironically, these beliefs then make teachers less effective than they want to be, which can further discourage them.

Generalized negative beliefs about our students are bad enough. Even more troubling are several recent studies that reveal the negative consequences when biases about students are rooted in race, like the experiences that Angie and Christina describe earlier in this chapter. For example, a 2016 study by Seth Gershenson and his colleagues at Johns Hopkins University investigated how teachers form expectations for students and whether those expectations are influenced by racial differences among their students. Both White and Black teachers in the study who taught the same students were asked to predict how far their students would go in school. The findings show that the evaluations of White students from both teachers were about the same. But for Black students, White teachers had significantly lower expectations than Black teachers.[4]

Beliefs like these also shape how teachers view student behavior and the level of discipline that students receive. For example, Stanford University researchers Jason Okonofua and Jennifer Eberhardt found that both White and Black teachers in their study were likely to interpret students' misbehavior differently depending on the students' race, and that teachers were likely to discipline Black students more harshly than White students for being insubordinate or disrupting the class.[5]

Research also reveals that negative beliefs and biases are especially persistent among teachers who work with children living in poverty—no matter what the race of the teachers and students. For example, in a 2011 study, Columbia University researchers Douglas Ready and David Wright found that teachers underestimated the literacy ability of children living in poverty and were likely to hold even lower expectations for children living in poverty who also attended schools in lower income communities.[6]

Drawing on a national database from the National Center for Education Statistics, their study of over 9,000 kindergarteners across 701 public and private schools examined the accuracy of teacher ratings of children's language and literacy skills during their kindergarten year. Children's literacy skills were rated by their teachers and also assessed using a standardized measure. Teacher ratings were then compared to the actual student scores to determine how accurate they were. The researchers wanted to find out if teachers' accuracy varied based on teacher characteristics (such as their level of teaching experience or their racial background), student characteristics (race or socio-economic background), classroom characteristics (class size or the racial, economic, and academic composition of the class), or school characteristics (public versus private schools).

At the start of the school year, when compared to Black teachers, White teachers underestimated the literacy abilities of Black students as well as Hispanic and Asian students for whom English was not their primary language. However, by the end of the academic year the inaccuracies related to the race and ethnicity of students disappeared. The researchers attributed this finding to teachers knowing their students better as the year progressed.

But the most significant and enduring inaccuracies were related to the children's economic status. They found that both White and Black teachers underestimated the literacy abilities of children living in poverty, and especially those living in poor neighborhoods.

It can be challenging to fight these biases. But one of the best ways is to learn about our students' lives outside of school. That will help us to know them better—their strengths and their stressors. That knowledge tends to reduce bias and increase empathy. As you read the following excerpt in which Jessica Yauri, 18, describes her out-of-school life, imagine how much of her time and emotional energy is taken up keeping a secret for six years and feeling ashamed of her poverty—energy that could have been expended on schoolwork and participating in enriching after-school programs. Think about how easy it would be, for example, for a school staff member to jump to a conclusion when she shows up to school smelling like alcohol. Then notice how a perceptive teacher and her peers eventually help her:

> My family collects bottles from sunup to sundown all year long. I started when
> I was 12, watching my parents glazed in sweat, as if it just rained on them. Despite
> the aches and the tireless nights, their smiles shined as they worked.
>
> My mother leaves at dawn to collect cans, and when she returns 12 hours later,
> I help her pull the shopping cart the six long blocks to the recycling center. Three
> blocks before we reach the center, we are greeted by bees and the stench of beer
> and compost.
>
> Although this center has been like my second home for the past 10 years, I have
> kept it mostly a secret. I usually did this work after school, except for Mondays

when I would go early to bring my mom breakfast and supplies like gloves, tape, and boxes.

One morning in 6th grade, beer spilled on my school uniform and backpack at the recycling center. The smell followed me into the classroom. A chain reaction of "Eww" erupted from the students. I joined in trying to play it off, saying "Eww" too and fanning my face with my hand.

From that day on, I'd bring spare clothes, so my uniform wouldn't smell.

My mom often asked me, in Spanish, "Why don't you bring your friends here?" I smiled and said "*No lo sé*." (I do not know.) But I couldn't bear the idea of my friends knowing our family lived off other people's garbage. I felt guilty for being embarrassed, but I couldn't help it.

Eighth grade was even more financially stressful for my family because I had to pay senior dues—about $400. My parents argued late into the night about who pays which bills and expenses.

But at school, I still hid from my *amigas* how poor we were and what my family did for their income.

Every day after school my friends would go out to eat, but I couldn't afford to do that. So I'd say, "I am too good for fast food," or make excuses.

But these lies started wearing on me. I felt like I had to tell someone, so I chose my friend Kip. We were in the lunchroom, and I blurted, "My family collects cans for a living."

Kip responds compassionately to Jessica, and even wants to see the recycling center. However, she doesn't know what she's in for, like the unfamiliar smells and the buzzing bees. Kip is so freaked out she breaks off the friendship. Jessica continues:

It hurt that I finally trusted a friend and she reacted so horribly.

When I got to high school the secret was still in hiding. Even though I had a lot of friends and was a social butterfly, I was not ready to trust someone else.

Then in the summer before my senior year I took a college essay course. I chose to write about the impact my neighborhood's gentrification had on me, and how that led me to volunteer with officials in my community who were trying to fight it. At the end, there was just one sentence about can collecting. After class, my teacher asked me to schedule a one-on-one with him during lunch.

"Your story has potential," he said. "However it is not about personal growth. How about you tell me about the can collecting?" So once again, I was faced with sharing my secret. But he was my teacher and I trusted him so I rewrote the essay.

Two days later I found out we were expected to read our essays out loud after lunch, but I was ashamed for my peers to know. As I headed down to the cafeteria, I met up with a friend, Mason, who I always have lunch with.

I was less talkative, and Mason caught on that I had something on my mind. We sat down, and he asked me what was wrong. I told him I was embarrassed about my family's story and wasn't sure if it was significant.

Talking to him was the first step in a process of shedding my shame. "Every struggle makes us who we are," said Mason. "My aunt actually collects bottles and cans too, and you should be proud that your family is hustling to take care of their loved ones."

Then we hugged and I cried. This was what I needed to hear and I felt like I could finally breathe after all those years of hiding a part of myself.

Now, I am not ashamed to say that a sticky Heineken beer can holds enormous value. It is what feeds me every day and pays for my clothes. It unites my family and helps me understand the value of hard work. It represents my family's strong values and their dreams for me of getting the opportunity to go to college and lead a stable life.

Now when people ask me what my parents do for a living, I tell them not with embarrassment or shame, but with pride. My parents are can collectors. Because my friend is right; my family is hustling to take care of their loved ones. That is something to be admired.

The issue of bias and lowered expectations is complex. We know that biases exist—and that, despite our best intentions to expel them, biases can continue to live within all of us. Without knowing more about the life of a student like Jessica, we could easily develop a biased interpretation to explain why she never participates in after-school programs, hesitates to share about her family, or once came to school smelling like beer.

We know that our biases can harm our students. These biases and lowered expectations shape our beliefs about children and can cause us to treat students in ways that make them feel like they're "less than": less interested in school than other students, less concerned about their future than other students, and even less capable of learning.

The point of all this information on bias is not to make teachers feel bad or guilty. Rather, it is to encourage us to become more aware of our own explicit and implicit biases and those that form part of the collective unconscious of our society. After all, it is difficult to shake off our assumptions about poverty or race or ethnicity, or ones related to our own family dynamics, without admitting that unintentionally, and even unconsciously, we probably carry around those assumptions. So self-awareness is a first step, and it's a hard one.

Now for the good news: Perhaps the most revelatory part of the research is not that we *have* biases, but that a way to overcome them is right in front of us, every day: The most effective way to erase or minimize our biases is to get to know our students better. What teacher wouldn't be thrilled to learn that Angie's father teaches her vocabulary by reading the newspaper; that Christina has deep and complex ideas about race and representation, or that Jessica has the motivation (and time management skills!) to persist in school while helping her parents collect cans.

As I describe in Chapter 1, I suffered from unconscious bias in my first teaching experience in East Harlem. It was listening to my students talk about their neighborhood that helped to undo my unconscious biases about them. And even when we have little control over the things that can chip away at our best instincts, like inadequate school budgets or overly large class sizes, we can fight against the feeling of powerlessness by remembering that we have agency within our classrooms. Instead of falling prey to negative beliefs and cynicism, we can work to understand our students as best we can.

Moving toward Understanding Our Students

Knowing something about a young person is not the same as understanding why or how that thing affects them as a student. For example, we may know that our students are living in poverty, but we may not understand how the experience of poverty has influenced their learning and behavior in school. We may know that a student is Asian, Black, or Latinx, but may not understand how being Asian, Black, or Latinx has shaped their development and educational experiences. Jessica and Giselle were both poor, for example, but experienced poverty very differently. Jessica had the support of a strong extended family, while Giselle was largely left to her own devices.

Educators have attempted to bridge this gap in understanding by preparing prospective teachers to better support racially, ethnically, and linguistically diverse students. Many educator preparation programs now include courses on diversity and multicultural education, and some programs prepare educators to teach in ways that are culturally responsive. Many states even require prospective teachers to demonstrate multicultural competence as a requirement for teacher certification.[7] But working to value the culture of others or gaining some knowledge about culturally responsive teaching practices is very different from doing the work of study and introspection needed to fill gaps in our knowledge and to change our negative beliefs. And increasing our knowledge of ourselves and other people, while an important first step, is also far different from using that knowledge to develop practices that are responsive to the demonstrated needs of the children we teach.

Some of our students may come from backgrounds very different from our own. Others may superficially seem similar to us but be contending with challenges they are unwilling to reveal unless they feel like we really want to know who they are. With limited time, how can we understand their lives? One important way is to ask questions to get to know them as individuals whose prior experiences have shaped them, and which shape their engagement in our classrooms. Asking the following questions of just a sampling of your students, at any grade level, can help sensitize you to the broad contours of what most of them experiencing:

- Which adults in your lives can you count on when you need help with a personal or school challenge (parents, siblings, grandparents, guardians, etc.)?
- What do you find beautiful about your neighborhood?
- What would you like to learn more about?

The first question is important because we want to know who plays a parental role in their lives. That person can be an ally in helping students succeed. It also reminds students that help-seeking is a normal and positive activity. Some students have been raised by a single parent and some have been raised without their biological parents. Rather than assume that they've experienced a deficit because a biological parent might not be present, they can tell us about who plays that role in their lives. This can help us to learn who acts as their sources of strength. We could learn who might be their advocates and who we might appeal to for more insight into them as learners. Some students might even mention you, or another staff member, which is a good indication that your school is a welcoming, supportive place.

Facing mounting troubles in school, Danica Webb, 19, writes about a meeting to discuss transferring out of a large, impersonal high school that is not meeting her needs. The meeting with her distracted and apparently disinterested counselor includes her grandfather, who was encouraging her to make a change. Danica says that ultimately her own fears prevented her from taking her grandfather's advice, but one wonders whether that is the full story. Was the counselor aware that her grandfather was her most trusted adult and was best acquainted with the personal toll that the school was taking on her?

> I was living with an alcoholic uncle and another verbally abusive uncle who was loud and destructive. The combination of home problems and lack of care from the school sent my situation from bad to worse.

> I stopped applying myself because I felt no one cared. Even though education was valued in my home, no one helped me with homework. At school, if I asked for help, teachers would dryly tell me to go to after-school tutoring, but no student at that school wanted to stay after school. No teacher took the time to tell me that I wasn't passing the class or to give me options to improve my grades.
>
> During my junior year, my grandfather talked to me about changing schools. Though he was in poor health, he walked up three flights of stairs just to talk to my counselor about me transferring. I felt good that he cared enough to come, but I wasn't ready for change. Being at my high school was like being in a bad relationship: You know that things aren't good but you try to stick it out, hoping for better and afraid to change.

Later that year, Danica's grandfather died. She resolved to change "to make him proud." A more responsive counselor helped her to transfer to a school that was a better fit. She significantly raised her average and learned "that I wasn't dumb and that if I worked hard enough [I would] be in charge of my destiny."

The second question—about the beauty of students' neighborhoods—is important because many of our students have gotten explicit and unconscious negative messages about where they live. And we know from the research that teacher bias is strongest regarding poor students in poor neighborhoods. Some of our students may live in public housing or in neighborhoods viewed as unsafe. They've also been taught, implicitly or explicitly, that the purpose of school is to help them go to college, get a good job, and escape their neighborhood.

Over time, we may also begin to internalize these messages and even unknowingly reinforce them when we interact with our students. Asking them to find beauty in their neighborhoods reminds us that our students have a sense of pride about their neighborhood. It also helps to highlight the strengths and assets in their community that we might not be aware of. If we find ways to use that information in designing lessons, it helps students feel respected and supported and builds trust.

Like the "caring adult" question, the "neighborhood" question can tell you things about your students that are very important to them but that you never imagined—and that you can use in building relationships and in tailoring lessons to their interests. Here are three examples that show the diversity of students' experiences of place that teachers would never know unless they asked.

Sheila Maldonado, 17, lives in a housing project on the "bad" side of Coney Island.

> Every summer, millions of people come to ride the Cyclone, and Deno's Wonder Wheel and to go to the beach. Hordes of them come rushing out of the Stillwell Avenue station and invade the neighborhood. They come in waves—wearing swimsuits, tank tops and sandals, with a cooler in one hand and a portable speaker in the other. The cars swarm down Surf Avenue near the boardwalk, fighting each other over a handful of parking spaces.

> When they leave, they leave a mess. On the wooden planks of the boardwalk they leave chewed up ears of corn, greasy wooden shish kabob sticks, half eaten candy apples, and paper plates with leftover shrimp and French fries. The sidewalk outside Nathan's (the original hot-dog stand) is littered with napkins smeared with ketchup, mustard, and relish. And the wood of the boardwalk next to the kiddie park is stained with all the oil and grease.

> Still, I've always thought if you have to live in a "bad" neighborhood, live in Coney Island. Sitting on the boardwalk or walking on the beach, you can see the entire sky. There are no buildings to block the view, no car exhaust or smoke to fog up the sky, just the sun, wrapped in a patchwork of bright colors and pastels, nodding off into the sea. At least they can't tear down our sunsets.

Unlike Sheila, Sung Park, 18, lives in Forest Hills, one of New York's safest and most beautiful neighborhoods; but it's not as perfect as its reputation, at least not for Sung:

> It's very pretty here. Small, quaint houses are lined with either white picket fences or sturdy black metal ones. In the southern part of the neighborhood, the houses are at least 100 years old, although some are newly renovated. The old is blended in with the new and all the houses are tasteful, not tacky-looking.

> The streets are paved with cobblestones. It's got greenery and big bushes dotted with small rosettes in the spring and there are little pots of Swedish Ivy on every

corner. In the winter, the terrain is perfect for sledding. It reminds me of the New England scenery I see on postcards.

The neighborhood is also very safe compared to other places I could be living in—no burglaries or drug addicts hanging out on street corners. I don't have to worry about getting mugged, like I would in many of the neighborhoods where Asian immigrants live. Flushing, for example, is full of gangs that bother people on a daily basis.

My neighbors are the Arnolds. That is not their real last name. I don't know their real name, so I nicknamed them the Arnolds. They've lived right next door to me for the last seven years. [But] I don't know much about them.

No one knows each other here. Correction: My family does not know anyone here. Maybe it's because we don't fit in. After all, we must be the only Asian people within a one-mile radius.

One summer a few years back, my family had planted tomatoes in our backyard. The plants exploded with them at the end of the summer and we had more than we knew what to do with.

My parents filled a basket with them, and I mean it was big—they had a hard time carrying it out the door. They casually sauntered over to the Arnolds and offered them some of our "harvest." The Arnolds just gave them a look that said, "We wouldn't touch that stuff with a 10 foot pole."

My dad looked sort of depressed and upset. [After many years of trying to reach out] he was really offering an olive branch to our neighbors and they were nothing but ungrateful, prejudiced people. Still, in spite of the way our neighbors have treated us, I can't stand the idea of leaving Forest Hills.

And then there's Fabiola Duvalsaint, 17. She lives in a neighborhood that a teacher from the suburbs might consider very rough. But even she has stereotypes about a nearby housing project that mirror those I had of East Harlem:

The projects. A year ago I would have shuddered at the thought of visiting one and being around the people who live there. I didn't know anything about public housing projects because I had never been to one. But that didn't stop me from imagining what they were like. I mean, people in the housing projects are mostly drug dealers and prostitutes, right? Basically, they were forbidden territory.

Now, my neighborhood wasn't the kind with white picket fences up and down the block either. For a while, my neighborhood was thought of as dangerous, but at least it was changing for the better.

Fabiola then makes friends with a girl named Maria.

One day I asked if I could come over to her house.

"You want to come over to my house?" she asked, looking like I was talking in a foreign language.

"Yeah," I said. "What's the matter?"

Maria just looked at me and smiled. "I live in the projects," she said. I looked to see if she was kidding, but deep inside I knew she was dead serious. How was I going to get myself out of this situation?

I guess she could tell how I felt by looking at my face, because Maria told me right away that I didn't have to go if I didn't want to. I wanted to back out, I really did, but I sensed that not going would mean my friendship with her wasn't real.

When my last class ended that day, I went to meet Maria at our usual spot (the locker room). As we started to walk, Maria looked at me and started laughing. I asked her what was so funny (because at this point I sure needed a good laugh).

"You're scared to go to the projects!" she said.

I turned toward her and looked her straight in the face. "I'm not scared. Why should I be?"

> Great! Not only was I a coward, but I'd turned into a liar, too. I wanted to turn back, and had almost decided to, but just then Maria pointed to an orange building surrounded by other orange buildings.
>
> "Here it is," she said.
>
> I had been so filled with dread and my thoughts were so locked on turning back that I didn't even realize that we had already arrived.
>
> When I looked around I was shocked. There were no drug dealers on the corners and I certainly didn't hear any gunshots. This neighborhood was quiet and calm—as if all the people who lived here were hibernating inside their apartments. Was this what I was afraid of?
>
> We crossed the street and went inside her building. When we got upstairs to her apartment, I met her mom and sister. I got so comfortable in her apartment that my fears melted away. My worries were all just gone!

While the neighborhood question gives us an (often unexpected) view of our students' lives outside of school, question three—What would you like to learn more about?—directly relates to our work with them as subject teachers. It empowers our students to feel as though they can actively contribute to and shape the content that we discuss in class. Hearing what they would like to learn helps us see them as intellectually curious and eager to grow as learners. It is almost always possible to select some things from among their ideas to include in lessons, which further demonstrates that you see them and care about their concerns.

Fifteen-year-old Layla Hussein's teachers were unlikely to know that she might be interested in coding; in fact, she had rejected that interest years earlier:

> I was first introduced to coding in 4th grade when all math classes were assigned to do Hour of Code activities for one day. These beginner activities were fun and easy, but my journey with code ended on the same day it started because math was my least favorite subject. I had the wrong idea that I had to be a master at math to understand code.

But people change, and social conditions change, which is one reason we want to ask students—and keep asking them—what they want to learn. In Layla's case, it was her brother's persistence and excitement that ignited her interest in coding:

> In a year or two, I've watched him blossom from a person who couldn't understand the basic concept of data structures to a person who eats, sleeps, and breathes coding.
>
> His motivation and passion influenced me. I watched his frustrations when he couldn't understand a concept or spot an error in his program; he'd slap his head a lot. But then he'd dance around the house when he figured it out or when his result turned out exactly like his original vision. Watching his rollercoaster of emotions with computer science made me want to join the ride.

Layla signs up for a coding class during the pandemic. Neither Layla nor her teachers would have predicted what happened next.

> I researched coding opportunities and applied to Kode With Klossy, an organization that offers free coding scholarships for girls and non-binary individuals to learn web or mobile app development during a two-week summer camp. I researched alumnae from the program and learned that one had created a mobile app for survivors of sexual assault, and another had made a website full of resources for the Black Lives Matter movement. These girls were from backgrounds and with interests just like me! I applied and was accepted.
>
> On my first day, I was nervous. Not only would this be my first time learning computer programming, but it would also be my first virtual program and my first time meeting girls across the world. Yet all my worries vanished as soon as I saw the other girls' faces on Zoom.
>
> Over those two weeks, we learned HTML, CSS, and JavaScript, which are the languages needed to create content and functionality on a webpage. For our final projects, we were asked to design websites and apps to raise awareness about social justice issues, such as the Black Lives Matter movement, climate change, feminism, abortion rights, and mental health.

My group wanted to promote female empowerment by sharing stories by young women of color who are not often heard from on big media platforms. We named our website GenZGirls. We also learned about social media promotion, marketing, and entrepreneurship.

We created a Google form to encourage women of all ages to share how they overcame a challenge. In just three months, we've published numerous stories written by women across the globe, including an entrepreneur in India, an activist in Turkey, and a teen author in Florida.

Imagine what Layla's teachers would learn about her if they asked what she wanted to learn. Her answers would open up a world of possibilities for linking required subject matter to her interests—not just in coding, but in math, social studies, history, English, and other topics.

There are plenty of other ways we may get closer to understanding our students, and more suggestions will appear throughout this book. When in doubt, remember to return to the students themselves. Ask yourself what assumptions you are making about their clothing, manner of speaking, religiosity, social media use, home neighborhood, friends they hang out with, or other characteristics that you may not fully understand.

This is especially important for any students who seem to be struggling or acting out or who just get under your skin. There are always reasons behind behavior and reasons behind our responses to it, as we see in the case studies throughout this book. So observe and ask questions of your students and of yourself. You will get a deeper understanding of students who initially confound you. And they will notice that you're looking beyond their behavior to the reasons underlying it. That's another part of building the trust that will increase their desire to do well in your class.

As teachers and youth workers, beliefs and expectations about our students matter more than we may think. These beliefs are the lens through which we see our students, their families, and their community. In turn, they influence how students behave in our classrooms and the effort they expend on academic work.

When I was in elementary school we learned about the way light traveled through a lens to form an image of an object. We learned that concave lenses were referred to as being negative because they spread light out in ways that make it difficult to focus on an image. We also learned that convex lenses were thought of as being positive because they focused light in ways that made things clearer.

As I think back on that, I see direct connections to my work as an educator. My beliefs can shape my lens in a negative way, resulting in me making broad judgments about my students based on unfocused and limited information. Or, my beliefs can shape my lens in ways that focus my attention on students in a way that helps me to understand and appreciate them as individuals. When we're able to see students more clearly as individuals, it's easier to stop seeing their negative behavior as a personal insult and understand it as a response to an unfulfilled need.

Whatever lens we use, students notice. They can sense when a teacher believes in their potential and believes that they're intelligent just as much as they can tell when they're being judged as a "bad seed" or part of a "bad crowd" or living in a "bad neighborhood." And they certainly notice when we seem to have given up on them.

In the following excerpts, Selena Garcia, a 16-year-old writer from Brooklyn, describes how some teachers made her feel unwelcome in school. We can imagine the lens that those teachers are viewing her with:

> One day I sat down in 9th grade math class and started the work written on the board. The teacher took attendance and when I said, "Here," she said, "Wow, you are actually in class."
>
> "Don't get used to it," I said, feeling irritable.
>
> I finished the work on the board and handed it in. I got some of the answers right.
>
> She said, "You got almost all of the problems wrong. Go to your seat."
>
> "Obviously I got them wrong because I haven't learned any of this material."

> She then said, "How can you learn if you never come to class? Why do you even come to school if you're not going to do anything? You should just stay home."
>
> I then said, "Obviously you're not smart enough to be a teacher, ho." And I walked out.
>
> Other teachers began to ask why I bothered to show up to school. I told them to leave me alone and mind their own business. One teacher said sarcastically to a class full of students, "You don't want to be like her, never coming to class and getting all zeros. Yeah, that will definitely get her to college."
>
> I wished those teachers knew the real me and my potential. I can't blame them; they only saw the bad side of me. But I was going through so much. I wish they had taken the time to get to know more about me and my situation.

Selena could tell that her teachers only saw her "bad side" and responded to that "bad side" in ways that didn't address her true needs. Unfortunately, when faced with students like her, it's easier to respond to the student as we believe them to be rather than to the real needs of that student. If Selena's teachers had approached her differently, they may have discovered the real reason she had missed so much school and understood her apparent lack of motivation.

In her story, Selena explained that there was a lot leading up to that bad day in math class:

> Up until 5th grade I lived with adoptive parents, who were abusive. When I was 9, my adoptive mother died, and I was put into foster care. I got placed in homes with foster parents who ranged from pretty bad to bad. I often fought with the other foster children. By age 12, I'd been in over 16 foster homes.
>
> All that moving meant I was transferred from school to school. I didn't feel like I belonged anywhere. It was hard for me to fit in and make friends. I got bullied because I wore hand-me-downs and glasses. I probably looked weak to bullies because I cried a lot due to the abuse at home.

Even so, I was interested in learning new things. But I often couldn't complete my homework because my foster homes didn't have a quiet space for me to work. Few of my foster parents helped me with my schoolwork or encouraged me.

Yet I still did my schoolwork and managed to get acceptable grades. In 8th grade, I spent about three months at a school I really liked. Unlike my previous schools, the teachers reached out to me and encouraged me. They said I was a smart kid.

For instance, once my math teacher noticed I was upset because I had done poorly on a math test. I usually got As or Bs. She pulled me aside after class. "It's OK that you didn't do well. I know if you just study a little harder next time you will," she said. I felt better because she had faith in my capabilities.

I also made a few friends. I finally felt a sense of belonging and it felt good. But when I got the news that I was moving again, I got fed up. This was my 11th placement; I was sick of moving. Having to change homes again and leave a school I liked made me feel like it didn't matter if I did well or not. I figured I might as well stop trying. In a few months, I went from conscientious student to barely attending. I cut class and hung out with friends, smoked, and drank. When I did go to school, I cursed out teachers and students and got into fights. All the sadness I felt when I was younger now manifested itself as anger.

The summer before high school, I was placed with the Garcia family: Mom Jenny, Dad Jose, and six kids, some adopted, some foster, and some biological. They were kind and loving, but I didn't know it for a while, so I kept acting out.

I had so much built-up anger and frustration that disrespecting teachers and fighting felt like the only way to release it. Because I'd been bullied, I didn't want anyone picking on me or thinking I was weak, so I acted tough.

But deep down I felt bad. Looking back, I don't think it was the teachers I was mad at. In some cases, they were right: I should have gone to class and showed them that I am smart and capable.

After I had been living with the Garcias for a while, my life got better. My foster mom paid attention to me and knew I was smart. She didn't like the school

I was in because she felt it was too riled up and loud. She began researching other schools for me.

In the beginning of my junior year my foster mom found a new high school for me that was supposed to be better. Around the same time, my foster mom told me she wanted to legally adopt me. When the adoption went through, I felt loved and safe for the first time.

I am stable in both home and school, where I fit in well with both the students and the teachers. I don't see the teachers as adults harassing me or ignoring my pain anymore. Because I feel more comfortable and welcomed in school, I can appreciate them pushing me to do my best. I feel valued because they are interested in my academics and help me. I went from being a kid who didn't care about classes to a kid who participates and focuses on her academics. Now teachers push me forward, instead of trying to push me out.

Selena's description indicates that many of her teachers wrote her off, but we don't know whether those teachers didn't believe Selena was capable of learning (they didn't have a growth mindset) or if they believed that her behavior was an inherent part of who she was rather than a reaction stemming from her environment. It's all too likely that they didn't know the details of the struggles she was experiencing. We do know that the teachers' belief that Selena didn't care made a bad situation worse. We also know that teachers at her new school seemed more invested in Selena and her potential—and, importantly, after she felt safer and more comfortable in school she began to thrive.

What Teachers Can Do

Acknowledging our biases and preconceived notions about students' backgrounds and potential is a first step to becoming developmentally and culturally responsive educators. Whether those biases are negative or positive, they shape our perspective on our students and affect how we engage with them. Ultimately, biases obstruct our view and limit what we know and understand about our students.

So, once we acknowledge that, yes, just like everyone else, we have biases, how do we change?

1. Learn to accommodate new information that challenges our assumptions.

The developmental psychologist Jean Piaget theorized that when we encounter new information, we respond in one of two ways. If it is consistent with what we already know, we assimilate (or add) that information into our current way of thinking. If the new information is inconsistent with what we know, we can accommodate to it and change our way of thinking.

Similarly, when we encounter information about our students that matches our biases or preconceived notions about them, we are in danger of using it as another piece of evidence for holding that bias in the first place (what psychologists refer to as confirmation bias). For example, if they don't do their homework, we might think, "Of course they didn't do their homework, I knew they didn't care."

Think about how some of the examples in this chapter might require us to accommodate and change our way of thinking. Is Sheila depressed about living next door to a dirty amusement park or is she a budding poet who pays more attention to how the sun, "wrapped in a patchwork of bright colors and pastels," nods off into the sea? (She actually became a published poet.) Is Sung a relatively privileged Korean girl enjoying the benefits of an upscale neighborhood or someone who regularly experiences painful anti-Asian prejudice there? Is Layla a math-phobic girl or someone with a passion to learn coding for social justice? Is Selena an indifferent student, more interested in skipping class than studying or a girl fighting heroically to maintain focus on school despite steep odds?

If we want to change our beliefs and biases about our students, we need to encounter information that causes us to accommodate, challenges our assumptions, and changes our behavior. We need to have experiences with our students that reshape our lens from one that focuses on their limits to one that focuses on their possibilities. Asking them questions, like the three previously discussed, is one way to do that.

2. Broaden our assessment of competence.

Another way is to rethink how they can demonstrate their competence. For example, if we only allow students to demonstrate their competence through written tests that they always do poorly on, we ensure that we will continue to see them only as lower-performing students and poor test-takers (and they will also see themselves that way).

This anonymous writer, 17, fled Guinea in West Africa when his conversion to Christianity put his life in danger. After a harrowing journey across the Atlantic, and then through Colombia, Mexico, and California, he ended up going to school in a shelter for unaccompanied minors in Chicago where he struggled with the usual subjects. But noticing his interest in art helped a teacher get to know the writer much better. The student improved his speaking and abstract thinking skills as he translated his ideas into images. The anonymous teen writes:

> There were no art classes in the Chicago shelter, but Nidia and my English teacher, Mr. Tyler, got me paint and canvas or watercolor paper to paint on. I painted a portrait and some fashion ideas for Nidia and a painting of a nun holding a Bible for Mr. Tyler.
>
> Mr. Tyler used to call me in his office and ask me where I got my ideas for my paintings. I told him about my ambition of fashion design and how that motivated me to paint. He encouraged me to do it all. He said drawing, painting, and fashion go together, and that my art could inspire my fashion.
>
> Mr. Tyler told me what he saw in all of my creative work, including my logos, poems, spoken word pieces, paintings, and drawings.
>
> I got better at talking about my work from my conversations with Mr. Tyler. Others had praised my work and supported me, but nobody had ever taken my work as seriously as he did.

Another anonymous writer found connection and academic motivation through sports. He writes:

> The coaches made us take football seriously. They wanted us to learn how to be disciplined, and to strive for excellence on the field and in the classroom.
>
> After three weeks of tryouts, the coaches said that a list of players who made the team would be posted on the wall outside the main gym.
>
> When I went to check the list the next day, I was nervous. I didn't want to be disappointed if I didn't make the team. When I saw my name on the list, I was so happy that I called my mother at her job to tell her the good news. I believed in myself from the start.

Though his team lost its final game and did not make the playoffs, it was still a valuable experience for the writer—with lessons that he carried back to the classroom:

> Playing football is the best thing that ever happened to me. I realized that God had given me a talent that I never knew I had until I walked on a football field. I learned how to work hard and how to be on time. I worked hard in both my classes and on the field.
>
> Playing football has motivated me to study harder, because I want to get a scholarship to a good university with a top-rated football team. I'm planning to major in pre-law, but I will also work hard to make the team.

If we provide students with other ways to demonstrate their competence, such as through coding and creating social justice web pages as Layla did, or through the arts or sports as the two anonymous writers did, then we create new opportunities for them to reveal their strengths. Once revealed, this new information about our students represents the counter-narrative that forces us to adjust our preconceived notions.

Focusing on helping students discover their competence and their strengths is not just good for them, it's good for us. Regularly calling out our students' strengths inevitably leads to viewing them in a more positive light, which helps us maintain that perspective when we're faced with challenges that might potentially reaffirm our implicit biases. It helps us to continually guard against looking for that one negative thing about a student that confirms the bias that we already held. When students sense that we have that habit of mind, they tend to respond more positively and to give us the benefit of the doubt when we make a mistake or make an assignment that feels irrelevant or overwhelming to them. That sense of trust contributes to increased learning.

3. Honor students' strengths by giving feedback on process, not just product.

In most cases, we have to assess our students and ultimately assign them a grade. However, we need to continually reflect on the value we place on their work *product* versus the value we place on their work *process*. If they've had to navigate multiple stressors outside of school, yet still strove to complete the assignment but got it wrong, how do we respond? What message does a low grade tell them about how much we value their resilience? On the other hand, how does minimizing their incorrect response support them academically?

To solve this riddle, we can think about all the skills that our students must demonstrate to successfully complete a task. For some students, the skills are exclusively academic and for others the skills are social, emotional, and organizational as well as academic. We need to provide positive feedback for the demonstration of all these skills rather than exclusively academic skills. That way, students will recognize that we value these skills as well. Remember that in writing about Ms. Stanford, Giselle observed that she was respected even by students she had failed multiple times. Ms. Stanford clearly held to her grading standards, but it's highly likely that she recognized and praised her students' efforts, even if they weren't yet up to passing standards.

One way to praise students' efforts is to intentionally use academic language to describe valuable non-academic skills that we notice. For example, if students found a way to navigate challenges at home, like preparing breakfast for younger siblings, and still make it to class on time, we might say that we appreciate their organizational skills. If they use social media to analyze their relationships with their peers or to learn about current events, we could praise their analytical skills. If they chose to avoid becoming involved in a potentially problematic situation, we might say that we appreciate their logical reasoning skills. When teachers use language that's typically reserved to describe academic skills to describe other strengths, it helps students to see the academic competencies they already have—and can build on. Once they can see that they possess the skills, then our job becomes guiding them to apply those skills to their academic work.

4. Use what we've learned about our students to make lessons more meaningful.

Being developmentally and culturally responsive isn't simply about what we know about our students. It's about what we do with that knowledge. It's important that as we work purposefully to learn more about our students' lives and concerns, we integrate that knowledge into our lessons, making them more meaningful to students. In the short run, this takes work and imagination, but in the long run it develops a more productive classroom that is focused more on learning and less on behavior management. Here are two examples of responsiveness. In the first, a teacher simply notices something about an individual student and deftly uses it to increase understanding and motivation. In the second, the teacher creates a more engaging lesson for an entire class.

Ebony Coleman, 18, writes:

> In global history, my teacher taught a lesson about feudalism and the caste system, comparing it to a typical high school's cliques and hierarchies. Since she knew that I dislike cliques, she used me to explain those who rebelled about the clergy, nobility, and feudalism in general. Because she put our lives—and me—into her explanation, I will remember that lesson on feudalism forever.

A chemistry teacher at a school where I was working on a research project said that she had been struggling to get her students to understand chemical reactions and had tried everything that she could. Her students were failing her tests and starting to skip class. She felt that there was little she could do to get them to care about chemistry.

One day she was so frustrated in class that she essentially stopped teaching and just let her students "do whatever they wanted to do as long as they weren't killing each other." What she noticed was that a few students got up from their seats and started singing and dancing. She didn't say anything and then noticed more and more joining in. Within a few minutes she noticed that most of her students were dancing and she "saw more smiles in that one period than I had seen the entire year in my class."

Out of desperation, she wondered if she could incorporate dance into her chemistry class. After searching the internet for ideas, she found that other chemistry teachers were also searching for ways to help their students better understand chemical reactions and better appreciate and enjoy chemistry. Amazingly, some had already found success by incorporating dance into their lessons. Since then, her students have been participating in their version of the Chemical Reaction Dance (there are numerous examples of this dance online) and she discovered a level of engagement and excitement in her class that she didn't think was possible.

In a moment of frustration, this teacher chose to observe and learn about her students rather than just judge them. She was also willing to modify her method of teaching and take a risk—one that made her lessons more meaningful for her students. By doing so, she not only was able to view her students in a new and more positive light, but she also provided opportunities for them to demonstrate their competence and reshape their perspective of themselves and their abilities.

Of course, one sensitive assignment won't change Ebony's life, and one lesson won't magically transform a chemistry class. Fortunately, an amazing thing about working with students is that small gestures can have very large payoffs. Ebony's "unforgettable" experience and the chemical reactions dance built trust and motivation that can last for a semester. Ironically, even a creative lesson that fails can succeed in the long run; students respect teachers who take risks that show respect and understanding of them.

5. Celebrate the victories.

It absolutely goes without saying that teaching is hard work. Most of our time and energy as educators is spent focusing on the needs of our students. Yet, sometimes we feel like we haven't helped them as much as we hoped and haven't made a difference. It's precisely in those times that we have to remember to celebrate our victories. Our students might not increase their grade in our class, but they might be building the habits that will support future success. They might try to answer a question when in the past they kept their head down. They may start an assignment that they used to avoid or ask for help when in the past they would just have quietly failed.

While none of these immediately lead to better grades, they're necessary steps on the path to improved learning. We must recognize this, take credit for how we've helped them, and take satisfaction in these accomplishments. By doing so, we not only reshape the way we think about our students but also reshape how we think about ourselves, our impact, and even our abilities as teachers.

What Schools Can Do

Researcher Dona Kagan has identified three things that schools can do to help teachers make positive changes in their beliefs about students. First, they can help teachers to make their preexisting personal beliefs explicit. Second, they can challenge the adequacy and accuracy of those beliefs. Finally, they can provide teachers with opportunities to examine, elaborate, and integrate new information into their existing belief systems.[8] It takes support at the school level.

1. Schools provide safe spaces where teachers and school leaders can share and reflect on their beliefs about teaching, learning, and their students.

The goal of reflective conversations is to identify beliefs that align with creating developmentally and culturally responsive learning experiences for all students and build school-wide consensus around them. Making those beliefs explicit enables the school community to assess whether they are teaching in ways that align with their beliefs. It also helps them identify how to better align their practices with their beliefs.

In several schools that I've worked with, Professional Learning Communities (PLCs) have been helpful mechanisms for advancing this work. Professional Learning Communities are comprised of educators who meet regularly, share expertise, and work collaboratively to improve their teaching skills and the academic performance of their students.[9] They promote deep conversations needed to strengthen developmentally and culturally competent education practices.

Richard DuFour, who has written extensively on PLCs, notes that effective PLCs inspire educators to focus on answering core questions like: "What school characteristics and practices have been most successful in helping all students achieve at high levels? How could we adopt those characteristics and practices in our own school? What commitments would we have to make to one another to create such a school? What indicators could we monitor to assess our progress?"[10]

I have worked with teachers and administrators in PLCs that have included training in implicit bias, participating in reading groups on culturally responsive teaching, and activities where educators articulated and reflected on their values, beliefs, and expectations for themselves, their administrators, and their students. An advantage of PLCs that are facilitated by teachers who are recognized and valued as leaders is that the recommendations are more likely to respond to the needs and conditions of the school or district. This makes them more likely to gain traction across the entire school community. (Reading this book and discussing the relevance of its research, teen stories, and recommendations could be the basis for a rich PLC at your school.)

2. School leaders are open to responsive and flexible teaching.

In many cases, teachers fear being reprimanded if they teach in ways that deviate from typical instructional methods. But as the anecdote about the teacher who taught chemistry through dance shows us, teachers may need to adopt nontraditional teaching practices to reveal students' strengths. Maybe a particular class requires more student movement, student voice, and student choice to promote student engagement and allow them to show what they know in new ways.

At times, this can cause classrooms to appear less disciplined and teachers seem less able to manage their classrooms. School leaders can show that they value such experimentation and risk-taking as teachers learn new ways to be developmentally and culturally responsive and praise those teachers for their ingenuity. Here's an example I heard recently: A new elementary school teacher, Sr. Benedicta, was teaching her class early in the year when the principal suddenly opened the door to her room with a look of concern. "Why is it so quiet in here?" the principal asked. The principal's simple question reset and expanded Sr. Benedicta's idea about what was expected of teachers in her new school.

3. Schools develop both support systems and accountability systems.

Once the school community has identified shared beliefs and identified practices that align with those beliefs, they must provide systems of support to ensure that all school stakeholders (teachers, school leaders, counselors and social workers, nurses, after-school staff, parents, and others) can address the needs of students. These support systems must address the diverse levels of skill and commitment among school staff. For example, teachers who exhibit the will and skill to teach in developmentally and culturally responsive ways may be encouraged to serve as instructional leaders within their school. Alternatively, those teachers who exhibit the will but lack the skill may need targeted support to adjust their current teaching practices. Finally, those who lack the will but are identified as being skilled teachers may need encouragement and reassurance that they can be leaders.

Ultimately, to ensure that all school stakeholders engage in practices that align with their shared beliefs, schools must also develop ways to gather information and hold themselves accountable. These could include regular school climate surveys of students and teachers that identify specific practices to be enhanced or reduced, a revised disciplinary code, changing parent-teacher conferences from reports on students to learning about parents and their challenges, and more. Regardless, accountability systems should inform stakeholders of the beliefs for which they're willing to be held accountable and establish ways to measure progress toward the goals related to those beliefs.

Here's an example of new accountability systems that a Brooklyn high school put into place after students issued a manifesto about the school's weak or nonexistent responses to racist behavior at the school. The writer, E.N., 15, contributed to the manifesto:

> [In response to the manifesto] the adult staff organized a town hall with student leaders. The staff acknowledged their negligence and assured us that our voices would be heard. We expressed our concerns and together we came up with consequences for racist behavior. For example, initially, there would be a mandated discussion with the student, their parents, and the dean. The punishments start with a one day in-school suspension and then the suspension levels become progressively more severe depending on the racism that took place. It was the end of the school year, so an email went out that summer with the new rules.
>
> When school re-started in September, there was an orientation reviewing them. The school also hosted mandatory events about bullying, cyber bullying, and racial awareness to prevent racist behavior. Other positive changes that came out of the town hall: The history curriculum was shifted to be less Eurocentric. We learn about how inaccurate and missing coverage of Black history perpetuates racism today.
>
> We also get thoughtful messages from school leaders and teachers. One teacher wrote to the whole school, "Right now, so many people are speaking up, spreading awareness, and going out on the streets to demand justice. We are all feeling the momentum of the Black Lives Matter movement. These protests are a result of years of oppression and feeling unheard emotions that are commonly expressed by students of color in the classroom."
>
> BLM news and resources are now part of every school announcement, along with info about awareness groups at school and in the community that students can participate in.

Before, I had not been outspoken about racism. I'm still kind of shy and have some social anxiety, but I'm a lot more comfortable now and able to express myself better, whether verbally or in writing.

I want readers to know that your voice can be valuable in ways large and small. Speaking my piece to some of my peers exposed their ignorance, which changed *something*, even if it was on a small scale. I brought awareness, and rebuked that racism in my own little way, while also being a part of bigger change.

Notes

1. Dweck 2015.

2. De Kraker-Pauw et al. 2017.

3. O'Rourke, Haimovitz, Ballweber, Dweck, and Popović 2014.

4. Gershenson, Holt, and Papageorge 2016.

5. Okonofua and Eberhardt 2015.

6. Ready and Wright 2011.

7. The overwhelming majority of prospective teachers in the United States (residing in 41 states and the District of Columbia) are now required to earn a passing score on the edTPA (a teacher certification exam) in order to be certified to teach. The edTPA is a teacher certification exam in which prospective teachers must (among other things) demonstrate multicultural competence and knowledge of children's cultural assets.

8. Kagan 1992.

9. https://www.edglossary.org/professional-learning-community/.

10. DuFour 2004.

References

DuFour, R. (2004). What is a "professional learning community"? *Educational Leadership* 61(8): 6–11.

Dweck, C. (2015). Carol Dweck revisits the growth mindset. *Education Week* 35(5): 20–24.

Gershenson, S., Holt, S.B., and Papageorge, N.W. (2016). Who believes in me? The effect of student–teacher demographic match on teacher expectations. *Economics of Education Review* 52: 209–224.

The Glossary of Educational Reform. https://www.edglossary.org/professional-learning-community/ (accessed 15 January 2019).

Kagan, D.M. (1992). Professional growth among preservice and beginning teachers. *Review of Educational Research* 62(2): 129–169.

Kraker-Pauw, D., Van Wesel, F., Krabbendam, L., and Van Atteveldt, N. (2017). Teacher mindsets concerning the malleability of intelligence and the appraisal of achievement in the context of feedback. *Frontiers in Psychology* 8: 1594.

Okonofua, J.A. and Eberhardt, J.L. (2015). Two strikes: Race and the disciplining of young students. *Psychological Science* 26(5): 617–624.

O'Rourke, E., Haimovitz, K., Ballweber, C., Dweck, C., and Popović, Z. (2014, April). Brain points: A growth mindset incentive structure boosts persistence in an educational game. In *Proceedings of the SIGCHI Conference on Human Factors in Computing Systems*, pp. 3339–3348.

Ready, D.D. and Wright, D.L. (2011). Accuracy and inaccuracy in teachers' perceptions of young children's cognitive abilities: The role of child background and classroom context. *American Educational Research Journal* 48(2): 335–360.

CHAPTER THREE

How Schools Influence Our Beliefs about Ourselves

In 9th grade, my algebra teacher encouraged me to apply to [a highly competitive enrichment] program, which helps students get into and through college. I filled out my application and a while later I got an email inviting me for an interview. I was ecstatic yet nervous because I'm a better writer than speaker. The morning of the interview, I practiced words that I pronounce with an accent like "water," "thought," "park," and "dog." I also planned not to talk with my hands by sitting on them. Although my father had raised me to be myself and not act a certain way to appease others or fit in, I knew I had to for this interview.

For me, code-switching is more than changing some words that you use and slightly altering your accent. When I code-switch, I am abandoning a piece of my identity. People's accents and dialects often represent where they are from. I feel like a part of me is trapped when I code-switch.

—Meagan Zullo, 15, "Why Do I Have to Change How I Talk to Sound 'Professional'?"

What Is Identity Development?

Who am I? It's a question that we've all asked at one time (and may continue to ask). At times, it seems like a question without an answer. At other times, it seems like a question with multiple answers. As scholar Beverly Tatum wrote,[1] identity is a complex concept because it's influenced by multiple factors that operate simultaneously, including our gender, race, and nationality. These factors enable us to define our own identity. But they also shape others' perceptions of us and can even impose an identity on us that we may not choose. For example, whether you identify as Cuban American, Haitian

American, or Nigerian American, in the United States, you might be categorized simply as Black by a teacher or store clerk. It's this combination of both internal and external factors that makes the study of identity and identity development so complex.

Our identity represents the categories that we're placed in, the categories we choose, and the categories we value and ultimately internalize. This interplay may cause us to hold multiple identities at any one time. For example, I'm a husband, father, university professor, and a person of Afro-Caribbean descent who identifies as Black. Each of these identities shapes how I see myself, how I interact with others, and how they interact with me. There's no priority placed on any one of these. They are all aspects of who I am. What makes any one of these more salient than the others is often influenced by the setting I'm in. When I'm at home, my professor identity is less important, and my husband and dad identities matter more.

The development of identity is typically associated with adolescence, a period marked by the onset of puberty and dramatic physical and cognitive growth. This cognitive growth prompts adolescents to think deeply about who they are and where they fit in the world. This process of self-reflection is also influenced by their interactions with others. Through these interactions, they begin to understand how they're perceived by others. They also become aware of the labels imposed on them by the outside world. It's through the synthesis and integration of these multiple sources of information that adolescents begin to clarify their "sameness" and "oneness," and ultimately, develop a coherent sense of who they are. For example, my behavior at work aligns with my professor identity, while I may act at home in a way that aligns with my identity as a dad. But, at my core, I'm the same person regardless of the setting.

We attribute much of our understanding of identity development to the work of developmental psychologist Erik Erikson.[2] Erikson viewed psychological development as moving through eight stages from infancy to late adulthood. At each stage, we're faced with a defining moment or "crisis" which (depending on how we resolve it) shapes our future psychological development. The more successfully we resolve these crises, the healthier our conscious sense of who we are will be.

Erikson viewed identity development as occurring during the fifth of the eight stages. During this stage (which he referred to as the stage of identity versus role confusion) adolescents approximately between the ages of 12 and 18 begin to explore their independence. They engage in self-exploration and self-reflection, asking themselves "Who am I?" and "Where do I fit in?" Erikson viewed this period of introspection as reflecting an internal crisis between the development of a coherent sense of who they are versus a lack of understanding of who they are.

This role confusion can make adolescents feel insecure and anxious as they try to figure out who they are, what they're good at, and where they're going in life. To resolve some of these internal questions, adolescents often try out different roles, engage in new kinds of activities, and experiment with different behaviors. As a teacher, I'm sure you've noticed how cliques in your class change over the course of a school year. Students who may have spent most of their time with peers who liked the same type of music may now hang out with a different group of students who share a similar focus on academics or who share a similar faith. Students who spent most of their time with other "good" and "smart" kids may now spend time doing "bad" things with the "bad" kids in a quest for popularity.

Parents and teachers might view teen experimentation as problematic and sometimes dangerous, but Erikson views it as a critical developmental process that results in the formation of a clearer sense of self and a more defined sense of purpose.

In the following excerpt, teen writer Jennifer Ramos, 17, reflects on her period of experimentation when she goes to live with her dad for a while:

> My parents separated when I was 1, and I grew up as an only child with my mother and grandmother. Life with them was boring. I had no one to play games or hang out with. Sometimes I'd catch Mom on a good day, usually on weekends, and we'd bug out together. We'd put on some music and start dancing around the house as if we were on Broadway. Other times, I made believe I was two people and played games alone.

> I didn't even have friends in school. I wasn't used to being social with people my age and I was too shy to talk to anyone I didn't know. No one bothered to ask me to be their friend, either. I was the fat, shy, smart girl in class that no one noticed. At least no one picked on me, though.

I dreamed of being cool. I imagined how my life would be different if I were in the "in" crowd; I'd know the good gossip and I'd say "hi" to everyone when I walked down hallways. I envied the attention they got.

When I saw my father though, on occasional weekends, he paid attention to me. When I was little, he'd swing me around and carry me on his shoulders. We played kiddie games and laughed at silly jokes. He treated me like a princess.

Then, the summer after 7th grade, I got to move in with my dad in Pennsylvania, where he lived with his girlfriend and her two kids, Sandra and Luis. I didn't get to see my father much, though. I only saw him at night and on weekends because he worked long hours during the week.

But to my surprise, I had a lot of fun. I was able to hang out with actual people and not just myself. I went to parties with Sandra and Luis, who were a little older than me, and my two cousins, Cara, who was 16, and Adam, 17. They became my buddies.

Being social was a new experience for me. My new buddies took me to my first club on my 12th birthday. I had a blast. I hung out, met guys, and afterwards we got wasted on beer and hard liquor. That began my phase of trying drugs like alcohol, cigarettes, and marijuana, which I'd never even thought of doing before.

I was curious and excited to be experimenting. I thought I was cool. I felt like I belonged. Even though I was heavy, it didn't seem to matter to my buddies. I felt like an adult. No one told me I couldn't do something because I was too young.

Daddy wasn't aware of what we did. He worked all day and came home too late to worry. And when he was suspicious of us smoking, we lied about it. But I think if he'd found out, he'd have been furious.

I had arrived at my Dad's house a shy and obedient child, but by the end of the summer I had changed into a social and wild adolescent. For the first time in my life, I felt included and free.

But after six months at my Dad's, my buddies started to treat me differently. It was a shock to me because it came out of nowhere. I still don't know what happened. They made fun of my squeaky voice, my non-hip-hop style, my weight, my glasses, and my frizzy hair.

I felt like I was thrown into a desert and vultures were surrounding me, waiting for me to let my guard down. I felt alone in a house full of people. It was like I wasn't even part of their family. I was an outcast.

I started to take drinking and smoking pot and cigarettes seriously. I started depending on them. I kept telling myself that being high would take away the madness. I smoked every day so that I didn't have to recognize when I was being teased.

Sometimes one of my cousins or step-siblings acted nice to me so that they could smoke, too. Then the next day they'd start teasing me again. But the more I smoked, the more I forgot about everything around me. I called Mom many times to ask her to take me back, but every time she gave me an excuse.

Jennifer's experience of trying on new roles and new behaviors as she enters adolescence is not uncommon. Notice the yearning for belonging, acceptance, and status that underlie her actions. As teachers of adolescents, we must realize that these needs are a natural part of their development and satisfying these needs can take various forms—some healthy, others less so. So, it's important to create opportunities and structures for adolescents to satisfy those needs in healthy ways that make them feel cared for, affirm their voice, and help them feel good about themselves.

How We Can Shape Our Own Identity

Jennifer describes her transformation from a "shy and obedient child" to a social adolescent and eventually to a "wild adolescent" trying to figure out where she fits in. At first, she tries to fit in with her dad's new family by being "obedient." As she connects with her new stepsiblings and cousins, she becomes more social. To maintain the social connections that made her finally feel accepted, she ultimately becomes what she refers to as the "wild" child. As she tried to figure out where she fit in and who she connected with, she experimented with different "roles" (obedient, social, wild) and tended to "act" in a way that matched each role.

Psychologist James Marcia proposed a helpful extension of Erikson's theory of identity.[3] Rather than viewing adolescence as a time in which we develop a fully formed identity or we suffer identity confusion, Marcia theorized that identity development was related to whether we experience an identity crisis and what we do after we live through one. For Marcia, the term *crisis* represents a period in which adolescents are exploring roles and then committing to ones that are most personally meaningful.

Marcia found that identity crises are resolved in one of four ways: (1) identity diffusion, (2) identity foreclosure, (3) identity moratorium, and (4) identity achievement. We may find ourselves working with students in any one of these states.

Identity diffusion represents a time in which adolescents have not yet experienced an identity crisis, and as a result, have not made a commitment to any particular role.

Identity foreclosure is a period when adolescents have committed to a role but haven't experienced an identity crisis. For example, if an adolescent was raised by a family that ran a business, they may feel pressured to take over the business when they're older. If they accept this as their only possible role, they don't experience a crisis, but they've made a commitment to that role.

During identity moratorium, adolescents are experiencing an identity crisis, but have not made a commitment to any role. During this time, adolescents are grappling with critical questions (such as "Where do I fit in?" and "What do I want to do with my life?"). They may gravitate toward peers who share similar interests and may seek the advice of teachers or counselors about possible vocations.

Finally, identity achievement results from an adolescent experiencing an identity crisis and making a commitment to an identity. This commitment might be to join a school team or club. Or it could be volunteering at a local congregation or even joining a gang. Each of these is a commitment to exploring a particular role.

So, what does that crisis and commitment look like for real teens? In this excerpt, Marlo Scott, 19, reflects on the choices he made in order to be accepted by his peers, and the personal commitment he made to redefine himself and find a sense of purpose:

My mother died from cancer when I was 11. I was sad, then angry. I was angry that her death left us without a stable income, and I missed having my mother around to support me. During my sophomore year in high school, I was living with my father and brother, and we were in and out of shelters.

One day, a month after my mother's funeral, I was in the cafeteria at school. I was in the 6th grade. I usually sat at the table with the cool kids, mostly because some of them paid me to do their homework. One kid in a different 6th grade class yelled to me, "Hey, can you do my homework too?"

I said, "There is a small fee of $5 involved."

He threatened me, "I'm broke, but you're still gonna' do my homework."

I replied, "Just ask your parents for $5, and then we can do business."

He said, knowing I had just lost my mom, "Forget it then. I'll just go ask your mother for help with my homework."

Adrenaline and rage shot through my body. I stood up and hit him so hard his glasses broke and his eye started bleeding. "Now go ask your mother to buy you a pair of new glasses, punk!" I yelled.

All the cool kids and even some of the 7th and 8th graders ran over and asked what happened. My homeboy, the one whose homework I was doing, said, "Just don't disrespect his mother and you won't end up blind, like that kid."

Everyone started laughing and high-fiving me. Many of the 8th graders complimented me for sticking up for myself. Talk of me hitting this kid spread throughout the school.

This group of nine homeboys who hung out on my block also heard about the fight. They were boys ranging from age 13 to 18 who mostly grew up in single-parent households. They cut school and hung out a lot, and even though I was only 11, I joined them. We were not part of a bigger gang, so we called ourselves a crew. We robbed people but did not really get into fights over territory like a gang.

When an argument arose among the homeboys, we would fight each other. We lived by the rule, "No talking, just fight it out." I was a good fighter. I began to receive respect from my homeboys and from some kids at school for being tough and fearless.

I liked the principles of the crew: confidentiality (telling anyone what we did could lead to arrest), toughness, and progress. Progress to us meant getting money, which we imagined would eventually buy expensive cars and big homes. My crew's version of progress was simple, and for a while, that was enough for me.

We mostly fought each other, but if someone jumped a homeboy of ours, we would retaliate. I would fight anybody, anywhere, at any time. I would try to scare strangers or insult them by cursing a lot. Feeling as if I could beat the world turned me into a thug.

Society saw me as a menace. People would clutch their belongings tighter when I passed them on the street. I liked that "looking-glass self" of threatening thug. In the eyes of the other punks on the block, I was the man. Being tough impressed certain girls and earned the respect of my homeboys. I had money and nice clothes. I now had two mirrors reflecting back to me: scared strangers and admiring homeboys and girls. I liked the way I looked in both of them.

Still, while I talked back to my teachers, I always did my homework. I was rebellious, but I was not stupid. I knew school could be a key to success. Most of the older men on the block, who had also been in crews, suggested I stay in school, but they also applauded me for being a fighter.

When I was a freshman in high school I realized for sure that I did not want a thug life. I was a strong student in algebra and the teacher applied math to real-world topics. One day he asked me to solve a statistics problem, and I did within minutes. He was surprised and praised my accounting skills.

Ever since that moment, I have wanted to be an accountant. And that meant changing my behavior, attitude, and appearance. In the corporate world you cannot impress people by how many people you can beat up: You impress them with your intellect and skill. I stuck with school through many obstacles and enrolled in a business college.

I studied hard and did all the work, but I had not completely left my thug self behind. In my first-semester computer class, I was very disrespectful to the professor. He wanted all eyes on him, but I wanted to talk to girls in the back of the class. When he reprimanded me, I told him to shut up.

I was still attracted to the hood reflection of myself as a wise guy. Unfortunately, the computer professor started to view me as a menace, and I knew I had to change. I wanted a corporate looking-glass self, not the hood version. Therefore, I had to do things to impress corporate society, not hood society.

The inner change had already happened. I had already embraced the principles that accountants must follow: confidentiality, honesty, accuracy, and faithful representation. I like that in accounting the path is clear, because there is a specific way to succeed. Good accountants are smart, responsible, diligent, logical, stable, and most importantly, honest. Besides accounting, I am also studying general theories of business and management, which teach that the most ethical leaders are the most successful.

Making it to college a year early and making the dean's list my first semester helped me believe I had all those good accountant qualities. I liked these better than the qualities that made me chief of the homeboys.

Consistent with Marcia's theory, Marlo's experience of a crisis (in this case, using an unhealthy strategy to satisfy his need to be accepted) and his personal commitment to change from a "hood looking-glass self" to a "corporate looking-glass self" helped him develop a sense of his identity. In the end, he's able to experience the value of making that commitment to change as he reflects on his success in college.

But what happens when an adolescent doesn't move through the stages of identity development in the way that both Erikson and Marcia describe? More importantly, if an adolescent doesn't move, does it always result in a negative outcome?

Marcia's theory says that if adolescents lack opportunities to explore different roles, they may experience confusion because they're unsure of who they are and what their future path might be. But in some cases, not following the stages as Erikson and Marcia describe them doesn't cause negative consequences. For example, what if a child knew from an early age that he or she was going to be responsible for continuing a business that his or her parents started and was happy to do so? What if, as a result, the child didn't explore different roles, but simply focused on one that his or her parents defined for him or her? This type of identity foreclosure is often viewed as a negative, but it could be perceived by the child as a sign of honor and a sign of his or her parents' belief in their ability to continue their legacy.

While Erikson and Marcia could very well be right that this foreclosure could influence how a teen thinks about their future, it doesn't always mean that those thoughts are negative. For example, teens experiencing role confusion might not be interested in applying to college or exploring certain vocations. The key question is why? From a developmental perspective, it could be that they simply haven't reached that level of maturity (but we assume they have) or it could be that they accept a role bestowed on them by their parents and haven't felt the need to explore other roles.

It's important to note that theories of human development, such as those regarding identity development, have traditionally reflected Western cultural values of independence and individualism. Several scholars have noted that these values stress creativity, curiosity, assertiveness, and self-esteem.[4] However, cross-cultural studies of human development find many non-Western cultures more highly emphasize and reward the collectivistic values of responsibility, honesty, politeness, respect for elders, and loyalty to family. The field of cultural psychology has shown that typical interdependent and collectivist values in many cultures may be viewed as atypical when viewed through the Western lens that emphasizes individualism and independence.[5]

As a teacher, I've come to view these theories as something that should inform my teaching but not constrain it. I've learned that there will be exceptions—students who don't follow the typical developmental path—and it's important for me not to make negative assumptions about them simply because their path to identity achievement might differ from my own or from the implicit standards of Western culture.

The Power of Peers and Identity

For most of us, our teens were a time when our parents' influence waned and our peers' influence gained. We began questioning our parents' rules and adopting ideas, fashion, and other tastes that were more similar to the attitudes of our peers rather than our parents'. We looked less often to our parents and caregivers for comfort and support, and instead sought out our friends. This age-old pattern can make parents (and perhaps teachers) feel rejected, but that adolescent connection between peers is an important aspect of development.

In fact, recent research has found that positive relationships with peers, both romantic relationships and platonic friendships, can bolster adolescents through their process of identity exploration.[6] According to this research, peers provide each other with everything from companionship and social support to physical and psychological safety.[7] These connections are important to how adolescents come to understand who they are and what they're good at. But while peers can provide a powerful positive impact, of course, sometimes peer relationships can have a negative influence.

In the following essay, an anonymous 17-year-old from the Bronx reflects on his behavior in elementary, middle, and high school and discusses how his relationships with his peers influenced not only how he behaved, but how he felt about himself:

> When I was ages 10 to 14, I was a monster. It was as if my conscience had taken a long vacation. I did horrible things to people and didn't care.
>
> I ripped into other kids and mocked them till they cried. My friends and I called one kid "Bobby the Beaver" because of his teeth. We gnawed on pencils in front of him, making him squirm. And the other kids would laugh. We thought we were funny.
>
> At school, I went into people's desks or bags and took things. I stole from stores for the fun of it, too. I did it once and I got away with it, so that inspired me to do it again.

I enjoyed going into nice neighborhoods, like the Upper East Side, and scratching up expensive cars. I'd find a big gaudy car, like a Benz or a Lexus. Then I'd wait until no one was looking and scratch my initials on the trunk and put "album coming soon."

I never stopped to think why I did these things. I did them because I could.

I think I got so mean because when I was younger, people in school picked on me. I had a bit of a stammer, and I was taller than most of the class. I was a very hyper but nice kid, but I got the vibe that people didn't like me and thought of me as stupid. We played charades once in class and though the correct word was "stupid," several kids called out my name as the answer. That hurt.

I had one close friend, but he left in 4th grade, and then I didn't have any friends. The other kids in school avoided me and the girls ran away from me in the play yard. I felt alienated.

Since people didn't like me, I thought I might as well give them a reason. I started chasing the girls around and making monster noises. They hated it. But I thought it was funny.

Being picked on made me angry, and I turned being bigger to my advantage. My favorite activity was sitting on people. If someone said or did something to me, I'd push him on the floor and sit on him. "I could do this all day," I'd say. "I'm not getting off you until you apologize to me." I got my apologies.

I wanted respect, and I discovered that if I was tough, people respected me. Or maybe they feared me—I didn't understand the difference.

I fought over anything. I'd take on kids younger than me, my age, or older, whole groups, girls—anybody, as long as I thought I could win.

I liked the power I commanded over the situation and that made my actions bolder over time. I took things up a notch. A stare deserved a smart-ass comment, a smart-ass comment deserved a push, a push deserved a few punches, a few punches deserved getting stomped.

When I got to junior high school I was able to use my "talents" to acquire a group of like-minded friends. I was in charge. I admired my friends' humor, though. I'd point someone out and they would start dissing them.

But then there was Lisa. She was different from the other girls at my school. She was into art, books, classical music, and school—everything I wasn't. She was the first girl I fell in love with.

In my last year of junior high, I asked her to tutor me in math because it was the easiest way to start talking to her. I acted really nice toward Lisa and we talked a lot during our tutoring sessions. Our conversations brought out my intellectual side. I came to really love her and enjoy her company.

But when Lisa caught on to how I felt for her, she totally crushed me. She sat me down one day and said she could never see herself with me. "I think you're a horrible person," she said.

It surprised me, because she was the first person I was ever really good to and I thought she at least liked me as a person. She stopped tutoring me and we stopped talking. And whenever her friends were around, she'd make a negative comment about me loud enough for me to hear it. I couldn't say anything back because I cared about her too much to hurt her. I felt the way I must've made people feel, small and hurt.

Around the same time, I had another experience that threw me off course. My friends and I were hanging out with some girls from school, and one girl was hanging on my friend Tommy. Suddenly, some high school guys ran up. They were a lot bigger than we were. The girl with Tommy was seeing one of them, and he walked up to Tommy, punched him and pushed him on the ground.

I ran. I left out of fear. I picked fights I could win, and I didn't think I could win this one. Some of my friends were mad at me. They questioned my loyalty. The incident polarized my group of friends. While some supported me, I stopped hanging out with most of them.

These combined dramas took all the joy out of my work of being nasty. I got really depressed in the last couple of weeks of junior high school. I felt heartbroken by Lisa and bummed by what happened between my friends.

Then I started at a different high school than my friends, and I didn't know anyone. I got really reclusive and I sank into a depression. I didn't have my heart in harming people anymore. I tried it a few times, just to get my confidence going, but it didn't work.

In junior high I had so much power, but in high school I was nothing. I was anonymous and, more than anything, that drove me crazy.

I had no meaningful contact with anyone for two years. I felt that I didn't really know how to act toward people if they weren't in fear of me. I became very brooding and quiet. But eventually I realized I wanted a change. The first thing I did was change schools. I applied and got into an alternative school.

My goal when I left my old high school was to learn how to be social and to interact normally with people my own age. I had to learn how to communicate my feelings and ideas without being mean or aggressive. I also had to learn to respect people and not to insist on what I wanted.

First, I started observing people. When I used to pick on people, I'd study them to see where they might be vulnerable. So I thought I should also study people I wanted to be my friends.

I'd watch people and the way they interacted. I made mental notes, like, "This girl touches her friends as she talks to them; she's outgoing and seems well-liked."

Then, I tried striking up conversations on the train or bus, and in school. Sometimes people would open up to me during these encounters and I began to see people in a whole new light.

I began to see the beauty of people, something that never really struck me till I started to interact with them. I saw how frail a person can be, or honest, or compassionate, or smart or funny. I developed a sense of empathy. I started to understand what people are going through and have been through to act the way they do.

One person who helped set me on my current path was Anna. I met her on the bus. It was the first time I'd ever talked to a girl outside of school.

She had headphones on and I could hear the music, so I decided to ask her about it.

When I introduced myself, I said my full name and she said, smiling, "I am Anna and the rest of my name I can't pronounce." She was funny and had a sarcasm that made her approachable.

I told her I was 16, and she said, "Aww, you're a baby." (She was 20 but looked younger.) If someone had said something like that to me before, I would've gotten upset, but the way she said it sounded like a compliment.

Anna was from Europe and would fall into an accent when she told stories about life in her country. We didn't spend much time together, but we'd talk on the phone once or twice a week. Then, for a week, I tried calling and couldn't reach her.

When I did, she sounded sad. She told me her best friend had died and she was too depressed to do anything. It bothered me hearing her upset. But during our talk, I was able to make her laugh a few times and she told me that was the first time she'd laughed since her friend's death.

Making her feel better made me feel good. I was happy I could do that for her. Even though she moved away soon after that and we lost touch, my friendship with Anna made me realize how good it felt to help someone.

Then, I decided to talk to Shelly, a girl in my class, because it seemed that no one else was paying attention to her. I thought she was smart, but she later told me that people talked down to her. I knew what that felt like.

She reminded me of myself. I know what it's like to be alone and I don't like thinking that other people are alone. Most people have their issues, but they're good at heart.

With Shelly, there's a high level of trust—I can tell her things and be vulnerable to her in the way that she can be vulnerable to me. She helps me feel better about things, too.

Now, a lot of people see me as Mr. Rogers because I'm mostly friendly and unassuming. I do well in school. I'm helpful and polite. Most people assume that I've always been a good guy, but I know that's far from the case.

I know what I did in the past can't be erased, but these days what makes me happy is relating to people, having them trust me and letting them know that they're not all alone.

This excerpt describes how the writer's experiences in elementary and middle school influenced his identity development. His early rejection by his peers left him feeling alienated and powerless. These feelings prompted a need to be noticed by his peers that resulted in negative behavior as a way to establish his status. From his perspective, being noticed by his peers for doing something bad was better than going unnoticed. Unfortunately, these negative behaviors toward others made it hard to build positive relationships with his peers. Ultimately, this lack of positive relationships stunted his ability to make friends and maintain friendships.

After reflecting on his negative peer experiences and switching schools, his goal was to "learn how to be social" and how to "interact normally with people [his] own age." He then realized that he could use his skill at observing people to interact with others in positive ways. These positive connections with Anna and Shelly helped him learn that caring, trusting relationships with others made him happy. He also learned that the respect that he thought he could gain only by instilling fear in others could now be won by helping others.

Like most adolescents, the writer's identity development was largely influenced by his experiences in school: losing his one close friend in 4th grade, finding a like-minded peer group in junior high school, and redefining himself after transferring to a new high school. These school experiences helped him become someone whose strength and power could be demonstrated through his care for others.

What Teachers Can Do

1. Create safe spaces for students to explore their identity.

An important way that teachers can help their students develop a sense of who they are is by creating what Becki Cohn-Vargas and Dorothy M. Steele refer to as "identity safe classrooms." These are classrooms that promote a sense of belonging and value for students of all backgrounds.[8]

Their research found that to create identity safe classrooms, teachers should: (1) teach in student-centered ways that promote autonomy, cooperation, and student voice; (2) convey high expectations for all students; (3) ensure that students treat each other kindly and fairly; and (4) support the social and emotional well-being of students through social skill building activities designed to promote positive peer relationships. Sites such as @TeacherToolkit (https://www.teachertoolkit.co.uk) and Identity Safe Classrooms (https://www.identitysafeclassrooms.org) provide useful and practical information on how to structure identity safe classrooms.

The Youth Communication resources, https://www.youthcomm.org/curriculum-training/#curricula, are designed to help students explore their identities while helping teachers create more student-centered classrooms, build a climate of trust and support, and strengthen social and emotional competencies.

2. Help students see their strengths.

Another way to create identity safe spaces is to help students to get a better sense of their strengths. Teachers can help students realize what they're good at by providing them with multiple ways to demonstrate their academic competence beyond grades.

Some students might simply believe that they lack the ability to succeed in school because they earn lower grades. One way to counteract that mindset is to provide a variety of ways for students to demonstrate their competence. For example, a high school teacher I work with provides students with options for being assessed. They can write a paper, give an oral presentation, or propose a project. These options provide students with the chance to identify the assessment format that they're most comfortable with and choose different ways to demonstrate what they've learned. These options also help students to identify strengths beyond the classroom. For example, a student who prefers oral presentations may see themself as a talented public speaker. This teacher provided her students a way to try on different roles and supported their identity development.

3. Help students establish goals.

These spaces also help create classroom cultures where students feel safer opening up to us in ways that help us support them in determining how to achieve their goals. As teachers, we often post learning goals for our students that are tied to the curriculum. However, supporting positive identity development involves guiding students in developing their goals. One common goal-setting strategy is the creation of SMART goals (Specific, Measurable, Attainable, Realistic, Time-bound). SMART goals help students identify specific steps that they can take to achieve a personal objective.

I recently sat down with a middle school student who I have worked with for many years. He had just failed a test. Before I could say a word, he said, "I know, I know, I'll do better the next time," and then began to walk away. I stopped him and asked, "What exactly are you going to do?" He replied, "I'm not gonna lie, I have no idea." Rather than having the goal of "doing better the next time," SMART goals might include meeting with his teacher after school twice a week for a month to review his notes, asking questions prior to each test, getting help from peers on taking better notes, and resolving to pass the next test. This specific step-by-step plan helps students to see their goals as more attainable and increases their chances of success.

Here's an example of that kind of determination and its payoff. In 8th grade, Edgar Lopez visited Lincoln University in Pennsylvania. He was shocked to learn that even though the professors were not looking over their shoulders every minute, students still did huge amounts of studying. He realized that his style of working only when he was closely watched and supported was not going to work in the future. He called it "being babied." He talked with a teacher who, with some trepidation, agreed to monitor him from afar as he tried to become a more independent learner.

At first, he failed several classes because he no longer felt the watchful eye of his teachers but hadn't grown into his new identity as an independent learner. Then, after a year of floundering:

> I decided to cut out the baby in me and do what I needed to do to improve my grades. I developed a study schedule. Every day I devoted no less than 30 minutes to every subject I received homework for, instead of not studying at all, like before. Instead of complaining that I didn't know about a topic, I began to read more about it.

> And instead of spending money on expensive sneakers or clothes, I invested in myself. I went to Barnes & Noble and found biology textbooks that targeted standardized tests and went into more depth than my schoolbooks.

> By the end of my freshman year, I realized I was working independently. My study habits were now a part of my routine. My greatest moment was seeing my report card that June.

> I had done better in all of my classes. I was most excited to see an 85 for my French class, the hardest class I had. Through my own persistence I had improved my grade by 15 points.

4. Help students to develop positive peer relationships.

Peers help adolescents develop a sense of purpose by helping them to better understand who they are and what they're good at. To help promote positive peer relationships, teachers should create lessons that promote interdependence among students. These lessons might include activities that require students to work together to achieve a goal. These activities can be peer-to-peer, small group, or large group.

While peer-based activities are common in many classrooms, I've noticed that effective teachers help students strengthen skills that will enable them to develop and sustain positive peer relationships. These skills include active listening and responding with empathy. The George Lucas Educational Foundation's Edutopia site has resources that teachers can use to foster active listening and empathic responding skills (https://www.edutopia.org/article/value-active-listening).

What Schools Can Do

1. Help students develop their sense of purpose.

Throughout this chapter, we've discussed that a key feature of adolescence is developing a sense of who we are, what we're good at, and what we'd like to do with our lives. This process of self-exploration can also be viewed as a search for a sense of purpose (involving determining life goals, setting short- and long-term objectives that align with those goals, and engaging in behaviors to achieve those goals).[9] In this way, a sense of purpose helps adolescents better understand who they are and also helps guide where they're going.

Having a sense of purpose benefits adolescents in many ways. Adolescents with a sense of purpose report feeling more in control of their daily lives and are more likely to engage in activities that align with their short- and long-term goals.[10] They also tend to feel more capable of navigating life's challenges.[11] This sense of purpose has also been found to be a protective factor for youth as they face the typical challenges of adolescence. In examining the development of purpose among adolescents, researchers Patrick Hill, Anthony Burrow, and Rachel Summer reported the following:

> Adolescents with greater purpose appear less likely to drink alcohol and use drugs. In addition, teenagers in high-risk environments report less use of violence when they have a sense of purpose in life. Finally, youth with purpose in life are less likely to be depressed or to have suicidal thoughts. Therefore, not only does purpose promote positive outcomes during adolescence, but it also may reduce risk for maladaptive outcomes. (p. 234)

A sense of purpose provides adolescents with a "North Star"—a destination to focus on as they navigate the inevitable pitfalls of life. As we've discussed, this destination can be a short-term one (like making the honor roll at school or excelling in a sport) or it can be more long-term (like becoming a teacher or a professional athlete). A sense of purpose helps adolescents to be more self-reflective about how their behaviors relate to their goals.

A sense of purpose doesn't eliminate peer pressure, the desire to fit in, or the other challenges of adolescence. It doesn't stop an adolescent from feeling insecure about their appearance or their intellect. However, it does help adolescents reflect on the outcomes of their decisions and how those decisions impact their ability to achieve their goals. In this way, a sense of purpose helps adolescents refine their understanding of who they are and supports their identity development.

Schools can support the identity development of students by providing them with opportunities to explore their areas of interest, by creating a learning environment that redefines and broadens students' definitions of what it means to be competent, and by creating a culture that respects and values all students.

To help students develop a better sense of who they are and what they're good at, schools should provide opportunities for them to explore content beyond the traditional academic subjects. For example, elective courses and internships can provide students with opportunities to explicitly apply the academic skills and knowledge they've developed in their core classes to areas of special interest. They also provide students with opportunities to choose what they would like to learn more about, and often give students the chance to connect with teachers who share their interests.[12]

Here's a classic example described by Amanda Slamin, 17. After doing poorly in a traditional high school, she transferred to a school that allowed students to earn some of their credits through internships:

> For once I am enthusiastic about school, an enthusiasm I thought didn't exist in me—I love what I am doing. I look forward to going into work at the newspaper and the radio station. I found out that I learn better from hands-on experience, from seeing a job through from beginning to end.
>
> I like completing assignments that I carry out on my own, such as booking guests for a show at the radio station or thinking of my own ideas for stories.
>
> I am learning more in this one year than in the three years at my other high schools. It is really preparing me for the future.

> The skills I am learning will continue to help me. I've learned technical skills, like typing, recording, editing, and taping. But I also have learned assertiveness, how to deal with people, patience, how to meet deadlines, self-confidence, and responsibility.

This school experience directly influenced Amanda's purpose and motivation; she became a radio and TV producer.

2. Develop diverse opportunities for students to see themselves as competent.

Another way in which schools can promote positive identity development is by helping students to see themselves as competent. Because schools tend to focus on grades in core subjects as the primary way that students can demonstrate their skills, they may unintentionally restrict other ways students can see themselves as competent.

While honor rolls or other academic awards are important ways to recognize and reward students for their academic success, expanding the ways we formally recognize achievements helps to broaden their definitions of competence. For example, in addition to academic recognition, schools might formally recognize students for their leadership, citizenship, service, teamwork, or other positive experiences, such as the internship that showed Amanda a whole new side of herself.

In the final story in this chapter, Daniel Kingsley describes how the opportunity to participate on a debate team helps him overcome the feeling that he was an undesirable loser and brings out a different side of himself:

> In gym, whenever teams were selected, I was picked last, along with other socially undesirable people. I was the laughingstock of gym class. Being athletically hapless made me feel inferior. Deep down, though, I knew that not knowing how to balance myself on a bicycle or roller-skate faster than an old man with a walker did not define me as a human being.
>
> But my athletic limitations also limited my outlets for competition. Although I couldn't connect a bat to a baseball or sink a basket, I still had a strong desire to compete.

When I was 14, I gained that true sense of competition. Not on the athletic fields, but on the sacred floor of speech and debate.

There, I competed against other debaters as I tried to advance my position on different issues, from gay marriage to affirmative action.

When I attended my first debate at Christ the King HS. The topic was the outlawing of public breastfeeding.

"Of all the issues in the modern world," I'd thought when I'd first heard the topic, "I can't believe they chose public breastfeeding for discussion." What could I, an adolescent boy, say about this issue, and how would it ever affect me?

But then I learned that a woman had been either fined or threatened with arrest for breastfeeding her newborn child in the subway. As I listened to my teammates discuss the topic, I realized that I didn't see anything filthy about a woman breastfeeding her child.

In the evening, I talked to my father, who is from Africa, where women breastfeed in public more often than they do here. He said he thought we must live in a sex-crazed society if people see a woman breastfeeding in public as somehow unclean.

I felt pretty badly afterward, and humiliated too. But, unlike gym, where I tried and tried again and never got any better, I believed I could master debate. I had strong opinions, and I'd made clear arguments plenty of times before for class papers and in the school newspaper.

In the weeks before our second debate, I paid attention to Mr. Russo's advice and tried to emulate the speaking styles of my teammates every time we had practice. Sometimes I became the butt of their jokes. But other times I got positive feedback.

From them, I learned how to pace myself and use emotion to emphasize my point. I'll never forget the day Mr. Russo explained to me that it's not good to leave my mouth hanging open when I forget what I was going to say. After that, I learned how to just go on talking.

At home, I wrote out speeches on the subjects we'd be debating, which included whether the U.S. should continue to give aid to Israel, and what the effects of the Internet are on democracy. I recited them in front of my mother and the mirror, making sure to speak with clear and precise pronunciation.

At my second debate, I scored an eighth-place trophy. True, it was a plastic trophy. But I am proud of it.

Notes

1. Tatum 1992.

2. Erikson and Erikson 1998.

3. Marcia 1966.

4. Gallimore and Goldenberg 2001; Rogoff 1990; Tomasello 1999.

5. Berry 2005; Berry et al. 2002; Cole 1998; Rohner 1984.

6. Luyckx, Klimstra, Duriez, Van Petegem, and Beyers 2013.

7. Klimstra 2013.

8. Steele and Cohn-Vargas 2013.

9. Hill, Burrow, and Summer 2013.

10. Burrow, O'Dell, and Hill 2010.

11. Damon, Menon, and Cotton Bronk 2003.

12. Wolpert-Gawron 2018.

References

Berry, J.W. (2005). Acculturation: Living successfully in two cultures. *International Journal of Intercultural Relations* 29(6): 697–712.

Berry, J.W., Poortinga, Y.H., Segall, M.H., and Dasen, P.R. (2002). *Cross-Cultural Psychology: Research and Applications.* Cambridge, UK: Cambridge University Press.

Burrow, A.L., O'Dell, A.C., and Hill, P.L. (2010). Profiles of a developmental asset: Youth purpose as a context for hope and well-being. *Journal of Youth and Adolescence* 39(11): 1265–1273.

Chavez, A.F. and Guido-DiBrito, F. (2002). Racial and ethnic identity development. *New Directions for Adult and Continuing Education, 1999* 84: 39–47.

Cole, M. (1998). *Cultural Psychology: A Once and Future Discipline*. Cambridge, MA: Harvard University Press.

Damon, W., Menon, J., and Cotton Bronk, K. (2003). The development of purpose during adolescence. *Applied Developmental Science* 7(3): 119–128.

Erikson, E.H. and Erikson, J.M. (1998). *The Life Cycle Completed (extended version)*. New York: W.W. Norton & Company.

Gallimore, R. and Goldenberg, C. (2001). Analyzing cultural models and settings to connect minority achievement and school improvement research. *Educational Psychologist* 36(1): 45–56.

Hill, P.L., Burrow, A.L., and Sumner, R. (2013). Addressing important questions in the field of adolescent purpose. *Child Development Perspectives* 7(4): 232–236.

Klimstra, T. (2013). Adolescent personality development and identity formation. *Child Development Perspectives* 7(2): 80–84.

Luyckx, K., Klimstra, T.A., Duriez, B., Van Petegem, S., and Beyers, W. (2013). Personal identity processes from adolescence through the late 20s: Age trends, functionality, and depressive symptoms. *Social Development* 22(4): 701–721.

Marcia, J.E. (1966). Development and validation of ego-identity status. *Journal of Personality and Social Psychology* 3(5): 551.

Rohner, R.P. (1984). Toward a conception of culture for cross-cultural psychology. *Journal of Cross-Cultural Psychology* 15(2): 111–138.

Steele, D.M and Cohn-Vargas, B. (2013). Identity safe classrooms: Places to belong and learn. Thousand Oaks, CA: Corwin Press.

Tatum, B. (1992). Talking about race, learning about racism: The application of racial identity development theory in the classroom. *Harvard Educational Review* 62(1): 1–25.

Wolpert-Gawron, H. (2018). The Case for Electives in Schools, https://www.edutopia.org/article/case-electives-schools (accessed 25 April 2019).

How Schools Shape Gender and Racial Identity Development

I started to express my newfound self-love at school. I wore African head-ties, clothing, and jewelry. My friends complimented me a lot and it helped me make new friends with people in my school who saw that I was celebrating my culture and admired me for it.

—Aishamanne Williams, 16, "Dashikis and Dreadlocks: Learning to Be Black and Proud"

Fortunately, I had supportive friends and teachers. My guidance counselor didn't tell my family I was trans. She encouraged me to join our school's GSA (Gay-Straight Alliance). By talking to people in GSA, I learned that not every LGBTQ+ kid has a family that accepts them and goes to the Pride parade decked out in rainbows and glitter. It was a relief to know I wasn't alone.

—Anonymous, 17, "Not a Girl at All: Teachers Make Me Feel Safe Expressing My Gender Identity"

That summer I began to analyze my life, trying to have a better understanding of my real happiness, fears, and wants. Playing Darnell [a macho older man in August Wilson's *Jitney*] and looking at my father, I concluded that I didn't want to wear the mask of masculinity and hide my true self.

—Melvin Pichardo, 17, "Removing the Mask"

IN CHAPTER 2, we discuss the importance of our beliefs and how beliefs about our students often influence our relationships with them. We also discuss how our beliefs are related to what we know about our students and that gaining more knowledge about them can change our beliefs. Chapter 3 looks at what children think about themselves and how schools shape their perceptions of their abilities. We explore the concept of identity development by examining students' own accounts of how they grappled with the questions "Who am I?" and "To what group do I belong?"

In this chapter, we continue to explore identity development by focusing on gender and race, two categories that are used especially frequently to put people in boxes that can constrain how we view them. We talk about how awareness of these constraints, knowledge of how gender and racial identity develop, and skill in supporting that development are essential aspects of developmentally and culturally responsive teaching.

The Pressure to Conform

I visited my first-born son in the neonatal unit only a few hours after he was born. Two nurses were caring for several babies. As I stood at the window staring in amazement at my newborn son, he lifted his head. One of the nurses said, "Look at how strong he is." Within seconds, a girl lying in the crib right next to him also lifted her head in an almost identical way. The same nurse said, "Look, she's showing her pretty face to the world." Within a few hours of birth, the same behavior was viewed as a boy's sign of strength and as a girl's attempt to gain attention for her beauty.

One of the earliest categories in which we place ourselves is gender. It is perhaps the most important way in which we sort ourselves and each other and may be the earliest identity and social category to emerge in human development.[1]

Even as infants, children receive messages about gender from their family, their peers, and the media. At six months, infants can distinguish between male and female faces. By the time they reach kindergarten, children have learned to label themselves and others as a "boy" or a "girl" based on external characteristics, like hair length or clothing.[2] For most children, their sense of gender identity (their sense of belonging to a gender category) is fairly firm by the time they are two or three years old.[3] For other children, gender identity may be fluid until adolescence or later.[4]

Supporting Gender Identity Development

The two most common gender identities are girl and boy (or man and woman). Traditionally we've viewed these as the only two gender identities, a notion referred to as the "gender binary." But children may not identify strictly as a boy or a girl—they could identify as both, as neither, or as another gender entirely. We call this range the gender spectrum. This view of gender as a spectrum, rather than a binary construction, has become more accepted in recent years, particularly by young people.[5]

Still, children traditionally have been taught to connect particular behaviors, activities, or interests with being either masculine or feminine. These gender norms reflect what society considers appropriate male and female behavior. And, as my experience with my newborn son shows, people apply these norms to us from the time of our birth. The messages can be overt (like when a young boy is told to "Man up" when he's about to cry after falling down), or they can be subtle (like TV commercials that incessantly convey traditional gender roles). These messages then influence how we define femininity and masculinity and become the standard by which we judge the behaviors of those we've categorized as being female or male. Many young people feel a great deal of pressure to conform to these norms and often experience negative consequences for not conforming.

Here, 17-year-old Selena Garcia describes her experiences of feeling pressured to conform to a gender role and how she responded:

> I never wanted to be a boy; I just wanted to be able to do what they did. Being a boy seemed more fun. Boys didn't care about the way they looked. No cherry Chap-Stick and pink clothes for me: I was snapbacks and basketballs, climbing trees and having adventures. My brother and I are only one year apart, and we would ride bikes, play basketball, and play with his Hot Wheels together.
>
> The girls I knew didn't like to get their hands dirty. I remember when four guys and I needed one more player for a three on three basketball game. I asked three girls I thought of as "the pretty princesses" if one of them would play. One said,

"I don't want to get sweaty" and the rest agreed with her. The guys and I had to play three on two.

The pretty princesses said mean things about my lack of nice clothes and shoes. I tried to ignore them because it didn't matter to me what I wore. I cared about the person I was. They didn't know me and they didn't understand my life.

For the first 10 years of my life, my adoptive parents physically and verbally abused my brother and me. I felt more safe, tough, and powerful dressed as a tomboy. I wanted to protect my brother and I wanted to protect myself. Girls seemed like easier prey because they were soft and showed their feelings in front of others. I never thought anyone would care or try to understand my feelings, so I hid everything like a guy would do.

Then, when I was 13, my foster mother made me put on a dress and do my hair to go to a wedding. To my surprise, I liked it. I liked the attention. My guy friends who were at the wedding would usually give me a high five or a pound, but now they hugged me and called me pretty. It made me feel special.

After that day I still mostly dressed sporty, but I switched it up occasionally. I'd sometimes go to the basketball court in cute shorts and a pink or purple top. The boys paid more attention to me that way. When I felt like getting attention, I would look like a girl with skirts or dresses. However, when I wanted to play around and have fun, I would put on my shorts and my snapback. I felt more like myself that way.

I began to merge my two looks into something I call "tomgirl." I would wear skinny jeans, some cute retro Jordans, a tank top, and a snapback. In outfits like that I get the respect and the attention from boys. Girls like my tomgirl look if it's on the girly end of the spectrum.

I used to be mad at the pretty princesses for the way they acted. Now I think it's because of how they were raised and everything around them—from TV shows to videos to books to stores, and especially advertisements. There are so many messages for girls to be feminine that it is more of a requirement than a choice.

I see all the magazine covers say, "Look like this!" or "Tips on how to have a beautiful body" and I sometimes feel the pressure to measure up. Having a big butt and nice curves is considered beautiful, and I do not have a Kim Kardashian or J. Lo body.

However, I know I should not believe those messages, and I am happy with my freedom to mix it up like a tomgirl. I wear baggy pants, run around, and get sweaty, but I am also sensitive. When things get tough, I cry; I let it out because bottling feelings up only makes it worse. I'm lucky that I'm part of a good family now, and it feels safe to show my emotions.

Girls are expected to be weak and kind, successful but not too successful because then it will make men look bad. Guys are expected to be dominant and have no emotion. But can't I be kind and strong? Why do girls have to "act like a lady?" Why are guys who show their feelings called "gay" or "feminine"? Neither the male nor the female gender box defines me. I was always in between.

Likewise, boys face similar constraints, but in a different direction. Called the "gender straitjacket"[6] or the "mask of masculinity," young men are traditionally pressured into rejecting their more vulnerable and emotional sides and acting tough, stoic, and independent. Here, high school student Melvin Pichardo, 17, describes the stress he feels trying to conform to traditional masculine roles, and even how it affected his course selection:

I grew up believing that to be a man I had to be macho. My father wanted me to learn that men must be strong and valiant for themselves and women—and that men should be closed-minded, emotionless, and always winners. He seemed to think that the only acceptable time for a man to show emotions like sadness was if he'd been drinking. My father would criticize me when I showed my vulnerabilities, so I showed them only when I was alone or with my mother.

My father wasn't the only one I saw acting macho. In my neighborhood, young men hid their vulnerabilities by acting tough. I saw that when a guy was upset, he kept his body still, wore a blank expression, and reacted to nothing around him.

Instead of expressing his real feelings, he would become verbally aggressive and loud so he wouldn't be seen as weak.

By the time I was 14, most of the young men my age were trying out this act. We were starting to go through puberty, and many guys became defensive if they didn't have facial hair or their voice hadn't changed. There was huge pressure for guys to get into relationships and have sex, wear the right clothes, and have money. To express their masculinity, many guys started to make fun of others, and to speak badly to girls. Other boys got into sports to fit in. But I wanted to think differently, and I did.

At the beginning of my sophomore year of high school, I aspired to have high grades, but none of the subjects I was "supposed" to like as a guy interested me. I wasn't determined to become a great student in math, science, and engineering. That year, I was more interested in theater.

In theater class, I learned to take on other's emotions when I played someone on stage. It made me want to better understand my own emotions—the things that made me happy as well as those that scared me. What was happiness to me? It was when I wasn't trying to be anybody but me. I didn't want to have to worry about appearing intimidating or tough.

Sometimes I slip back into the mentality of what society believes men should be because everyone around me thinks that way. When someone asks what I want to be, sometimes I lie and say "businessman" or "cop" because I think the real answer—an actor or writer—might make people think of me as less of a man. But those moments of trying to fit society's idea of masculinity happen less and less frequently.

Melvin's story describes his internal conflict between feeling pressured to conform to his father's and peers' versions of masculinity while also trying to express his masculinity on his own terms. Like many adolescents, he learned that there were negative consequences for not following the "gender rules." Fortunately, through theater, he was able to express, and ultimately, affirm a masculinity that felt right for him.

All adolescents experience the developmental challenges of physical maturation, managing sexual interests, forming new kinds of relationships, and planning for their future. Like Melvin, their gender affects how they manage these challenges, with biological and socially constructed differences that often guide boys and girls in different directions. For example, researchers have found that boys' same-sex friendships are typically characterized by friendly competition, risky activities, and discomfort with intimacy. Girls' same-sex friendships are typically characterized by greater intimacy, self-disclosure, validation, caring, and relationship repair, but also more co-rumination (sharing of woes) and jealousy.[7]

Biological and social factors both contribute to differences between girls and boys. But it's often the case that the social factors can be the most impactful, and not always for the best. Socially defined gender roles and gender norms can limit the development of children and affect their self-confidence. This effect can be debilitating when girls receive messages that their looks are more important than their intellect or boys hear that showing empathy and revealing their vulnerabilities make them less than a man. These messages about gender can have unintended, and sometimes, tragic consequences.[8]

I was recently preparing a lecture on mental health and wellness for one of my classes and was trying to find some images to put on a PowerPoint slide to introduce the topic of teen depression. I searched in Google Images and was immediately struck by how many of the images had female faces. Out of curiosity, I searched under the word *trauma* and found a similar pattern. I then tried *fear* and again a similar pattern of disproportionately female faces emerged. I then tried the word *strength*, and surprise, overwhelmingly male faces!

Numerous recent studies have confirmed what we already know intuitively—depression, trauma, stress, and fear do not have a favorite gender. Terrance Real, co-founder of Harvard University's Gender Research Project, argues that because society places a female face on depression and trauma, males tend to experience what he refers to as "covert depression." Rather than internalize their pain, men externalize it through aggressive acts.[9] Since we tend to focus on the outward acts of aggression, we tend to miss the root cause. This is particularly important for adolescent males whose outwardly aggressive behavior in school may more likely provoke a disciplinary reaction rather than an attempt to understand and support their emotional needs.

Societal messages concerning gender norms can be harmful. However, when peers deliver these messages, they're even more impactful because children and adolescents tend to hold more "rigid" definitions of boyhood and girlhood. This rigidity makes it more likely for adolescents to have negative reactions to behaviors that do not conform to these definitions.[10]

Parents and teachers can also reinforce narrow messages about what is gender appropriate for young people, which can have additional damaging effects on their self-esteem. A 2019 national survey of school climate found that the vast majority of LGBTQ+ students experienced harassment or assault based on personal characteristics such as sexual orientation, gender expression, and gender.[11] Here, a recent nonbinary high school graduate, age 19, writes about why daily roll call was mortifying, and how teachers' inconsistent use of their preferred name affected their ability to do well in school:

> I sat in the back of the classroom during my sophomore year of high school, groggy from lack of sleep. I was anxious as the teacher began attendance. Minutes before, I had practically begged her to call me Scott, the name I felt more comfortable with. "OK, sure," she'd responded with an exasperated sigh and a wave of dismissal, like she couldn't be bothered.
>
> Then I heard the name that didn't feel like mine.
>
> The teacher blinked back at me with indifference. She repeated my birth name again. My heart sank and I felt the heat in my cheeks. Reluctantly, I raised my hand and whispered, "Here."
>
> Attendance was the worst part of my day and I had to experience it in every class.
>
> After class, I got up the nerve to approach my teacher again. She didn't make eye contact with me. When I finally stopped stuttering, she looked at me and said, "Scott is a boy's name. Are you a boy?" I heard hostility in her voice, like I had done

something to personally offend her. My fingernails dug into my palms, and tears welled in my eyes.

I was silent. I wasn't sure if I was a boy or not, and I was afraid of saying yes. After all, I had breasts that even the elastic binder I wore under my shirt couldn't cover. "I'll see you tomorrow," she said, repeating the name that was not my own.

Since freshman year, I'd been unsure of my gender identity and therefore what my name should be. People saw me as a girl, but I didn't identify that way. I struggled enough to explain it to myself, let alone to my friends, family, and teachers. The only thing I was sure of, since the early days of 2nd grade, was that when I heard my birth name, it felt like a paper cut: a tiny, seemingly insignificant thing that bleeds and hurts more than it should.

After the humiliating response from that teacher, I was too afraid to confront most of my other teachers about using the name I preferred or the pronouns he/him. I decided it'd be better to keep quiet and subject myself to discomfort.

On the rare occasion I was comfortable enough to come out to a teacher, I still felt hesitant. In some classes, teachers called me Scott, and in others, they called me by my "dead name"—the one I'd been given at birth and no longer identified with. And my classmates noticed.

"So which one is it?" one girl asked, in a demanding tone.

"Yeah, why do you have two names?" the boy next to her asked.

"Is this one your *real* name?"

I kept my eyes glued to the math handout. I scribbled random numbers. I felt my cheeks flame. I didn't like to be confronted by anyone, let alone people I rarely associated with. "My name is Scott," I said. I tried to tune out the snickering behind my back and the looks that felt like they left holes in my skin.

This affected my ability to do well in school. I avoided being called on in class. I feigned sickness to stay home. After a while, I told my friends not to call me anything. Being nameless was better than hearing the wrong name and feeling awful or being called the right name and receiving glares.

For most people, their gender identity aligns with their sex.[12] However, for some people their gender identity and sex at birth do not align. The most recent U.S. government statistics suggest that about two in every 500 people identify as transgender.[13] Though this frequency suggests that there are transgender students on the register in most average-size schools, they often are not acknowledged. Many of them feel that they must hide their identity until they get older.

Transgender children like the preceding writer have an almost 50% chance of attempting suicide at some point in their life and an 80% chance of being the victim of violence while in school.[14] These rates are both much higher than rates of attempted suicide and bullying for cisgender youth. Still, when they can find an accepting community, gender nonconforming youth can thrive. Chris, 19, is a recent transgender high school graduate. He describes how good it felt to find acceptance and support from a school counselor:

> When I was around 15, my counselor sent me to an LGBTQ+ group.
>
> When I first went, I was scared and shy because most of the people in the group were a little older. In that group, I first heard the term "transgender," and I overcame my shyness to ask questions. "How do you become that? How do you change your name? When can you get the surgery?"
>
> For the first time, I understood what I was. I had been waiting to outgrow being a tomboy, but now I realized this was not a phase. It was me.
>
> I had a chance to start high school with my new identity. It was a school for kids who had behavioral problems or were in special education. Before I could start at that school, the woman who would become my counselor had to interview me. First, she interviewed me with my mother, then by myself. Without my saying anything, I guess from my clothes, she said, "Would you rather be called 'he' than 'she'?" and "Do you have a nickname you like to be called?"

> It felt good that she figured out I was transgender. I asked her if I could be called "he." She said yes, so I needed a boy name. All my brothers' names start with a C, so I settled on Chris.
>
> The teachers and students called me Chris and "he," and it felt good that they respected me. One kid asked, "What are you?" but when my counselor said, "Leave him alone; he's new to the school," the kid backed down.

For Chris, a supportive counselor and joining an LGBTQ+ group were instrumental in helping him to feel supported and connected to others in school. Several studies have demonstrated how the school climate can impact the experiences of nonconforming youth. University of Arizona researcher Russel Toomey and his colleagues surveyed over 1,400 students from 28 high schools to ask how safe they thought their school was for gender nonconforming peers. This research found that "when schools included lesbian, gay, bisexual, transgender, and queer (LGBTQ) issues in their curriculum and had a Gay-Straight Alliance, students perceived their schools as safer for gender nonconforming male peers."[15] This work also found that students experienced greater negative consequences for breaking male gender norms than for breaking female gender norms, so school efforts to support nonconforming youth particularly helped males. As was the case with Chris, other studies have also found that when schools took explicit steps to reduce harassment, students reported greater connections to school personnel. Those connections were, in turn, associated with greater feelings of safety.[16]

Supporting Racial Identity Development

I remember vividly the day that I picked up my son after his first day of preschool. I was standing with a few other parents and I could hear their children excitedly describe their first day. "My teacher is really nice," one child said. Another ran to his dad saying, "We got to play with a bunch of cool toys." Finally, another told her mom, "I really liked the book we read."

My son then walked up to me with wide-eyed exuberance and said, "There's another Brown boy in my class, Dad!" It wasn't his teacher, or the toys, or the books that caught his attention. Of all the things that he could have reported about his first day, the thing that was the most important was that he wasn't the only Brown boy. As I stood there excited about how happy he was on his first day, I was also saddened by how quickly and deeply his awareness of being different due to his skin color had impacted him.

As teachers, we often work to protect our students from the problems that plague society. We work hard to create safe and supportive classrooms and school environments where all of our students feel capable of learning and capable of being successful no matter what color their skin is. As they try to create these types of learning environments, however, teachers sometimes interact with their students in ways that unduly minimize the impact of race. While well-intended and designed to promote the belief that all students should be treated equally, statements such as, "I don't see color," or "I treat all my students the same," ignore the crucial ways in which students view themselves and their world through a "racialized" lens.

When people say "I don't see color," they generally mean that they don't let a person's color influence how they think about that person or how they interact with that person. However, what they fail to realize is that this self-professed color-blindness comes from a position of privilege. My son didn't have the privilege of color blindness because his eyes had been trained from a young age to notice his color and to notice how he was different. Whether it was through the commercials and shows he saw on television or the toys he saw in our local stores, he realized that he didn't "match" the images he often saw around him. At home, my wife and I surrounded him with images, games, and books that included people who looked like him. But outside of our home, he saw continual reminders of his difference.

For students who must confront racial discrimination in many aspects of their daily lives, the notion that race doesn't matter directly contradicts their lived experiences. More importantly, when we ask our students to accept that race doesn't matter and that as teachers we "treat all of our students the same," we're telling them that we can't see part of who they are.

As adolescents try to answer the question "Who am I?" they become more aware of their membership in certain socially constructed groups, such as racial and ethnic groups. They begin to evaluate themselves based on the value they place on group membership. As they begin to self-identify as being part of a racial group, they begin to develop their sense of racial identity. Rather than defining racial identity in biological terms (with respect to group affiliation based solely on skin color), racial identity has been defined "as a social construction, which refers to a sense of group or collective identity based on one's perception that he or she shares a common heritage with a particular racial group" (p. 40).[17]

Scholars studying racial identity development have proposed several models to describe the process by which we develop a sense of racial identity. Based on Erikson's theory of identity formation, William Cross developed a model that has helped shape the field of racial identity development (and particularly, the study of Black identity development in the United States).[18] Cross's model describes five stages of racial identity development: (1) pre-encounter; (2) encounter; (3) immersion/emersion; (4) internalization; and (5) internalization-commitment.

Cross's model views racial identity development as typically beginning in later adolescence or early adulthood. During the pre-encounter stage, adolescents tend to be unaware of the significance of being part of a particular racial group. Essentially, it represents their identity before having an encounter that alters their identity. In the second, encounter stage, they experience something that makes them aware of their race and aware of their vulnerability because of their membership in a racial group. This encounter is the first time that they become aware of being treated differently because of their race.

Cross describes the third stage of immersion/emersion as being a time in which Black adolescents have a strong drive to adopt visible symbols of "Blackness" while simultaneously rejecting White culture. For adolescents at this stage, "being Black" is interpreted as not "acting White." Children in the first part of this stage (immersion) may be adamant about proving their "Blackness," but may judge their Blackness against superficial and stereotypical media representations of Black culture. As they proceed within this stage to emersion, they engage in a more nuanced analysis of what it means to be Black. They are more inclusive in their views on "Blackness," and are less likely to define themselves by stereotypical depictions.

The fourth stage, internalization, marks a period in which individuals are secure in their racial identity. As a result, they can develop and sustain relationships with people from other racial or ethnic groups.

Finally, during the internalization-commitment stage, they have not only internalized their racial identity but have made a commitment to supporting members of their racial group.

Cross suggests that individuals may revisit stages throughout their lives as they encounter new information and have new experiences. Importantly, he views this revisiting as a positive process that builds a more coherent sense of racial identity.

In the following essay, Gabrielle Pascal, 16, describes the challenges she faced in school, where peers questioned her racial identity. She struggles to reconcile the differences between her perception of herself as a Black girl and her peers' criticism that she "acts White":

> "Gaby, why are you such an Oreo?" one of the girls in my 8th grade class asked out of the blue. I was reading the final book in *The Chronicles of Narnia* series and sitting alone at my desk during a free period. Everyone else was either talking to their friends or doing schoolwork. I was the only girl who read the *Narnia* series and it was a borderline obsession. The other Black girls in my class didn't sit quietly and read by themselves and I guess they didn't know other Black girls who did.
>
> I mumbled quietly, "I don't know."
>
> "Really? You don't know why?" Now, the conversation grabbed the attention of a few other classmates, who looked at me, waiting to hear what I would say. I felt embarrassed. I wanted to say, "Why would you even ask me something like that?" But I was too intimidated by her question.
>
> An Oreo is a term that is used to describe Black people who act in ways that are not stereotypically associated with Black culture. They are labeled as being White on the inside, Black on the outside.
>
> I was a goody two-shoes and one of the highest-achieving kids in the class, so other kids called me Oreo too. I enjoyed reading fantasy novels and Edgar Allan Poe.

I loved classical music and the Icelandic indie-rock band Of Monsters and Men. I usually kept to myself. All of these things combined made those girls think that I acted "too White." Too White to be Black.

When the TV show *Empire*, which is about a hip-hop mogul and his family, came out, all of my friends were talking about it. I didn't want to be left out, so I marathoned the first few episodes.

During lunch, I told one of my classmates that I'd started watching *Empire*. "You did? That's surprising," she replied. When I asked her why, she said, "Well, it's just that I didn't think it would be the type of show you'd be into. You usually watch shows White people watch." Whenever these kinds of comments were made I wanted to stick up for myself. But the words never made their way out.

I've watched every single episode of the anime *Your Lie in April* twice, which isn't popular among Black kids, but have yet to finish a full season of *The Boondocks*, a show that most of my Black friends have watched.

I began to feel like an outsider in my own race. Whether it was the books I read, the TV shows I watched, the way I talked, or the type of music I listened to, it was as if everything I did was the antithesis of what it meant to be a Black girl.

Rather than confront my peers' expectations, I escaped to my books where none of the characters could jump off the page and judge me. Through reading, I could transport myself to a different place where I didn't have to worry what people thought of me. Fictional characters can't call you an Oreo.

After I switched schools to one that was more diverse, I was never referred to as Oreo again. But the stigma stayed with me and I began to question what it meant to be Black. Was there a rulebook that I hadn't read? Is the type of person I am not what Black people are supposed to be like?

With the posing of one question, "Why are you such an Oreo?" Gaby moved from the pre-encounter to the encounter stage of Cross's model. She moved from not thinking about herself as a Black child to realizing that, in some way, her race mattered to those around her. That one question forced her to begin to think deeply about her race, but also forced her to think about what it meant to be Black. Was it a more inclusive term that welcomed people with varied interests and experiences? Or was it a restrictive term that meant that being Black essentially meant not being White? In contrast, her peers appear to be in the immersion portion of the immersion/emersion stage.

So what does this mean for educators of Black students and other students who may be moving along Cross's continuum?

It means that some of your Black students, for example (or some of your Asian or Latinx students), may be at a stage where they define their racial identities as simply not being White. They may chastise and even reject other peers from their own racial group who, from their perspective, "act White," and they may reject teachers (particularly White teachers) whom they feel do not embrace their "Blackness" or other salient racial identity.

It is important for teachers to understand that this isn't a personal attack against them. Rather, it is a stage in a typical developmental process as their students come to develop a healthy sense of their racial identity. Rather than interpret these behaviors as signs that their BIPOC students are rejecting them, rejecting school, and are uninterested or unmotivated, teachers can recognize that these are normal stages in racial identity development and can take explicit actions to help students develop a positive racial identity.

Drawing on the work of Cross, scholars within the field also view racial identity as being multidimensional.[19] In much the same way that Marcia's idea of identity statuses extended Erikson's theory of identity development, the work of Robert Sellers extends Cross's model to include the concept of racial identity statuses.[20] For Sellers, each status represents the "significance and meaning of race" in one's self-concept. His model includes four dimensions: (1) racial salience; (2) centrality; (3) regard; and (4) ideology.

Racial salience refers to how much one's race is a relevant part of one's self-concept at a particular moment or in a particular situation. For example, in the following excerpt, Sayda Morales, 16, describes her first day in a new all-girls private high school, when her race suddenly became much more salient to her:

It was my first day of high school and already I felt like an outcast.

I was standing in a corner with the other new girls, marveling at the sight of so many White people. The Nightingale-Bamford School was an all-girls private school on the Upper East Side, one of the richest neighborhoods in Manhattan. It went from kindergarten through high school, which meant most students had already known each other for nine years. As if that didn't intimidate me enough, I was also on scholarship. Most of the other girls were rich, and I mean really rich.

If you had asked me before high school to describe myself in one word, "Hispanic" would have come nowhere near my lips. I attended a public middle school in the South Bronx where most of the students were Black or Hispanic like me, and I took my ethnicity for granted. It just didn't seem important. But when I entered private school and found myself in the minority for the first time, I had to figure out what it really meant to be a Latina from the South Bronx.[21]

That first day, I arrived in my navy blue kilted skirt that reached my knees, shoes I got on sale at Macy's and a book bag. Most of the girls wore skirts that ended right underneath their butts, so that you could see their shorts or underwear. They wore Lacoste polo shirts and Coach flats and carried LeSportsac bags. I felt like a penguin in the middle of the Sahara.

Some girls asked me where I lived, and when they heard the words "South Bronx," their eyes widened and their faces elongated in shock. They wanted to know if I had seen people get shot, if I had seen people do drugs, if I had been to any wild parties. I chuckled to myself—did they really think that the South Bronx was that dangerous?

It was only 8 a.m. and I was already being exposed to ignorance I'd never thought possible. But what happened later that day was even more eye-opening.

Next thing I knew, Soulja Boy's "Crank That" was pumping from the homeroom stereo and girls were imitating the dancing from the music video. I hadn't heard the song before because I didn't listen to hip-hop that much. Out of nowhere one of my new White friends, Delilah, pulled my arm and begged me to dance with her. I shook my head "no" because I had no clue how to crank that soldier boy or even what it looked like. But the other girls started begging me, too, and I was thrust to the front of the room.

I feebly tried to explain I didn't know how to dance to that kind of music, but the girls started saying things like, "C'mon, that's ridiculous. Of course you do!" and, "Just try it, it probably comes natural to you."

I'm sorry to say that I didn't stand up for myself at that moment. I just tried to remember my friend Ashley from middle school, who knew how to dance hip-hop, and I attempted to imitate some of her moves. It was quite pathetic, but surprisingly all the girls thought it was amazing. I was ashamed of myself for trying to fit into their stereotype instead of correcting them.

After that, I became known as the ghetto girl from the ghetto neighborhood with ghetto friends. It didn't really bother me that they called me "ghetto." But it bothered me that they didn't recognize my Hispanic culture. Then again, I guess I didn't bother to recognize my Hispanic culture.

If we return to Gaby's story, we see a young girl struggling to reconcile her beliefs about her "Blackness" with the opinions of her peers who have a very different view about how Black people act. Feeling "like an outsider in her own race," she grapples with either holding firm to her more inclusive conceptualization of Blackness or following the "rulebook" for Blackness—a book that she neither helped to write nor ever read.

For both young writers, it was a particular interaction (in the case of Gaby, being asked a racially charged question) or a particular context (Sayda entering a new school on the first day) that forced them to confront the reality that, in some way, they were different. More importantly, it forced them to acknowledge that being different was related to their race. These incidents made their race salient and forced them to consider how they saw themselves, how they saw others, and how others saw them. This influenced how they interacted with the world (such as trying to adopt certain practices that they believed would "affirm" their race and connect them to their peers) and how they interacted in the world (such as by switching schools to make race less salient). Importantly, both writers' experiences occurred within their schools. In this way, their experiences highlight the important role that schools play in racial identity development.

Gaby's story highlighted how her racial identity development was shaped by her schoolmates. For others, their racial identity development was supported more directly by their interactions with their teachers and other school staff. The following excerpt describes how a teacher and peers supported Christina Oxley, 17, an African American student, as she struggled to figure out where she fit in after transferring to a mostly White school from a mostly Black school:

> By 7th grade I had subconsciously mastered the art of codeswitching—changing the way I speak and act based on whether I am around White people or not. I started caring more about grammatically correct sentence structures, even in casual conversations, and using different slang: "Y'all" became "you guys."
>
> I also had to learn what not to speak about: where I live, the ways I was punished as a kid, hair care, or even getting tan in the summer. These topics set me apart. I kept this filter on constantly as I went about my life at school, and my White peers got more comfortable around me. I noticed that I was more accepted when I erased aspects of myself that made me different.
>
> But that same year, some peers and teachers convinced me to join the Black/Latinx affinity group at school. For the first time since switching schools, I was sitting in a room with people who looked like me and understood me. The Black and Latinx teachers who led the group listened to us and taught us how to recognize microaggressions and other acts of subtle (or not-so-subtle) racism that we face both in school and in the world. They introduced us to art as a means of self-expression and activism.

The Importance of Positive Racial Identity

Scholar Janet Helms has described racial identity as a sense of group identity that is based on a perceived common heritage with a racial group.[22] When we take pride in our membership in that racial group, we are viewed as having a positive racial identity.

Numerous studies have identified the benefits of a positive racial identity. Positive racial identity has been found to promote positive outcomes and protect against adversity (such as bigotry, racism, and discrimination).[23] For example, a review of research findings regarding the impact of a positive Black racial identity on youth found that a positive and more developed Black racial identity has been associated with increased self-esteem, enhanced interpersonal relationships, reduced levels of anxiety and depression, greater resilience and coping skills, and higher academic achievement.[24]

Additionally, a review of research on how racial and ethnic identity development supports positive youth development found that feeling positively about membership in one's racial or ethnic group is associated with positive outcomes among Latinx, Asian, Black, Native American, and multiethnic youth.[25]

The researchers also found that adolescents' racial identity attitudes are often related to their racial socialization. This is the process through which caregivers convey implicit and explicit messages about the significance and meaning of race, teach children about what it means to be a member of a racial and/or ethnic minority group, and help youth learn to cope with discrimination.[26] They note that there are a number of ways in which racial socialization can occur, including:

- cultural socialization (teaching children about their racial and ethnic heritage and history, and promoting cultural, racial, and ethnic pride);
- preparation for bias (highlighting the existence of inequalities between groups and preparing youth to cope with discrimination);
- egalitarianism (emphasizing individual character traits such as hard work over racial or ethnic group membership); and
- self-worth messages (promoting feelings of individual worth within the broader context of the child's race-ethnicity)."[27]

While caregivers may be the primary source of socialization, peers also provide an important role in reinforcing positive attitudes. In the following example, we return to Sayda's story as she discusses how her connection to peers helped foster her sense of positive racial identity:

I had slowly assimilated into White American culture over the years. I started listening to pop music and watching American TV shows until my Spanish was terrible and I became too embarrassed to speak it. In kindergarten, before I knew English, my name, Sayda, sounded to me like steamed rice, platanos and beans. By the time I entered high school, my name sounded more like hot dogs and hamburgers on the Fourth of July.

After about three months of comments from my classmates, I finally realized that if I didn't stand up for myself and my culture, my classmates would continue to live in ignorance. But what was my culture, exactly?

I started thinking more about everything that made me Hispanic. For example, I still spoke some Spanish and ate Spanish food at home. I danced bachata and merengue at parties, and I had been to Mexico and Honduras several times. I was Hispanic at home, but not in school, and I realized that for years, even before high school, I'd been keeping that part of myself separate from who I was at school. But there was nothing to be ashamed of. So what if I watched telenovelas as well as Gossip Girl? So what if I loved listening to Anthony Santos and Ricardo Arjona as well as 50 Cent and Rihanna?

I began talking to my friends at school about my life and culture. I told them about how I had been in a bilingual class in kindergarten and wasn't fluent in English until 3rd grade. I told them that in my house we eat foods like *platanos, arroz con habichuelas* and *tamales*.

Some girls thought I had an attitude problem and was being arrogant for talking about myself. But the girls who were genuinely interested in learning about Hispanic culture and were sincerely sorry for stereotyping me became my close friends.

I learned to embrace my ethnicity even more by getting involved with school organizations for students of color. That spring, I signed up for a one-day workshop with an organization called Diversity Awareness Initiative for Students (DAIS). Hundreds of other students from private schools in the New York area got together to attend sessions on topics like identity and homosexuality. It was good to talk to other private school students from all different backgrounds who cared about the same issues I cared about.

> After that, I joined Cultural Awareness for Everyone (CAFE), a club at my school where Black, White, Asian, and Hispanic students come together and talk about our cultures. Talking to other Hispanic students who had gone through similar experiences at my school made me realize I wasn't alone.

Throughout this chapter, you've had the opportunity to hear first-hand accounts of how students navigated the challenges of finding their sameness and oneness. As they tried to figure out who they are, what they're good at, and where they fit in, our young writers also describe the adversity they faced for being different.

Some of your students may follow a process of identity development that you find familiar and that you understand and are prepared to support. But other students' processes of identity formation may differ from what you're used to. It's important to be aware that identity development is difficult for all adolescents regardless of their gender or racial identity. As whiteness is decentered in American society, even White students are now having to be more conscious of their own racial identity development. When we keep this in mind, we're more likely to empathize with them when they seem unsure of themselves, we're more likely to try to support them as they struggle to fit in with their peers, and we're more likely to seek to better understand them when they don't fit our expectations and beliefs about typical adolescent development.

What Teachers Can Do

1. Create environments that support gender identity development.

It's critical that educators create spaces in which children can safely explore gender identity. Consider how you challenge or reaffirm gender stereotypes when interacting with children as they discuss career choices, play interests, clothing preferences, and other gendered areas of their life. Include examples of gender nonconformity in books you read and topics you cover so all students see themselves reflected in the world around them, including nonconforming students. Celebrate instances where children make choices that allow them to be who they are and avoid being pigeonholed into roles that don't fit them.

One way in which we can support the gender identity of our students is by honoring their name. As we learned from Chris's story, finally being asked what he would like to be called was transformational and empowering. It was someone finally saying, "I see you the way you see yourself." So don't simply rely on the class roster. Showing our students the respect of asking them their preferred name helps to create a classroom environment where students are welcomed, respected, and safe.

Another way to support gender identity is to examine gendered language in your classroom. Ask: "Does my use of language demonstrate care and respect for all of my students?" This examination should consider both spoken and written language (such as the reading you assign). You may find the following reflection questions to be helpful:[28]

- Are masculine terms like *he* or *guys* typically used to refer to your entire class?
- Are gendered pronouns such as *she* and *he* used exclusively?
- Do you tend to use *man* or *men* or words containing them to refer to people who may not be men?
- Do you tend to use *he*, *him*, *his*, or *himself* to refer to people who may not be men?
- If you have mentioned someone's sex or gender, was it necessary to do so?

One increasingly common practice is to use *they* as the accepted third-person, gender-neutral pronoun both in speaking and in writing, which you will notice we sometimes do in this book.

Be prepared to be uncomfortable, but also be prepared to turn that discomfort into a teachable moment both for yourself and for your students. Long-held habits are hard to break, so periodically engaging in self-reflection using the preceding questions can be an important way to make sustainable change. As you know, students will sometimes say hurtful and offensive things. While it's completely natural to be angry with them, it's more important to teach them how their words impact others.

I've found the Human Rights Foundation's Welcoming Schools site (welcomingschools.org) to be particularly helpful. It provides tools (including curricula and videos) to help teachers engage in what can, at times, be uncomfortable conversations. Sites like Gender Spectrum (https://www.genderspectrum.org) and

GLSEN-Gay, Lesbian & Straight Education Network (https://www.glsen.org/) are also good sources for guidance on how you can create gender sensitive and inclusive classroom environments.

2. Teach in ways that promote positive racial identity.

Teaching in ways that promote positive racial identity requires awareness, knowledge, and skills. To support our students, be aware that their race influences how the world sees them and can also influence how they see themselves. Support includes having a positive perspective on their families and teaching them in ways that make explicit connections between their school and home lives so that we validate the importance of those experiences in shaping who they are as learners.

Teachers can also help their students develop a positive racial identity by learning more about the contributions from members of their students' racial groups and using that in teaching. One thing that I try to remember when doing this is to provide a variety of examples of positive contributions so that I don't inadvertently reinforce a particular definition of success. For example, my students often equated wealth and fame with success, so I made sure to seek out role models of people who are not famous or wealthy. I would ask my students for examples and even prompt them to ask their family members.

Teachers can also help their students in this area by becoming more skilled at creating respectful, supportive, and inclusive classrooms. One resource that I've found tremendously useful is the Southern Poverty Law Center's Learning for Justice website (https://www.learningforjustice.org). It provides an array of classroom resources and professional development tools for teachers seeking to promote social justice and anti-bias education.

What Schools Can Do

1. Prioritize staff diversity when hiring.

Diversity doesn't happen by accident. Schools need to be intentional in providing students with opportunities to interact with adults from underrepresented racial or gender identity groups. That includes deliberate hiring practices, such as expanding the pool of prospective hires through new outreach methods that emphasize teacher, counselor, and school leader diversity. Diversity may also require professional development work within the district to ensure that it is a workplace where staff from underrepresented groups feel comfortable and welcome for who they are.

Studies have demonstrated that BIPOC students benefit from having more diverse teachers.[29] As we discuss in Chapter 2, these studies have found that BIPOC teachers tend to have higher expectations for BIPOC students than their White colleagues. Other studies have emphasized the importance of providing BIPOC students with diverse teachers, counselors, and school leaders who serve as role models and examples of academic achievement. Still other studies have highlighted how learning from diverse teachers benefits all students and prepares them for the diverse workforce they will join.[30]

2. Develop a plan to recruit, hire, and retain diverse staff.

Increasing teacher, counselor, and administrator diversity requires schools to shift the focus from recruiting from a traditional pool of applicants (which in most districts tends to yield a low number of BIPOC candidates) to actively taking steps to enlarge the pool. School personnel involved in the recruitment process should be prepared to answer the following questions: What specific steps are we prepared to take to recruit BIPOC candidates? What unique opportunities does this school provide to BIPOC candidates? How might mentoring need to be reimagined to support BIPOC candidates? Does this hire represent an ongoing commitment to increasing staff diversity? Resources developed by the Learning Policy Institute (https://learningpolicyinstitute.org) can help to support both district and school-level efforts to recruit and retain teachers of color.[31]

We give the last word in this chapter to Will Lohier, 18, who has suffered from a lack of Black teachers and has ideas for change:

> In my 14 years of education, I have only had one Black teacher for an academic subject, 9th grade biology. My three other Black teachers taught physical education and dance. That means of the 80 or so teachers I've had, only around 5% have been Black.

I recently graduated from one of New York's top public high schools. Of the 213 faculty, just 10 are Black. Only four teach academic subjects like math, science, and English. This leaves Black students with few or no adults who look like them, forced to navigate microaggressive school environments largely by ourselves.

In my first year of high school, my world history teacher, Mr. Smith, who is White, decided that the entirety of our unit on the transatlantic slave trade would be an eight-minute clip from the movie *Amistad*. The scene portrays naked Black men and women crying and screaming in the hull of a slave ship. It shows them being whipped and beaten. It shows Black women chained together as they are tossed into the sea, dragged beneath the waves by each other's weight.

As I sat in the back of the classroom crying beneath the dimmed lights and covering my ears to block out the screams, Mr. Smith stood next to the screen, cracking jokes. I was the only Black person in the room.

In art history we didn't learn the name of a single Black artist. We learned nothing of the countless contributions Black people have made in STEM fields. My sophomore year English teacher didn't teach a single author of color. When teachers did introduce Black artists or writers, they often tokenized them, including them for diversity's sake while further marginalizing Black experiences and excluding them from the norm.

When the people in charge of our education and well-being don't look like us, don't understand our experiences, and don't try to make their classrooms more inclusive, Black students are the ones who suffer. While having more Black teachers would not have been a fix-all, it would have helped me feel safer in a school environment where I often felt alienated and misunderstood because of my race.

Numerous studies show the positive impact on Black students that comes from having role models of the same race in school. Research shows that teachers of color generally have higher expectations for students of color, leading to improved performance in class and on standardized tests. Having a Black teacher in elementary school reduces high school dropout rates among very low-income Black boys by 39%, according to a Johns Hopkins study. North Carolina public school data aggregated by Education Next shows that Black male teachers were significantly less likely to suspend Black male students than White female teachers.

The lack of teachers of color also hurts White students, who will enter an increasingly diverse workforce. Nearly half of White students in New York attend a school without a single Black or Latinx teacher. As Dr. Gloria Ladson-Billings told *Education Week*, "It is important for White students to encounter Black people who are knowledgeable and hold some level of authority over them."

At the start of my senior year I'd had enough. I scheduled a meeting with the assistant principal of the English department. I wanted to address the glaring lack of Black teachers at my school and make the case for hiring more.

"Especially in English classes, where we discuss so many issues related to race, having people who can understand and relate to the things they're teaching about is important," I said. "Of the 24 teachers in the department, only two are people of color! The vast majority of students here aren't White and the faculty should reflect that."

Mr. Brown paused for a moment, frowning as he laced his fingers together in front of his mouth. "William," he said softly, "I just want you to know that I hear you and respect your opinion. It is so important that students are bringing these kinds of issues to the attention of the administration."

He cleared his throat, leaning back in his chair. "I promise you, I'm dedicated to making the department more diverse. It's one of our top priorities. But let me explain to you how it works on my end." He went on to explain to me how, despite his many efforts to "boost diversity," there were just no "qualified Black applicants."

I was disappointed. He had taught *Between the World and Me* by Ta-Nehisi Coates. Yet here he was rehashing the "pipeline" excuse.

Research shows that people with hiring power, like my assistant principal, often draw on their pre-existing networks and unconscious biases to make new hires when an opening arises. This can include their friends, people they went to college with, or colleagues from previous jobs. In many professions, including teaching, those networks are often overwhelmingly White due to segregated social circles, generational privilege, and historic job discrimination. As a result, it can be hard to find applicants of color within traditional networks.

The solution is not to blame the pipeline, but to actively seek out and contact qualified people of color and encourage them to apply for open positions.

To anyone with hiring power in the education system: Make sure that you are doing the best you can to hire and train teachers of color and do your part to remedy the systemic inequalities that exist in your school.

To students: Hold teachers and administrators at your school to account. Bring up the issue of hiring practices to those in charge and talk with your principal about your experiences. You are who these institutions are meant to serve, and you have a voice. Don't be afraid to use it.

Notes

1. Maccoby 2000; Lewis and Brooks-Gunn 1979.

2. Quinn, Yahr, Kuhn, Slater, and Pascalis 2002; Kohlberg 1966.

3. Baldwin and Moses 1996; Zosuls et al. 2009.

4. It is important to note that gender identity is distinct from one's sex, which is determined by one's anatomy and chromosomes at birth.

5. The 2015 Millennial Poll revealed that more individuals aged 18–34 see gender as a spectrum than as a binary (Gender Spectrum, 2017).

6. Pollack 2000.

7. Benenson and Christakos 2003; Kokkinos et al. 2020; Rose, Carlson, and Waller 2007.

8. Hartley and Sutton 2013; Del Rio and Strasser 2013; Wolter, Braun, and Hannover 2015.

9. Real, T. 1998.

10. Weinraub et al. 1984; Miller, Lurye, Zosuls, and Ruble 2009.

11. Kosciw, J.G., Clark, C.M., Truong, N.L., and Zongrone, A.D. 2020.

12. The term cisgender is used to describe those whose gender identity and sex align. The term cis female refers to those whose female identity and female sex are aligned and the term cis male refers to those whose male identity and male sex are aligned. Cisgender people can be gay or straight, for example.

13. Meerwijk, E.L., and Sevelius, J.M. 2017.

14. Haas and Rodgers 2014.

15. Toomey, R.B., Ryan, C., Diaz, R.M., Card, N.A., and Russell, S.T. 2013.

16. McGuire, Anderson, Toomey, and Russell 2010.

17. Chávez and Guido-DiBrito 1999.

18. Cross 1995.

19. Ashmore, Deaux, and McLaughlin-Volpe 2004; Hughes et al. 2014; Rowley et al. 1998.

20. Sellers, R.M., Smith, M.A., Shelton, J.N., Rowley, S.A., and Chavous, T.M. 1998.

21. Sellers refers to the extent to which a person generally defines themselves with respect to race as racial centrality. Additionally, racial regard is the extent to which the person feels positively about their race. It includes both private regard (the extent to which people feel positively or negatively toward Hispanics as well as how positively or negatively they feel about being Hispanic) and public regard (the extent to which people feel that others view Hispanics positively or negatively). Finally, ideology represents a person's beliefs, opinions, and attitudes about the way she or he feels that the members of the race should act and interact with society.

22. Helms 1990.

23. Mandara, Maryse, Gaylord-Harden, and Ragsdale 2009.

24. Zirkell and Johnson 2016.

25. Neblett Jr., Rivas-Drake, and Umaña-Taylor 2012.

26. Ibid.

27. Neblett Jr., Rivas-Drake, and Umaña-Taylor 2012, p. 296.

28. Adapted from the American Psychological Association. 2010. *Publication Manual of the American Psychological Association*. 6th ed. Washington, DC: American Psychological Association.

29. Goldhaber, D., Theobald, R., and Tien, C. 2015.

30. Goldhaber, D., Theobald, R., and Tien, C. 2019; Lindsay, C.A. and Hart, C.M. 2017.

31. Carver-Thomas, D. 2018.

References

Albert Shanker Institute. (2015). *The State of Teacher Diversity in American Education*. Washington, DC: Author. https://www.shankerinstitute.org/resource/teacherdiversity.

American Psychological Association. 2010. *Publication Manual of the American Psychological Association*. 6th ed. Washington, DC: American Psychological Association.

Ashmore, R.D., Deaux, K., and McLaughlin-Volpe, T. (2004). An organizing framework for collective identity: Articulation and significance of multidimensionality. *Psychological Bulletin* 130(1): 80.

Baldwin, D.A. and Moses, L.J. (1996). The ontogeny of social information gathering. *Child Development* 67(5): 1915–1939.

Benenson, J.F. and Christakos, A. (2003). The greater fragility of females' versus males' closest same-sex friendships. *Child Development* 74(4): 1123–1129.

Carver-Thomas, D. (2018). Diversifying the Teaching Profession: How to Recruit and Retain Teachers of Color. Washington, DC: Learning Policy Institute.

Chavez, A.F. and Guido-DiBrito, F. (2002). Racial and ethnic identity development. *New Directions for Adult and Continuing Education, 1999*, 84: 39–47.

Cross Jr., W.E. (1995). *The Psychology of Nigrescence: Revising the Cross Model*. In: *Handbook of Multicultural Counseling* (eds. J. Ponterotto, J. Casas, L. Suzuki, and C. Alexander), 93–121. Newbury Park, CA: Sage.

Dee, T.S. (2004). Teachers, race, and student achievement in a randomized experiment. *Review of Economics and Statistics* 86(1): 195–210.

Dee, T.S. (2005). A teacher like me: Does race, ethnicity, or gender matter? *American Economic Review* 95(2): 158–165.

Del Río, M.F. and Strasser, K. (2013). Preschool children's beliefs about gender differences in academic skills. *Sex Roles* 68(3–4): 231–238.

Egalite, A.J., Kisida, B., and Winters, M.A. (2015). Representation in the classroom: The effect of own-race teachers on student achievement. *Economics of Education Review* 45: 44–52.

Ehrenberg, R.G., Goldhaber, D., and Brewer, D.J. (1995). Do teachers' race, gender, and ethnicity matter? Evidence from the National Educational Longitudinal Study of 1988. *Industrial and Labor Relations Review* 48(3): 547–561.

Gershenson, S., Holt, S.B., and Papageorge, N.W. (2016). Who believes in me? The effect of student–teacher demographic match on teacher expectations. *Economics of Education Review* 52: 209–224.

Goldhaber, D., Theobald, R., and Tien, C. (2015). *The Theoretical and Empirical Arguments for Diversifying the Teacher Workforce: A Review of the Evidence* (CEDR Working Paper No. 2015-9). Seattle, WA: University of Washington Bothell, Center for Education Data & Research. https://www.eric.ed.gov/?id=ED574302.

Goldhaber, D., Theobald, R., and Tien, C. (2019). Why we need a diverse teacher workforce. *Phi Delta Kappan* 100(5): 25–30.

Haas, A.P., Rodgers, P.L., and Herman, J.L. (2014). Suicide attempts among transgender and gender non-conforming adults. *Work* 50: 59.

Hartley, B.L. and Sutton, R.M. (2013). A stereotype threat account of boys' academic underachievement. *Child Development* 84(5): 1716–1733.

Helms, J.E. (ed.). (1990). *Contributions in Afro-American and African studies, No. 129. Black and White Racial Identity: Theory, Research, and Practice*. New York and England: Greenwood Press.

Hughes, M., Kiecolt, K.J., and Keith, V.M. (2014). How racial identity moderates the impact of financial stress on mental health among African Americans. *Society and Mental Health* 4(1): 38–54.

Kokkinos, C.M., Kountouraki, M., Voulgaridou, I., and Markos, A. (2020). Understanding the association between Big Five and relational aggression: The mediating role of social goals and friendship jealousy. *Personality and Individual Differences* 160: 109946.

Kohlberg, L. (1966). Moral education in the schools: A developmental view. *The School Review* 74(1): 1–30.

Kosciw, J.G., Clark, C.M., Truong, N.L., and Zongrone, A.D. (2020). *The 2019 National School Climate Survey: The Experiences of Lesbian, Gay, Bisexual, Transgender, and Queer Youth in Our Nation's Schools*. New York: GLSEN.

Lewis, M. and Brooks-Gunn, J. (1979). Toward a theory of social cognition: The development of self. *New Directions for Child and Adolescent Development* 1979(4): 1–20.

Lindsay, C.A. and Hart, C.M. (2017). Exposure to same-race teachers and student disciplinary outcomes for black students in North Carolina. *Educational Evaluation and Policy Analysis* 39(3): 485–510.

Maccoby, E.E. (2000). Perspectives on gender development. *International Journal of Behavioral Development* 24(4): 398–406.

Mandara, J., Maryse R.H., Gaylord-Harden, N.K., and Ragsdale, B.L. (2009). The effects of changes in racial identity and self-esteem on changes in African American adolescents' mental health. *Child Development* November/December 80(6): 1660–1675.

McGuire, J.K., Anderson, C.R., Toomey, R.B., and Russell, S.T. (2010). School climate for transgender youth: A mixed method investigation of student experiences and school responses. *Journal of Youth and Adolescence* 39(10): 1175-1188.

Meerwijk, E.L. and Sevelius, J.M. (2017). Transgender population size in the United States: A meta-regression of population-based probability samples. *American Journal of Public Health* 107(2): e1–e8.

Miller, C.F., Lurye, L.E., Zosuls, K.M., and Ruble, D.N. (2009). Accessibility of gender stereotype domains: Developmental and gender differences in children. *Sex Roles* 60(11–12): 870–881.

Neblett Jr., E.W., Rivas-Drake, D., and Umaña-Taylor, A.J. (2012). The promise of racial and ethnic protective factors in promoting ethnic minority youth development. *Child Development Perspectives* 6(3): 295–303.

Pollack, W. and Shuster, T. (2000). *Real boys' voices: Boys speak out about drugs, sex, violence, bullying, sports, school, parents, and so much more.* New York: Random House.

Quinn, P.C., Yahr, J., Kuhn, A., Slater, A.M., and Pascalis, O. (2002). Representation of the gender of human faces by infants: A preference for female. *Perception* 31(9): 1109–1121.

Real, T. (1998). *I Don't Want to Talk about It: Overcoming the Secret Legacy of Male Depression.* New York: Simon & Schuster.

Rose, A.J., Carlson, W., and Waller, E.M. (2007). Prospective associations of co-rumination with friendship and emotional adjustment: Considering the socioemotional trade-offs of co-rumination. *Developmental Psychology* 43(4): 1019.

Rowley, S.J., Sellers, R.M., Chavous, T.M., and Smith, M.A. (1998). The relationship between racial identity and self-esteem in African American college and high school students. *Journal of Personality and Social Psychology* 74(3): 715.

Sellers, R.M., Smith, M.A., Shelton, J.N., Rowley, S.A., and Chavous, T.M. (1998). Multidimensional model of racial identity: A reconceptualization of African American racial identity. *Personality and Social Psychology Review* 2(1): 18–39.

Steele, D.M. and Cohn-Vargas, B. (2013). *Identity Safe Classrooms: Places to Belong and Learn*. Thousand Oaks, CA: Corwin Press.

Tatum, B. (1992). Talking about race, learning about racism: The application of racial identity development theory in the classroom. *Harvard Educational Review* 62(1): 1–25.

Toomey, R., McGuire, J.K., and Russell, S.T. (2012). Heteronormativity, school climates, and perceived safety for gender nonconforming peers. *Journal of Adolescence* 35(1): 187–196.

Toomey, R.B., Ryan, C., Diaz, R.M., Card, N.A., and Russell, S.T. (2013). Gender-nonconforming lesbian, gay, bisexual, and transgender youth: School victimization and young adult psychosocial adjustment. *Developmental Psychology* 46(6): 1580–1589.

Weinraub, M., Clemens, L.P., Sockloff, A., Ethridge, T., Gracely, E., and Myers, B. (1984). The development of sex role stereotypes in the third year: Relationships to gender labeling, gender identity, sex-types toy preference, and family characteristics. *Child Development* 55: 1493–1503.

Wolpert-Gawron, H. (2018). The Case for Electives in Schools, https://www.edutopia.org/article/case-electives-schools (accessed 25 April 2019).

Wolter, I., Braun, E., and Hannover, B. (2015). Reading is for girls!? The negative impact of preschool teachers' traditional gender role attitudes on boys' reading related motivation and skills. *Frontiers in Psychology* 6: 1267.

Zirkel, S. and Johnson, T. (2016). Mirror, mirror on the wall: A critical examination of the conceptualization of the study of Black racial identity in education. *Educational Researcher* 45(5): 301–311.

Zosuls, K.M., Ruble, D.N., Tamis-LeMonda, C.S., Shrout, P.E., Bornstein, M.H., and Greulich, F.K. (2009). The acquisition of gender labels in infancy: Implications for gender-typed play. *Developmental Psychology* 45(3): 688.

How Stress and Trauma Affect Learning

In 5th grade I started getting into fights and arguments with teachers and girls at school. I would go on rampages—vandalizing bulletin boards, tearing apart displays, and cursing at anyone who crossed my path. I despised my teachers for not questioning my behavior. They never thought: "I don't think a kid wakes up in the morning intending to ruin everyone's day and tear everything apart. There must be a valid reason as to why a child is acting out like this."

—Amya Shaw, 16,

"Living in Shelter: It Took Time to Overcome My Anger and Regain My Confidence"

Stress Reactions Are Not "Logical"

I answered my phone and heard my son say the words that no parent ever wants to hear: "Dad, there's a shooter in my school!" I tried to be calm as I asked him, "Are you safe?" He paused for a few seconds and replied, "Yeah, Dad. I ran out of the school and went to the McDonald's. Can you come and get me?" I raced to get him. As I drove past his school, I could see officers gathered near the front entrance and the panicked looks of other parents.

In the car, my son told me that he and some friends had been near an exit when they heard a teacher shout, "This is not a drill!" Fearing for their lives, they decided it was safest to leave the building. They were met by an officer who said "Keep running!" Convinced that they were running for their lives, they ran to the nearby McDonald's where I picked him up. His other classmates were locked down for more than three hours, not knowing what was happening outside of their classrooms. Thankfully and simultaneously frustratingly, we soon were told that the reason for the lockdown was not a shooter but a computer malfunction.

The next morning, my son said that he didn't want to go to school. I reminded him that the scare was just a technical malfunction and that his school was perfectly safe. But upon hearing his loud protest, my wife reassured him that it was OK to stay home if he didn't feel safe. Seeing how calm he became in that moment, I realized that it didn't matter if the event wasn't "real."

To help him feel safe (and reassure myself), I had tried an "evidence-based" approach to show him that it was illogical to feel afraid. Thankfully, my wife responded in a way that focused on how being in school made him feel, regardless of what the "data" said. She helped him to feel a sense of calm and reduced his stress—so much so that he even asked me to take him to basketball practice at school that same afternoon.

As we have discussed in Chapter 1, DCRT is grounded in the belief that experiences both inside and outside of school influence how adolescents learn and behave in school—and that the relationship between those inside and outside of school experiences has a powerful impact on learning. This chapter will focus on the corrosive experience of stress and trauma on students, how schools contribute to stress, and how to create developmentally and culturally responsive classroom and school environments that reduce stress and support students who have experienced trauma.

Understanding the Differences among Stress, Chronic Stress, and Trauma

According to the Cleveland Clinic, "Stress is the body's reaction to any change that requires an adjustment or response."[1] As the American Psychological Association (APA) notes, when we experience stress, nearly every system of the body responds, and this influences how we think, how we feel, and how we behave.[2] We tend to think of stress as a response to something negative, but positive experiences can also cause stress. I remember how hard I worked to land my first teaching job and how stressed I was before my first class met.

Whether our students feel stress because of positive events, like finally getting into that honors class, or negative ones, like not being sure where they're going to be living from one day to the next, it is a normal part of the school experience.

However, it's important to distinguish among stress, chronic stress, and trauma. Stress is typically temporary and can result from a negative or positive event. Stress is also something we feel that we have some control over, like the stress of a big test. In addition to studying, you might do deep breathing exercises, or take a walk to calm down. The key is that these stressors are temporary and basically manageable.

Chronic stress is what we experience after prolonged exposure to negative stress. It also feels largely outside of our control. We can view it as an accumulation and compounding of negative stressors.

The 17-year-old anonymous author of this story experiences chronic stress from an all-too-common source: taking on parental responsibilities when parents are swamped by challenges. It affects her mental health and her ability to succeed in school:

> The amount of stress in my house is overwhelming. My stepmother can't deal with her rambunctious kids, and too often she either yells at them and hits them or she just leaves the house and all the responsibilities to me.
>
> My father works hard to support the family and pay the bills. He's a good dad when he's around, but he doesn't do much to change how my stepmother runs the household or treats their children.
>
> As for me, sometimes I feel so stressed that I want to scream or run away, but I don't. Instead, I take on many adult responsibilities. Sometimes I feel like the mother of the house.
>
> Every weekend my stepsister and I are supposed to clean the house. I sweep, clean one of the bathrooms, clean the kitchen, and mop. When my stepsister doesn't help out, I clean the entire house alone.
>
> Then there's my three younger half-siblings, ages 4 to 10, to worry about. Most of the time, my stepmother can't handle them. My stepmother was once addicted to

drugs and is incapable of taking care of anyone. She beat her addiction about seven years ago, but she has trouble dealing with her responsibilities.

Sometimes my stepmother is nice. She has a good heart. But other times she scares me. She can be happy one moment, then in the blink of an eye, she's screaming.

Any little thing can trigger her temper. If something bothers her too much, she gets angry at everyone in the house. Often she hits her children, too. When I see my stepmother hitting her children, it boosts my anger to high levels and I feel like calling child services on her. I feel like hitting her.

My stepmother doesn't have a job. Sometimes she just lies down in bed watching TV or sleeping. Other times she gets frustrated with the amount of work that needs to be done around the house and decides to go out. This happens several times a week. Usually I'm in my room doing homework and she comes in and tells me that she'll be right back.

She doesn't come right back, though. It's a routine. Usually she's gone for at least a couple of hours. Every time she leaves, I know that I have to get ready for the stress of watching my three little siblings. I'm so used to it now that I feel more resigned than bitter about it.

When my stepmother leaves, my stepsister, who's a year older than I am, usually just locks herself in our room and goes on the computer or plays a video game. I don't blame her. Because of her mother's addiction, she had to take care of the little ones while she was still very young herself. She had to grow up quickly, so I tell myself that she needs this time.

The most stressful part is when my little siblings don't listen to me.

"No" is my 4-year-old sister's favorite word. "Can you please stop jumping?" I ask her calmly, scared that she might slip or fall as she goes up and down on the couch. "NO!" she'll scream.

"Can you stop running down the hallway? Can you be quiet? I'm trying to talk on the phone. Can you calm down?" I ask her.

"NO! NO! NO!" is always her response. Sometimes I feel so frustrated that I want to scream.

Stress feels controllable. Chronic stress like this writer faces feel overwhelming.

Trauma is different still. It is typically regarded as our response to a deeply disturbing or even life-threatening event that is beyond our ability to manage and that causes some form of psychological impairment. So, while stress may not result in trauma, trauma is always stressful.

Chantel Jackson, 19, had a chaotic family, but it transcended the chronic stress of the preceding writer's family. She was abused by her parents and then placed in foster care, which was extremely traumatic itself. Then, she was further traumatized by abusive foster parents. These experiences profoundly influenced her ability to trust. Her story mirrors those of countless students who have suffered the trauma of everything from relationship violence to arriving in the United States as refugees from war or extreme poverty, to the loss of loved ones:

> Living with so many people who aren't what they seem makes me cautious with everyone. I have a fear of people hiding their real, selfish bad selves behind a nice façade; I'm always waiting for the other shoe to drop.

> I reject kind gestures and words because I don't believe them. Former friends who have seen me grow, change, and overcome trials reach out, and I respond, "I appreciate it but I'm OK"; "I'm fine"; "Thanks for the offer but I'm managing."

> I'm only 19, but I've accepted that I'll never have an adult take care of me. Instead, I hope to find a peer to trust. I'm looking for people who show compassion with their actions, not their words. I'd like a relationship with someone who doesn't make me feel like a burden. I want us to do and say meaningful things without expecting anything in return. That's the foundation of a trusting relationship.

> But my past experiences form a wall between me and other people: I have my guard up against everyone I come into contact with. I think if I were able to trust even one person, it would make me more sociable and less pessimistic.

> I know that my fear and suspicion will make me miss out on friends, jobs, and other opportunities. To try and overcome my past and learn to trust the right people, I've recently enrolled in psychotherapy and am working toward overcoming my mental health issues like anxiety, depression, and PTSD. I take part in supportive

> groups at a place called STEPS to End Family Violence. I can be opinionated and understood there, which makes it feel like a safe space.
>
> I try to stay open and converse. I join groups I wouldn't have joined before. I'm not ready to open all the way up, but I'm not ignoring and closing people off either. My path to finding someone to trust is to communicate with others who share my interests: music, art, books, photography, writing, and spirituality. I can't undo what's happened to me, but I'm moving forward with slightly open arms.

Sometimes when we reach out to young people like Chantel, we fail to connect with them. My "logical" explanation to my son about his school's safety did not connect with his emotions. Similarly, we may be perfectly well-intended in reaching out to a student like Chantel but be rebuffed. That's not because of who we are or our intentions, but because her experience has made her extremely wary of adults in helping roles. Students who have suffered trauma may push back, withdraw, or simply observe us and our actions for a long time before they trust us enough to engage.

The Adolescent Brain's Response to Chronic Stress and Trauma

Multiple studies demonstrate that the adolescent brain is in a development stage.[3] While adolescents may appear to be physically mature and even adult-like, their brains are still "immature." When I discuss adolescent development in my courses, I begin by displaying the word *adolescence* on the board, and then ask students to write down words that immediately come to mind. The most common words include *moody*, *emotional*, *risk-taking*, and *rebellious*. These aren't just clichés. New scientific tools like neuroimaging have enabled scientists to demonstrate that many emotional and behavioral characteristics of adolescents are closely related to typical changes in the developing brain.

One of the most important brain developments during adolescence is called synaptic pruning. As we move from childhood to adolescence, we experience a rapid growth of neurons and synapses, followed by a period of synaptic pruning. Similar to pruning a tree to strengthen its branches, synaptic pruning ensures that the most often used neural connections become stronger by eliminating connections that the brain uses less often.

Another typical change that occurs during adolescence is that neural connections become more refined and neural networks become more specified and localized. Brain functions grow more efficient as they become more associated with specific regions of the brain. For example, logical reasoning tends to be more associated with one region while emotional regulation is more likely associated with another.

The adolescent brain also becomes more stimulated by risk-taking. Numerous studies have demonstrated that, when compared to adults, adolescents experience a greater sense of pleasure from taking risks. But this risk-taking isn't just about fast driving or reckless posts on social media. It's also about speaking up in class or trying out for a school play or team. This willingness to take risks helps adolescents to gain a better sense of their limits and their possibilities; it is an important part of their social and emotional development.

As the adolescent brain matures, it is highly susceptible to being shaped by environmental stimuli. Increasing evidence shows that as children move into adolescence, they are more susceptible to the negative effects of stress.[4] Several studies have documented a rise in stress-related psychological disorders such as anxiety and depression as children transition into adolescence.[5] As we've discussed, stress during adolescence is typical. However, for some adolescents, the cumulative impact of stress and the duration of that stress doesn't just make them feel bad; it can also detrimentally affect their brain's development.

As you could see in Chantel's story, she has the intellectual awareness that her fear and suspicion stem from her experiences. She also knows that those experiences have emotionally changed her. She can't simply wish them away. But she is participating in programs that will enable her to begin to think and feel differently. In time, her thinking and emotions may change, which will probably reflect changes in her brain. It is helpful to know that many behaviors we consider challenging, like the vandalism and cursing that Amya describes at the beginning of this chapter, are not willful misbehavior. Rather, they are typical and even predictable biologically-based responses to stress.

Even more important, to the extent that we create safe and nurturing school climates, we can help to minimize or even reverse these effects.

Here is some basic information about brain science that has helped me take it less personally when students push my buttons and has helped me understand the importance of creating school environments that reduce chronic stress and are sensitive to the impact of trauma.

Studies examining the neurological impact of chronic stress have typically focused on three areas of the brain: the prefrontal cortex, the amygdala, and the hippocampus.[6] The prefrontal cortex is responsible for regulating our thinking, actions, and emotions. It plays a critical role in performing what are termed "executive functions" such as those involved in planning, reasoning, judgment, and logical decision making. The prefrontal cortex regulates these executive functions in flexible ways so that we're able to adapt to changes in our environment. For example, if we're trying to solve a problem, it enables us to monitor what we're doing and what is and isn't working. Then it enables us to shift to more successful strategies. So, the prefrontal cortex plays a critical role in helping us adapt when we encounter stressful situations, and ultimately, regulates how we respond under stress.

While the prefrontal cortex is a highly evolved region of the brain that is responsible for complex functions, research demonstrates that it is also the brain region most negatively impacted by exposure to stress.[7] In her study investigating how stress impairs the prefrontal cortex, Yale University School of Medicine researcher Amy Arnsten found that even mild forms of uncontrollable stress can cause significant loss of prefrontal cognitive abilities. More prolonged stress exposure causes changes in the structure of the prefrontal cortex.[8]

Mild forms of stress can temporarily impair our ability to think, plan, and make logical decisions. However, chronic stress can affect our thinking, our planning, our ability to make logical decisions, and our capacity to understand the consequences of our actions. Recent research demonstrates that cognitive impairments related to the prefrontal cortex are associated with several psychological problems, including depression and post-traumatic stress disorder (PTSD).[9]

Importantly, this research finds that since the prefrontal cortex of adolescents is not fully developed, adolescents may be more sensitive to the effects of stress. When they experience the same stressors that adults do, the negative effects may last longer.[10] (But just as important to teachers, brain plasticity means our actions can help mitigate or reverse those effects.)

Another brain area that is harmed by stress is the amygdala.[11] It plays a crucial role in processing emotions. Studies have demonstrated that the amygdala also regulates responses to stress. It helps us determine which situations are stressful and how to respond appropriately. It also plays a key role in what's commonly called our "fight or flight" mechanism.[12] Studies have also demonstrated that chronic stress causes the amygdala to become "overworked" (referred to as exaggerated amygdala activation), resulting in a number of psychological impairments.

For example, exaggerated amygdala activation is related to a higher general level of anxiety, PTSD, social phobia, and impulsive aggression.[13] It has also been found to switch the brain from thoughtful, reflective regulation by the prefrontal cortex to more rapid reflexive regulation by the amygdala and other brain structures.[14] As a result of this switch, students exposed to chronic stress may be more likely to respond to stress in reactive, uninhibited ways that lack a thoughtful analysis of the consequences.

In addition to the prefrontal cortex and the amygdala, the hippocampus is also adversely affected by exposure to chronic stress.[15] The hippocampus regulates ways in which we learn and form memories. It also plays an important role in how our emotions function and how we react to stress.[16]

Studies have demonstrated that exposure to stress causes structural changes in the hippocampus.[17] While unable to identify a direct causal relationship, researchers believe that this structural change "may be a mediating factor in the decreased learning and memory abilities and increased emotional reactivity seen in adolescents exposed to chronic stress."[18]

I remember working with a few middle school students who always seemed to "overreact" to things that I considered benign. Whether it was someone accidentally stepping on their sneaker or touching their book bag, they reacted in ways that were overblown for the situation. They treated routine incidents as acts of aggression.

When I talked with them and learned their personal stories I saw the stressors behind their reactions. One young man had been homeless for much of the school year. Another had regularly witnessed acts of violence in his home, and another had been the victim of violence in his neighborhood and feared for his safety outside of school. According to Cornell University researcher James Garbarino, traumatic experiences create a lens through which these young men view the world. This lens led to their developing "aggressive cognitions." They saw the world as an unsafe, aggressive place.

So, chronic stress and trauma don't just change behaviors; they can shape the brain in unfortunate ways. Researchers have found that chronic stress and trauma can cause neural connections to strengthen areas of the brain that are related to fear, anxiety, and impulsiveness. Unfortunately, trauma and chronic stress simultaneously weaken neural connections that are related to areas involving reasoning, planning, and behavior control. It also shapes brains in ways that make them highly susceptible to triggers.

In the following excerpt, teen writer Marcus Howell, 17, reflects on his elementary school years and how the trauma of moving between living with his mother and living in foster care shaped his emotional development and negatively impacted his behavior in school:

> Although I didn't know it at the time, my life changed on a cold winter day in the 2nd grade. I was 7 years old and had just returned to my biological mother after four years in foster care. I had left my mother when I was about 2. I was too young to remember why I had left her.
>
> I visited my mother from time to time while I was in foster care. She gave me the impression that she was the kindest, gentlest, and sweetest person in the world, but as soon as I returned to live with her again I found out that wasn't the case.
>
> Out of nowhere, she would change emotions in a moment. Kind, gentle, and sweet one instant, she would be angry and cruel the next.
>
> One day I was sitting with her as she helped my brother Brian with a school lesson. When she saw him write something incorrectly on the page, her calm mood turned violent. She slapped him hard on the side of his face. Tears poured from his eyes

and mine as she abruptly left the room. Thoughts of rage (that no child should endure) rushed through me, but there was nothing I could say or do.

Instead, I began to act out my rage in school. Anger at my mother was the fuel for the destructive power I unleashed on others. I punched, kicked, and cursed any person or thing that stood in my way. I caused my 2nd grade teacher, Mrs. H, a great deal of pain. I would pull away her chair when she went to sit down. I would trip her and laugh at her when she fell.

The worst day happened in the winter. The snow was fresh on the ground as I entered the round lunchroom. There was a short pause at each crowded table as my classmates stared at the School Terror. It was a trip day for our class, so I had been on relatively good behavior the prior week. We were going to a puppet show called Little Red Rocket Hood. As the day went by, I behaved myself pretty well. I sat silently through the show and then we returned to the school.

We filed back into the classroom. The air felt cool in the brightly colored room that was filled with the smell of clay and paints. I remember thinking, "The colors at the show were brighter." Then I quietly took my seat.

"Now just as I promised, class, I will give out the candy that I brought for you," Mrs. H said in her kind, gentle voice.

Candy. Even I, the School Terror, like candy, I said to myself as she gave it out. I quickly gulped down the caramel blocks. I licked my lips greedily and wanted more. So when Mrs. H turned her back, I stood up and grabbed the candy from her desk.

Naturally, some other kid told Mrs. H. She grabbed my arm and pulled me toward her. She stuck her face into mine, staring at me with her grey-blue eyes.

"Get your f-cking hands off me, b-tch!" I yelled at the very top of my lungs, "or I'll get my brothers to kill you!!!"

My voice was thick with rage. How dare she grab me in that way! Only my mother had ever done that.

> Mrs. H released her grip. Her face was in shock and wet with tears. For the first time my anger had completely broken someone. I returned to my seat, also in shock. It was the lowest, meanest, most heartless thing I had ever done. I looked at my teacher and, in the blink of an eye, for just a fleeting moment, I was filled with shame and guilt. Then, in another moment, the feeling of compassion left me.

The accumulated chronic stress and trauma of transitioning between living with an abusive mother and living in foster care shaped how Marcus saw the world. As we've discussed, experiences of chronic stress are often accompanied by feelings of powerlessness. These feelings of powerlessness caused Marcus to experience a heightened need to exert some control over his life. When his teacher grabbed him, she exerted her power over him and reinforced his powerlessness. Coupled with the accumulated chronic stress of experiencing the same feelings at home, the experience of being grabbed triggered his response. It's as though school became too much of a reminder of home.

Marcus's story also reminds us that students who experience chronic stress are more likely to have parents or caregivers who are also experiencing chronic stress. So, the people who students may typically turn to for support (like a parent) may not be prepared to provide that support because they're struggling with the same stressors.

In this story by a parent who wrote for *Rise,* a magazine by parents involved with the child welfare system that Youth Communication published for several years, Philneia Timmons writes about the stresses that contributed to her son acting out in school, and how that impaired her ability to respond appropriately, despite her best intentions:

> The problems started when my son was 10 years old and his grandfather died. His grandfather was more like a father to him than his own father. Many times when my son would visit their house, his father wouldn't be there, but his grandfather was, and they'd sit and talk and have fun.
>
> Before his grandfather died, my son was basically well-behaved. After, he had so many questions, like, "Where do people go when they die?" I could see the anger in his eyes and hear the fear in his voice. I believe his feelings were even stronger because losing his grandfather brought up the sad feelings he had about his father not being around.

My son began to get in trouble just about every day in school. He wasn't working and he was being disruptive. I was running to the school so often that I had to quit my job. I felt so frustrated, I didn't know what to do.

Even though I don't believe in hitting kids, one night I hit him with a belt because his teacher had called to say he had cursed in class. He screamed so loud when I hit him that I stopped, but the damage was already done. The next day the school informed me that they had found bruises on my son's body. [My son and my daughter were put in foster care.]

I felt like a piece of my heart was being ripped out. After my children were taken, I went through terrible pressure and depression, not knowing whether my children were safe. I could not eat or sleep many days and nights.

But when my son's behavior got so bad, I was angry and desperate and I just wanted to do something to stop it. I knew how I acted after my mom hit me—I was so hurt and afraid of another beating that I'd stop doing whatever it was I just got hit for. I thought a beating would make my son stop, too.

I never imagined it would mean I would lose my kids. I was so angry at myself because my children had to suffer for what I'd done. I cried myself to sleep many nights. My emotions were really running wild because I loved my kids so much and it hurt so much to lose them.

[After a period of rebellion, in meetings with the agency about getting my kids back] I spoke calmly but firmly and I carried myself in a way that let them know I was in control.

The agency began to look at me as a person, not as a caseload and docket number. It helped, too, that I began to comply more fully with their requirements. I went to therapy and I completed two parenting skills classes.

Because of all that, I gained permission to take my children to school every day. I took them to doctors' appointments and therapy, too. Eventually I was allowed to spend time with them on the weekends.

> One day my son said to me, "Mommy, you're always telling me what to do." He
> said, "Ma, I would feel better if you said, 'Just try to do it.'" When he said that I
> realized that maybe I was too demanding and I had to accept that my son had ways
> of his own.

Philneia and her son suffered tremendous stress, but his teachers saw only the bruises. Instead of intervening to reduce Philneia's stress, the foster care system inflicted additional trauma on Philneia and her kids. She eventually got help, got her children back, and became a parent advocate in the foster care system, but that didn't take away that her son suffered when Philneia's needs were not met or when he went into care.

Stress, Trauma, and Disproportionality

Between 1995 and 1997, the Centers for Disease Control and Prevention (CDC) conducted a study to investigate how negative childhood experiences affected health and behaviors later in life.[19] Over 17,000 adults were asked whether they had experienced certain Adverse Childhood Experiences (ACE) in the first 18 years of their lives. ACE were categorized in three ways: abuse (including emotional, physical, and sexual abuse), household challenges (having a family member incarcerated, experiencing parental separation, having a physically abused mother, or having someone at home with a substance abuse problem), and neglect (including emotional and physical neglect).

Among the study's key findings was that, "Almost two-thirds of the participants [experienced] at least one ACE while more than one in five reported three or more ACEs."[20] The researchers also found that individuals who had experienced four or more ACE, compared to those experiencing none "had a 4- to 12-fold increase in health risks for alcoholism, drug abuse, depression, and suicide attempts."[21] This study was groundbreaking in identifying links between childhood experiences and adult challenges, but it was limited because most participants were White, middle class, and college-educated.

To investigate the impact of ACE on the health and well-being of a more economically and racially diverse population, in 2012 the Institute for Safe Families conducted a study on the impact of ACE on 1,700 residents of Philadelphia. This survey included the same ACE categories as the original CDC study. However, it also asked about environmental stressors more prevalent in urban communities: feeling unsafe in one's neighborhood, being subject to bullying by peers or classmates, witnessing violence, experiencing racism, and living in foster care.[22]

In this study, almost 70% of respondents reported at least one ACE. They also found that the experience of environmental stressors varied significantly by race. Black respondents were much more likely than Whites to report having witnessed violence, been discriminated against, or felt unsafe in their neighborhood.

More recent studies confirm that Black and Latinx communities and those living in poverty are more likely to report ACE.[23,24] Significantly higher ACE exposures were also reported by those without a high school diploma, those living in poverty, and those who were unemployed or unable to work when compared to those completing high school or higher levels of education, those in higher income brackets, and those with jobs.[25]

These studies demonstrate that Black and Latinx children are more likely to experience multiple stressors caused by toxic and unequal social and economic environmental conditions. They also demonstrate that Black children are more likely to experience the stress and trauma of racism and discrimination. This inevitably places BIPOC students at a heightened level of vulnerability to ACE. They are also more likely to experience stressors linked to their living conditions, such as housing insecurity or community violence.

Hence, BIPOC students are more likely to experience certain stressors (racism), are more likely to experience combinations of stressors (such as housing insecurity coupled with racism), and are more likely to experience longer durations of certain stressors (lifelong experience of racism and discrimination). This disproportionate impact of stress on BIPOC students and students from economically struggling families means we must take extra steps to compensate for those multiple stresses.

Josiah Alexander, 17, experienced the ACE stress of racist taunts that also echoed the history of racist violence against young Black men like himself:

> "Hey Emmett!" a White kid yelled at me as we were playing dodgeball during my 6th grade gym class. I didn't think much of it. I didn't even know what the insult meant, but some kids on the other side of the court started snickering and repeated it. They also made jokes about my whistling. Our gym teacher didn't hear what was going on, so it continued until the period ended.
>
> Later that day when I arrived home, I looked up "whistling and Emmett" and learned about the Emmett Till lynching in 1955. I was obviously aware that Black Americans faced a history of racism, but not entirely aware of how it affected people today. My own experience made that racism real and it shocked me.
>
> I live in a culturally diverse neighborhood in Queens and have gone to predominantly Black schools, so this was my first racist experience. To think that kids thought it was OK to make fun of the lynching of Emmett felt awful to me.
>
> Following this incident, I [did more research on] Black historical figures and current day statistics. I was shocked to learn Black men are incarcerated at a rate of five times that of White men. Then I read about the tragedy of Kalief Browder, a 16-year-old boy from the Bronx who was accused of stealing a backpack. He was jailed on Rikers Island for three years because he didn't have enough money for bail—mostly in solitary confinement.
>
> Knowing that someone this young—close to my own age—had such a terrible experience, made me reflect somberly as I began relating to his story. Watching this young boy have one violent fight after another on the jail's surveillance video frightened me, because it was too close to home. I know men in my neighborhood who have served time and returned with a defeated, almost lifeless look in their eyes.

Fortunately, Josiah's school and neighborhood have created programs that help to buffer the trauma of racism. Josiah goes on to describe two activities that are helpful to him and that help to build a more supportive community:

> While racism and discrimination may not be solved overnight, the first thing I can do to prevent it is to help work towards reform. I am a chapter leader of My

Brother's Keeper, an organization dedicated to helping young men of color gain access to the resources and mentors necessary to thrive.

For example, I was mentoring a Black sophomore in my school, showing him the ropes around certain classes and tutoring him in Algebra II. Although the school year was cut short [by the pandemic], we developed a wholesome bond, and I still help him and talk to him. My Brother's Keeper helped establish a healthy environment for young men in my school.

I am also a mentor and student with Youth Justice Court, a program which allows teens to rule on petty cases and provide an alternative response to youth crime in their community. My Brother's Keeper and the Youth Justice Court help young people of color reach their full potential by supporting them and making them feel valued and heard.

Our Cultural Backgrounds Influence How We Cope

Race and poverty don't just impact the stresses people face. They also influence how we cope with stress and trauma.[26] A report published by the American Psychiatric Association (APA) in 2017 found that racial and ethnic minorities in the United States are less likely than Whites to seek mental health treatment. One reason is that the stigma associated with mental illness has been found to be greater among African American, Latinx, and Asian populations than Whites. For example, research on how African American college students cope with the stress of attending primarily White institutions[27] finds that they are more likely to rely on social support, spiritual and religious practices, and avoidance (such as mental distraction and mental disengagement) as coping mechanisms.[28,29,30]

Fears of racism and discrimination by health care systems also affect how people access services. For example, the lack of diversity among mental health care providers, and the lack of linguistically diverse and culturally competent providers have been associated with underdiagnosis and misdiagnosis of mental health symptoms among African American and Latinx populations.

Finally, economic barriers to care including no or inadequate insurance and poorer quality facilities and services have also been reported to disproportionately impact African American, Asian, and Latinx populations, thus contributing to the lowered levels of help-seeking.

Thus, it's important for educators to be aware that students' cultural and racial backgrounds play an important role in how they navigate stress. In this story, Gabrielle Pascal, 18, writes about how her ideas about therapy were influenced by her experiences as a young Black woman:

> One night when I was 14, I sat my parents down at the dinner table and told them there was something they needed to know. A silence fell over the room; I could hear the rattle of the fridge, birds chirping, and grasshoppers humming outside. I held my head down, terrified my parents would look at me and see a cracked glass, falling apart at the slightest touch.
>
> "I don't know why, but I'm sad and angry all the time," I finally said. "I'm tired, lonely, and I don't ever want to do anything. And it's getting worse. I thought that I could handle it on my own, but I don't think I can."
>
> My mouth started to tremble and tears fell down my face. My mother's hands cupped my cheek. Then she wrapped herself around me and hugged me tight.
>
> Opening up to my parents didn't automatically fix everything, but it helped me start feeling better. They didn't think I was crazy or broken, but they did begin to ask me how I was doing each day. [But] why was it so difficult to talk with my parents about mental health even though my father is a psychologist? I suspected it had something to do with being Black.
>
> According to the Health and Human Services Office of Minority Health, Black Americans are 10% more likely to report serious psychological distress than Whites, but many don't receive the help they need. Misconceptions and deep-rooted stigma surrounding mental illness often keep Black people from seeking treatment.
>
> Many Black communities emphasize recovery through faith and spirituality rather than medication and therapy. Whenever I was sad, upset, or facing any kind of an emotional issue when I was growing up, I was taught that prayer would solve the problem. As a Christian, I can attest to the benefits of prayer; it plays an integral role in my life. However, it shouldn't dissuade people from seeking additional professional help if necessary.

[I read an article] in which Kathryn De Shields, a writer in Atlanta, described her struggles with depression. She recounted holding her pain inside under the guise of being a "strong Black woman."

I can relate to feeling like I have to be "strong." My parents immigrated from Haiti in the 1980s. I grew up hearing stories of how hard they worked to create a beautiful life for our family.

My whole life, I've worked as hard as I could so I wouldn't add to the pressures my parents face. I got good grades, loved God, and kept up good behavior. So when I first started to feel depressed at 14, I tried to hide it.

For instance, when I first started having panic attacks, I would hold my hands over my mouth so no one would hear me hyperventilating. If I started crying, I would bury my face in my knees, sitting in the corner of my bedroom, hoping I'd calm down before anyone came inside. The door of my room was always closed, and eventually I started calling it my "fortress of solitude." Depression was a chip in the mold of perfection I'd worked so hard to cultivate, and I desperately hoped no one could see it.

Talking to my parents brought some relief, but it also felt like I was losing what made me strong. Back then, strength meant displacing myself from all I was feeling, locking it in a safe box in some distant, dark corner of my mind. If that lock were to open, it would mean that I was weak and a burden. So when my parents saw I was having a bad day, I'd say, "I'm just tired," or "I'm OK, don't worry about me."

Gaby and her parents continued talking and eventually helped her begin to look for a therapist:

I think the main reason I didn't open up for so long is the same one that keeps many Black people from seeking professional help: the feeling that I had to be strong. As the daughter of immigrants who have sacrificed so much for me, I felt guilty for being in pain, and I hated myself for feeling the way I did.

Reducing Institutional Stress Caused by School

Over the past six years, I've facilitated focus groups with hundreds of adolescents to talk about their experiences in school. Those conversations have taught me how stressful school and life can be for them. I've found that while students experience a variety of stressors, the majority fall into three categories: institutional (school) stressors, external stressors, and interpersonal ones.

Institutional stressors are imposed on students by how their school day is structured and the demands of their school. External stress stems from demands they face outside of school. Interpersonal stressors relate to students' relationships with peers and adults. Let's examine institutional and external stressors and their relationship to creating supportive classrooms and schools. In my conversations with students, I learned that a school's policies and practices can sometimes, unintentionally, make students' lives more difficult and cause institutional stress.

This anonymous student, age 17, describes stress related to academic achievement that many students feel:

> By the time I was a high school freshman, my anxiety—and my schedule—was out of control. A typical day went something like this: Wake up at 7 a.m. and grab a Red Bull to drink on my way to school. In class, I remind myself to raise my hand and force myself to concentrate. I solve an equation in Algebra 2, but I have the wrong answer, and my face flushes red with embarrassment as some other girl raises her hand and flawlessly corrects the mistake. Time for English, where I try hard to say something that will make my teacher exclaim, "Brilliant!" I fail.
>
> Walking to lunch, I hear a junior complaining about the SATs, which sends a wave of panic through me. Before I've eaten half my grilled cheese, the bell rings and my half hour lunch break is over. It's time for more tests, more hurdles for me to jump over, more chances for me to prove myself, though I never quite feel like I'm doing anything right.
>
> The stress doesn't end after school. I need to write articles for the school paper or volunteer at a homeless shelter or design a layout for the yearbook. I feel an intense

need to get into an amazing, impressive college, and in order to do that, I think I have to do a ridiculous amount of extracurriculars.

I finally get home at 7 p.m., watch TV while snacking, then take a nap until 10:30. I miss dinner, but I've filled up on Pringles so it doesn't matter. I wake up panicked, remembering the massive stack of homework I have sitting on my desk.

"We get way too much homework"—OK, the number of times I've heard a student say "I wish we got more homework" is zero. Having said that, the more I listened to what they were saying about homework, the more I understood just how stressful it can sometimes be. For most students, the issue was a combination of handling homework volume, the ebb and flow of due dates, and their schools' grading policies.

I once asked a team of high school teachers what they thought was a reasonable amount of homework to assign each night. Most said between 30 and 45 minutes. Since students in their school typically received homework from five classes, the average student would face 2½ to 3¾ hours of homework per night—assuming they attacked it highly efficiently.

For some students, that amount of homework was difficult but manageable. But for many students homework accentuated other stresses. The students shared stories of being responsible for siblings, working to help "keep the lights on," and participating in demanding after-school activities. One shared that she helped her younger brother with his homework, but in doing so often neglected to do her own. Each evening they faced stressful decisions about what assignments they would do, which teachers would be the most understanding if they didn't complete the homework, and how to manage domestic responsibilities including simply connecting with their families.

"It really seems like my teachers don't talk to each other"—Across all of my focus groups, one common question students asked was, "Why do we always seem to have things all due on the same day?" Students reported feeling the stress of having certain days when nothing was due and then days when they were inundated with assignments or tests. Collectively, students experienced challenges not simply as too much work, but as a reflection of how little teachers knew about them. "Don't they realize we have lives outside of school?" one student asked. "Either they don't know or they don't care," shared another.

Grace Garcia, 18, is not obsessed with being a top student or getting into an elite college, but like many of her peers, she still struggles to maintain balance and perspective about her schoolwork and needs help from teachers in managing those stresses:

"Did you know Lisa got a 97 average and her class rank is a 2?" my friend Kathy asked me.

"Oh my gosh, that's amazing!" I said excitedly.

"Yeah, but she was crying because she isn't ranked number one," said my other friend Elizabeth.

I was confused. Although I don't mind my 80-plus average, I'd be ecstatic to be in the top 10 of my class and have a 90 average.

I know a lot of teens like Lisa who are rarely satisfied with their grades and feel pressure from their teachers and parents to be perfect. But I've done fine in school with no burning desire to be the best. Most of my friends also get grades in the 80s and work hard like I do. We don't fall apart if we don't get the best grade on a test or assignment. But, in my school, we're a minority.

I value my free time to do things I love, like reading and writing. I try to keep a balance between work and fun. I don't like to be constantly busy—I need to do nothing sometimes.

I identified these priorities in middle school, and they keep me sane and calm. I don't do well under stress. Fortunately, my parents, teachers, and other adults respected these priorities and didn't try to change them.

But that all started to change in my junior year. The work piled on and I became overwhelmed. I had to study for hours for the SATs and ACTs, continue to study for tests for my classes, get in extracurriculars for my college résumé, stay after school for tutoring, and come in on weekends for mandatory extra help and test prep. I felt like if I stopped even for a second, my grades would plummet. I was terrified of that happening.

My teachers constantly reinforced how important junior year was and how much colleges would be looking at it, which placed a bigger weight on me. School was taking over my life.

I felt like I was losing my happy, free self. I couldn't do the things I love most, like hanging out with my friends, writing, reading, taking walks, or just doing nothing. My friendships became weaker. I started having chronic migraines, and I dreaded going to school. Rather than improving, my grades were getting worse because I was too stressed to focus well. I also felt depressed and unmotivated. Suddenly, my teachers were saying, "There's room for improvement," although in the past, my best had been good enough for them.

There was a particular class that put the situation into focus for me. I was in computer science, and we only had a few minutes left to submit our project. My group and I were racing to complete it. If it was a minute late, we would lose credit. Something wasn't working in the code that we had written and I grew frustrated as the clock ticked.

"Forget it! Let's just send what we have." And I hit send.

We went back to our seats and all I could think about was how it was incomplete, and then I suddenly realized what the problem was in the code.

But we had already submitted the project; it was too late. I tried my best to keep calm. My teacher was speaking, but it just sounded muffled to me. I had failed my group and myself because I figured out the solution to the problem too late.

As soon as class was dismissed, I dashed out, pushing past the people in the crowded hallway. I burst into tears and called my older sister. "I can't do this anymore. Can you please pick me up? I want to go home." My teacher saw me and took me into a quiet room. After catching my breath I ended up staying at school, but I felt lost. I was panicking over one group assignment? And for what?

Later I called my sister, who was in her junior year of college, and asked her for help. She said she was going through something similar. "It may seem like the end of the world with all the stress, but you have to push through it. Don't let it get to you because it's almost over. You're a smart girl, you can do it." Talking to her helped me. I knew school would be over in a few weeks, and then I could go back to my old life.

I recently read an article in the *New York Times* that linked suicides among college students to the pressure to be "'effortlessly perfect': smart, accomplished, fit, beautiful, and popular, all without visible effort."

I don't think there is one definition of perfection. Even if society sets out this idea of a perfect person, it's impossible because there are differing opinions about beauty and intelligence and even success. Asking someone to try to be all of this is like asking someone not to be human.

These expectations make young people feel like if we make even a minor mistake, it will greatly impact us. But I think it's important for teens to be allowed to screw up. I've certainly learned a lot by being allowed to do that.

Making a mistake gives you a chance to be a better person and get a clearer understanding of what you did wrong. Also, you will know what to do if you come across a similar situation again. For example, after getting a 65 on a trigonometry test once I felt defeated. But then I went to my teacher to ask him if there was any way I could bring up my grade. He said by doing test corrections I would get a few points back, so I did. The test corrections were also great practice and I understood trig better after that.

Students shared with me that they appreciated teachers' flexibility, like Grace's teacher providing an additional path to a higher grade in trig. They appreciated it when teachers gave them assignments ahead of time so that they could devote time to complete them based on their schedules. They also appreciated teachers who coordinated due dates for assignments so that they weren't overwhelmed on any one day.

"I Need to Get Up and Move"—I've found most schools underestimate the importance of physical comfort and the stress of discomfort. I remember as a young boy being reprimanded for leaning back in my chair. Because I was tall, I would bang my knees on the desk. To relieve the pain, I would occasionally lean back. I can still remember spending energy that I could have been applying to my lessons on trying to avoid chastisement for leaning back.

Numerous studies have demonstrated that the failure to address students' needs for physical comfort and movement causes stress,[31] and can lead to lower academic performance. Yet we seldom think about the physical environment of the classroom: the types of tables and desks, the quality of the chairs, or even the temperature of the rooms. (Wealthy private schools do pay close attention to reducing stress through the design of the physical space. The first impression I often have visiting them is just how comfortable and inviting they are as physical environments.)

A few years ago, I saw first-hand how adapting the physical environment of a middle school classroom improved students' engagement and persistence during a standardized test. I was working with a 6th grade teacher who was struggling to address classroom management issues. Several students would leave their seats without permission to walk across the room and a few leaned back in their chairs to the point of bothering students around them. A few others would simply stay in their seats but their fidgeting would distract students near them.

After a few frustrating weeks, she decided that rather than viewing movement as a violation of a class rule, she would reinterpret it as a physical need. Upon getting approval from her principal, she removed most of the desks and chairs and replaced them with yoga balls, yoga mats, bean bag chairs and tables of varying heights. Students could then sit on these things rather than classroom chairs.

One day I observed her students taking a computer-based standardized test on yoga balls. I had never seen this before, so I was curious to see how students would respond. Several would sit still on their yoga ball for a while as they answered questions, then pause and bounce for a bit, and then return to the questions. After the test, I asked one student if she realized she had been periodically bouncing and if she knew she was doing it, why she did it.

She said that when she got stuck on a question, it was helpful to "bounce it out." It helped her think more clearly. I asked, "Before you had yoga balls, what would you do when you got stuck on a question?" She replied, "I just skipped the question and if I had time I might go back and try to answer it." Simply being able to move during a test addressed a physical need that helped her to persist through a challenging question.

We Need to Be Attuned to the Impact of External Stressors

While the institutional stress of school can be challenging for students to navigate, some students see school as a safe space that provides them with a sense of structure and predictability that contrast with the uncertainty and instability they may experience outside of school. There are countless sources of external stress. I will address two—housing insecurity and lack of sleep—as examples of how we must be aware of external forces that impact our work with students and how we might address them.

Housing insecurity is huge and growing. Nationally, 1.5 million students experienced homelessness in the 2017–2018 school year[32] (the most recent year for which we have data). In New York City alone, 100,000 students—one in 10—experience housing insecurity in a typical year, including several of the teen writers in this book.[33]

Numerous studies have found that housing insecurity can have detrimental effects on mental health.[34] These studies have reported that children who experience housing insecurity are at greater risk of developing anxiety, depression, and symptoms related to PTSD.[35]

In the following excerpt, Amya Shaw, 16, writes about how living in a shelter impacted her social relationships, her mental health, and her school experience:

> Before I went into the shelter system, I was confident. I wanted to try new things and I was very loud. No matter what I was saying, I had to be loud about it. "THERE'S THE ICE CREAM TRUCK! CAN WE GET ICE CREAM PLEASE?"
>
> I was 9 years old and in 4th grade when I went into the shelter system after my family was evicted from our apartment where I had lived my whole life. The night before we moved into the shelter, my mom, dad, and two of my aunts and uncles were packing. I hid under the table and wondered where we were going.
>
> My mother said, "It's only for a little while. We'll be back home soon." And that's what I believed. Little did I know I'd live in and out of a shelter for the next five years.

After a few months in the shelter, I became closed off. I didn't yell when the ice cream truck came by anymore; I didn't announce my arrival home from school with loud laughs and giggles. I just came back to the shelter and curled up on the bed.

I became closed off because in my mind, whether it was true or not, all the other kids at school had a home to go to. And they had things that belonged to them. My bed didn't belong to me. I didn't have a room or a bookshelf or a toy chest. I figured other kids didn't live in one room with their parents and brother. I felt like an outcast.

The only comfort I got was from books. I was in love with *Harry Potter* and *The Hunger Games*. Reading books was like traveling to another world. Reading kept me occupied when my parents argued relentlessly and helped me block out their loud voices. I also wrote a lot. Being able to put my emotions into words relaxed me.

But I had always been a hothead, flying off the handle and having a temper, and this side of me got much worse once we became homeless.

In 5th grade I started getting into fights and arguments with teachers and girls at school. I would go on rampages—vandalizing bulletin boards, tearing apart displays, and cursing at anyone who crossed my path. I despised my teachers for not questioning my behavior. They never thought: "I don't think a kid wakes up in the morning intending to ruin everyone's day and tear everything apart. There must be a valid reason as to why a child is acting out like this."

I am self-aware—I knew what was wrong and why I was acting the way I was acting, but I didn't know how else to deal with it.

Finally, I was assigned to Dr. Morrow, a social worker at my school. Whenever my temper got the best of me, she took me to her office to talk. She let me draw and we ate tea biscuits and delicious muffins while we spoke. Sometimes she would bring me sweaters because she knew how much I loved them.

Dr. Morrow didn't give me exercises or coping skills to help me control my anger: she just let me talk. She didn't treat me like a troubled kid with anger problems. She treated me like a regular human being with a lot going on in her life.

Just being able to talk to someone who understood me helped reduce my lashing out.

I was close with my parents and brother before we went into the shelter system. But, as time went on, I became distant and angry and wanted nothing to do with them. I didn't want to help my mother clean on Sundays anymore. I didn't want to take trips to the library with my dad and read books with him until it closed anymore.

I had no goals and I criticized myself for it. But now I realize that when you are homeless and don't have a stable living situation, it's hard to focus on yourself or do anything well.

In my freshman year of high school, I started to change. I was in a new, healthier environment. This school had supportive teachers and I made more friends.

[I still got into some trouble] but that summer, I began to realize that I had great qualities like my brains, my writing talent, and my self-awareness. I recognized that my anger over being homeless for so long and the constant exposure to my family's violence was legitimate, but I was letting it get in the way of my ability to reach my full potential.

Over the last five years, I have lived in four shelters. But I know this is temporary. When I was younger, I thought my homelessness would be permanent.

I have often thought about Dr. Morrow over the last two years, but I did not feel comfortable reaching out to her. As I was finishing this article I decided to do so. I emailed her and got a response back a few days later. I was ecstatic to hear from her again. We both agreed that we would meet soon, and I can't wait. It will feel good to see the one person I felt was always there for me during those difficult years. I can't control my homelessness, but I can try to take care of myself.

In his research examining the impact of chronic stress and trauma on youth, Dr. James Garbarino finds that these experiences reshape the way youth view their world. He reported that youth experiencing chronic stress and trauma may initially develop coping skills that help them navigate their stressors, but ultimately, the accumulated chronic stress and trauma is beyond their ability to cope. We see this clearly in Amya's story. She became distant and angry and lost her motivation. If not for her exceptional self-awareness, a counselor who listened, and switching to a school with a healthier culture, her story could have ended on a much less hopeful note.

Exhaustion is another external stressor. Students in focus groups tell me that coping with multiple stressors simultaneously—schoolwork, relationships, home life issues—tires them out. I began asking them what time they went to bed on a school night and what time they woke up for school. I began to realize that many were getting as little as 7 hours of sleep per night with a smaller number getting as little as 6. This is far below the recommended 9 to 11 hours for middle school students and 8 to 10 hours for high school students.[36] When I asked them how fatigue affected them in school, they said it made it hard to focus in class (particularly morning classes) and that it made them "moody" and "irritable" at times. These were students who were talking about navigating what most might view as the typical stressors of adolescence. So, what do sleep habits mean for students experiencing chronic stress or trauma?

Lack of sleep doesn't just cause stress; it can be a consequence of it. Several recent studies have identified a link between chronic stress and trauma, and sleep deprivation.[37] People who are sleep-deprived also exhibit inattention, impulsivity, increased aggressive behavior, a loss of control of emotions, and an inability to concentrate.[38] These are the same characteristics associated with Attention Deficit Hyperactivity Disorder (ADHD).[39] In fact, several studies have found that parents of children diagnosed with ADHD often report that their children experience sleep disruptions. Some of these studies have also reported that addressing children's problematic sleep has been associated with reductions in ADHD symptoms.[40]

These findings provide clues for educators seeking deeper understanding of student behavior, especially given the overdiagnosis of ADHD reported by the National Institutes of Child Health and Human Development and the disproportionately high rate of ADHD diagnoses that have been documented in schools with predominantly African American and Latinx enrollments.[41]

A Developmentally and Culturally Responsive Approach to Understanding Student Behavior

As we have noted, being developmentally and culturally responsive involves reconsidering how we think about problematic student behavior. If we begin by viewing behavior as willfully disruptive, then we're more likely to consider punishment as our default response. However, if we view problematic student behavior as a response to stress, then we can try to help students identify and manage their stressors.

This isn't easy. If a student throws an object across the room or treats other students with disrespect, our first instinct is often to issue some negative consequence. I am not saying that students shouldn't be held accountable for misbehavior. What I am saying is that viewing misbehavior as a stress response means that we think about what we do in *addition* to the consequence. We have to recognize that if it worked to yell at students, or detain or suspend them, we wouldn't have to keep doing it.

A DCRT approach to classroom management means viewing student misbehavior as a response to institutional, interpersonal, and external stressors. Those students who become disruptive immediately after you've given them an assignment may not simply be "acting out," but may instead be trying to avoid the stress of an assignment that will make them feel dumb. Those students who seem to overreact to what you might consider to be "little things"—like when someone accidentally touches them or when you call them out to redirect their behavior—may view those things as acts of aggression toward them and they may respond aggressively to assert their power to protect themselves.

A DCRT approach to supporting students who experience stress and trauma involves understanding the sources of their stress, how stress shapes brain development, and how they behave in response to stress. As we've discussed, adolescents are typically exposed to multiple simultaneous stressors that they need to skillfully navigate to succeed in school. Thus, supporting students who've experienced chronic stress and trauma requires multiple layers of support at the classroom and school levels.

What Teachers Can Do

1. Rethink student behavior: Is it a stress response?

What if we thought of problematic student behaviors as how they respond to stress? I've learned that every student behavior that I might consider to be problematic has a purpose. Seeking to understand the purposes of their behavior can help us better support our students. A DCRT approach to classroom management means focusing on how student behavior is a response to unmet cognitive, physical, social, and emotional needs.

Most of the disruptive student behavior that I've witnessed tends to fall into four categories: (1) an attempt to gain attention; (2) an attempt to avoid something that makes them feel uncomfortable; (3) an attempt to assert power and control; or (4) a reflection of a lack of social and emotional competence. While I find this to be the case for most students, the needs may be deeper and responses to unmet needs even more pronounced for students experiencing the impact of chronic stress.

That student who you always must ask to be quiet could be trying to satisfy a need for attention. That student who always seems to get up to throw something in the garbage as soon as you hand out an assignment might be trying to avoid the task because not understanding the material causes him or her stress. That disinterested student who seems to never want to learn no matter how hard you try to make your lessons fun and exciting might simply feel defeated and powerless in your class and may indirectly be asking: "Why don't you ever ask me what I would like to learn about?" That student who mistreats classmates and even disrespects you might be "acting out" because they don't have the skills to cope with their stressors. Seeing it as a stress response, instead of a challenge to our authority, for example, can make our response more humane and effective.

2. Reflect on how our responses to student behaviors reflect our own needs.

If students' behaviors are linked to their needs, then wouldn't it make sense to think that our responses to their behaviors might be linked to our needs? As a teacher, I've sometimes found myself questioning whether I was somehow making my students' behavior worse. Was I doing things that were triggering negative responses? Most importantly, were these things that I was doing related to my unmet needs as a teacher? One important way that we can help students to manage their stressors is to try our best to avoid being stressors ourselves.

As we've discussed in earlier chapters, being developmentally and culturally responsive includes awareness, knowledge, and skill. An important component of how we support our students is knowing how our behavior reflects our unmet needs for attention, avoidance, or control. So being aware also means being self-reflective. Asking ourselves the following questions can help to end a cycle of misbehavior and punishment:

- Am I pushing my students too hard and getting frustrated when they don't meet my expectations because it's important for me to be recognized as a "successful" teacher?
- Am I ignoring or avoiding challenging students because they make me uncomfortable in some way?
- Do I try too hard to constantly be in control of my classroom because I feel powerless and unable to make a positive impact on my students?
- Do I need help to manage how I respond to stress?

Reflecting on our answers to those questions increases awareness of how our needs and behaviors may be contributing to our students' stress levels. For example, is it really that important for me to be in complete control? What would happen if I gave students more voice and choice in what we do as a class? How does my need to assert my power trigger their response to exert control over their own lives? Is my goal student compliance or having my students be excited about learning in school? We can use that awareness to develop more effective practices.

3. Teach in ways that reduce student stress.

One major stress point that students reported during focus groups was homework. Numerous studies have also identified homework as one of the leading sources of stress for adolescents.[42] These studies find that volumes of homework that aren't developmentally appropriate can stress out students. In response, both the National Education Association (NEA) and the National PTA (NPTA) recommend a standard of 10 minutes of homework per night per grade level with 6th graders receiving 60 minutes, those in 9th receiving 90 minutes, and seniors receiving 120 minutes.[43]

We also overrate the effect of homework. A study of over 4,300 students from 10 high-achieving high schools found that only 20% to 30% of students found homework to be meaningful or useful.[44] The researchers recommend that teachers focus on the quality of the assignments rather than the quantity of homework students are assigned.

Ask yourself: "What's the purpose of this homework?" If the purpose is for students to demonstrate what they can do independently without teacher support, does it always have to be completed outside of school? I'm a big proponent of incorporating independent practice activities within lessons. This is particularly important for students without internet access at home, a quiet place to complete homework, or who have competing demands on their time.

Another helpful question for making homework more strategic is: "What is the smallest amount of information that I need to see to know that my students are learning?" Asking that question can help tightly focus homework assignments.

A more collaborative approach that I've seen is when teachers coordinate some assignments across several content areas (such as through thematically oriented assignments that require students to draw on information they've learned across different subject areas). The Public Broadcasting Service's Learning Media site has resources for coordinating math, science, and art assignments (https://www.ny.pbslearningmedia.org/).

What Schools Can Do

1. Employ a multidimensional approach to examining student stress.

As we've discussed in this chapter, all students experience stress. They experience the stress of making and maintaining healthy relationships with their peers, managing schoolwork, and simultaneously navigating their school and home lives. Furthermore, the type of stress that students experience and the duration of that stress often varies based on race and poverty. We have also identified three categories of stress that students typically experience: institutional stress, external stress, and interpersonal stress. Educators have significant influence over institutional stress. For example, schools can establish policies for how many tests can be administered on a given school day or practices that reduce homework by including more opportunities for independent work within class.

Schools can also raise their awareness of the extra institutional stress experienced by BIPOC students by intentionally seeking to better understand their unique school experiences. Student surveys, focus groups, and written testimonials from students can provide critical insight into the school-based factors that contribute to stress. Asking the following questions can help identify sources of institutional stress and ways to address them:

- What are the typical sources of school-related stress that most students experience?
- Are there sources of school-related stress that BIPOC students are more likely to experience?
- What policies and practices do we have in place that unintentionally contribute to institutional stress? Which can we change?
- What do students say about how to reduce or eliminate institutional stress?

2. Identify the sources of teacher stress.

Teacher stress is a leading factor in decisions to leave the field.[45] While numerous factors have been found to contribute to teacher stress, they tend to fall into one of three categories: organizational factors (such as school climate); interpersonal factors (the quality of relationships between teachers and their colleagues or the challenges they experience when working with certain students); and intrapersonal factors (such as the personal strategies they use to cope with stress).

To reduce teacher stress, it's important to attack it from this multidimensional perspective. Efforts to support teachers in one category may prove unsuccessful due to the impact of stress in other categories. For example, practicing self-care will have little impact if the primary source of stress is ineffective school administrators or chronic lack of resources. The following questions can help guide an interrogation of teacher stress and how to mitigate it:

- How does our organizational structure and climate contribute to teacher stress?
- What aspects of our school climate do we need to address to decrease the level of interpersonal stress experienced by all school stakeholders?
- What professional learning opportunities can we provide to teachers to help them more successfully manage and cope with work-related stress?

Notes

1. https://www.my.clevelandclinic.org/health/articles/11874-stress.
2. https://www.dictionary.apa.org/stress.
3. Blakemore and Choudhury 2006.
4. Hollis et al. 2013; McCormick and Mathews 2010; Park and Schepp 2015.
5. Romeo 2017; Lindsey, Sheftall, Xiao, and Joe 2019.
6. Spear 2013.
7. Arnsten 2009; Heisler et al. 2015.
8. Arnsten 2009.
9. Heisler et al. 2015.
10. Niwa et al. 2013; Romeo et al. 2013.
11. Romeo et al. 2013.
12. Cohen et al. 2013.
13. Hölzel et al. 2010, p. 11.
14. Arnsten 2009.
15. McEwen 2001.
16. Fanselow and Dong 2010.
17. Carrion and Wong 2012.
18. Romeo 2017.

19. https://www.cdc.gov/violenceprevention/acestudy/about.html.

20. https://www.cdc.gov/violenceprevention/acestudy/about.html.

21. Felitti et al. 1998.

22. Research and Evaluation Group (2013). Findings from the Philadelphia Urban ACE Survey.

23. Wade Jr., Shea, Rubin, and Wood 2014.

24. Merrick, Ford, Ports, and Guinn 2018.

25. Ibid.

26. Knight and Sayegh 2010.

27. Shahid, Nelson, and Cardemil 2018.

28. Brown, Phillips, Abdullah, Vinson, and Robertson 2011.

29. Barnett 2004.

30. Brown et al. 2011.

31. Skoffer and Foldspang 2008; Haapala et al. 2014.

32. *Education Week* 2020.

33. *New York Times* 2020.

34. Sandel et al. 2018.

35. Cowan 2014.

36. National Sleep Foundation 2020.

37. Han et al. 2012.

38. National Sleep Foundation 2020.

39. American Psychiatric Association 2013.

40. Konofal, Lecendreux, and Cortese 2010.

41. Coker et al. 2016.

42. Pope, Brown, and Miles 2015.

43. American Psychological Association 2016.

44. Galloway, Connor, and Pope 2013.

45. Ryan et al. 2017.

References

American Psychiatric Association. (2013). *Diagnostic and Statistical Manual of Mental Disorders (DSM-5®)*. American Psychiatric Pub.

Arnsten, A.F. (2009). Stress signalling pathways that impair prefrontal cortex structure and function. *Nature Reviews Neuroscience* 10(6): 410–422.

Barnett, M. (2004). A qualitative analysis of family support and interaction among Black college students at an Ivy League university. *Journal of Negro Education* 53–68.

Bath, H. (2008). The 3 pillars of trauma-informed care. *Reclaiming Children and Youth*, Fall 2008, 17(3): 17–21.

Blakemore, S.J. and Choudhury, S. (2006). Development of the adolescent brain: Implications for executive function and social cognition. *Journal of Child Psychology and Psychiatry* 47 (3–4), 296–312.

Bottiani, J.H., Duran, C.A., Pas, E.T., and Bradshaw, C.P. (2019). Teacher stress and burnout in urban middle schools: Associations with job demands, resources, and effective classroom practices. *Journal of School Psychology* 77, 36–51.

Brown, T., Phillips, C., Abdullah, T., Vinson, E., and Robertson, J. (2011). Dispositional versus situational coping: Are the coping strategies African Americans use different for general versus racism-related stressors? *Journal of Black Psychology* 37: 311–335. doi:10.1177/0095798410390688.

Carrion, V.G. and Wong, S.S. (2012). Can traumatic stress alter the brain? Understanding the implications of early trauma on brain development and learning. *Journal of Adolescent Health* 51(2): S23–S28.

Chun, C.A., Moos, R.H., and Cronkite, R.C. (2006). Culture: A fundamental context for the stress and coping paradigm. In *Handbook of Multicultural Perspectives on Stress and Coping*, 29–53. Boston, MA: Springer.

Cohen, M., Jing, D., Yang, R., Tottenham, N., Lee, F., and Casey, B. (2013). Early-life stress has persistent effects on amygdala function and development in mice and humans. *Proceedings of the National Academy of Sciences* 110(45): 18274–18278.

Coker, T.R., Elliott, M.N., Toomey, S.L., Schwebel, D.C., Cuccaro, P., Emery, S.T., . . . and Schuster, M.A. (2016). Racial and ethnic disparities in ADHD diagnosis and treatment. *Pediatrics* 138(3).

Cole, S.F., Eisner, A., Gregory, M., and Ristuccia, J. (2013). *Helping Traumatized Children Learn, Volume 2: Creating and Advocating for Trauma-Sensitive Schools*, Massachusetts Advocates for Children.

The Council of School Superintendents. (2019). Ninth Annual Survey of New York State School Superintendents on Financial Matters, November.

Cowan B.A. (2014). Trauma exposures and mental health outcomes among sheltered children and youth ages 6–18. In: *Supporting Families Experiencing Homelessness* (eds. M. Haskett, S. Perlman, and B. Cowan). New York: Springer.

Davis, D. and Hayes, J.A. (2012). What are the benefits of mindfulness. American Psychological Association, *Monitor on Psychology*. July/August. http://www.apa.org/monitor/2012/07-08/ce-corner.aspx.

Dymnicki, A., Wandersman, A., Osher, D., Grigorescu, V., Huang, L., and Meyer, A. (2014). Willing, able→ ready: Basics and policy implications of readiness as a key component for implementation of evidence-based practices. *ASPE Issue Brief.* Washington, DC: Office of the Assistant Secretary for Planning and Evaluation, Office of Human Services Policy. Washington, DC: U.S. Department of Health and Human Services.

Education Week. (2020). https://www.edweek.org/technology/number-of-homeless-students-hits-all-time-high/2020/02 (accessed December 2020).

Fanselow, M.S. and Dong, H.W. (2010). Are the dorsal and ventral hippocampus functionally distinct structures? *Neuron* 65(1): 7–19.

Felitti, V., Anda, R., Nordenberg, D., Williamson, D., Spitz, A., Edwards, V., and Marks, J. (1998). Relationship of childhood abuse and household dysfunction to many of the leading causes of death in adults: The Adverse Childhood Experiences (ACE) Study. *American Journal of Preventive Medicine* 14(4): 245–258.

Frey, N., Fisher, D., and Everlove, S. (2009). *Productive Group Work: How to Engage Students, Build Teamwork, and Promote Understanding*. Alexandria, VA: ASCD.

Galloway, M., Connor, J., and Pope, D. (2013). Nonacademic effects of homework in privileged, high-performing high schools. *The Journal of Experimental Education* 81(4): 490–510. doi:10.1080/00220973.2012.745469.

Garbarino, J. (2001). An ecological perspective on the effects of violence on children. *Journal of Community Psychology* 29(3): 361–378.

Haapala, E.A., Poikkeus, A.M., Kukkonen-Harjula, K., Tompuri, T., Lintu, N., Väistö, J., . . . and Lakka, T.A. (2014). Associations of physical activity and sedentary behavior with academic skills–A follow-up study among primary school children. *PloS One* 9(9): e107031.

Han, K.S., Kim, L., and Shim, I. (2012). Stress and sleep disorder. *Experimental Neurobiology* 21(4): 141–150. doi:10.5607/en.2012.21.4.141.

Harris, M. and Fallot, R. (eds). (2001). *Using Trauma Theory to Design Service Systems: New Directions for Mental Health Services*. San Francisco, CA: Jossey-Bass.

Heisler, J.M., Morales, J., Donegan, J.J., Jett, J.D., Redus, L., and O'Connor, J.C. (2015). The attentional set shifting task: A measure of cognitive flexibility in mice. *JoVE (Journal of Visualized Experiments)* (96): e51944.

Hölzel, B.K., Carmody, J., Evans, K.C., Hoge, E.A., Dusek, J.A., Morgan, L., . . . and Lazar, S.W. (2010). Stress reduction correlates with structural changes in the amygdala. *Social Cognitive and Affective Neuroscience* 5(1), 11–17. doi:10.1093/scan/nsp034.

Hopper, E.K., Bassuk, E.L., and Olivet, J. (2010). Shelter from the Storm: Trauma-Informed Care in Homelessness Services Settings. *The Open Health Services and Policy Journal* 3: 80–100.

Hummer, V.L., Crosland, K., and Dollard, N. (2009). *Applied Behavioral Analysis within a Trauma-Informed Framework*. Presented at the Florida Center for Inclusive Communities "Lunch n Learn" Series. Tampa, FL.

Hummer, V.L., Dollard, N., Robst, J., and Armstrong, M.I. (2010). Innovations in implementation of trauma-informed care practices in youth residential treatment: A curriculum for organizational change. *Child Welfare* 89(2): 79–95.

Jennings, A. (2004). *Models for Developing Trauma-Informed Behavioral Health Systems and Trauma-Specific Services*. Alexandria, VA: National Association of State Mental Health Program Directors, National Technical Assistance Center for State Mental Health Planning.

Jennings, P.A., Frank, J.L., Snowberg, K.E., Coccia, M.A., and Greenberg, M.T. (2013). Improving classroom learning environments by Cultivating Awareness and Resilience in Education (CARE): Results of a randomized controlled trial. *School Psychology Quarterly* 28(4): 374.

Knight, B.G. and Sayegh, P. (2010). Cultural values and caregiving: The updated sociocultural stress and coping model. *The Journals of Gerontology: Series B* 65(1): 5–13.

Konofal, E., Lecendreux, M., and Cortese, S. (2010). Sleep and ADHD. *Sleep Medicine* 11(7): 652–658.

Lindsey, M., Sheftall, A.H., Xiao, Y., and Joe, S. (2019). Trends of suicidal behaviors among high school students in the United States, 1991–2017. *Pediatrics* 144(5): 1–10.

McEwen, B.S. (2001). Plasticity of the hippocampus: Adaptation to chronic stress and allostatic load. *Annals of the New York Academy of Sciences* 933(1): 265–277.

McFarland, J., Hussar, B., Wang, X., Zhang, J., Wang, K., Rathbun, A., . . . and Mann, F.B. (2018). *The Condition of Education 2018*. NCES 2018-144. National Center for Education Statistics.

Meiklejohn, J., Phillips, C., Freedman, M.L., Griffin, M.L., Biegel, G., Roach, A., . . . and Isberg, R. (2012). Integrating mindfulness training into K–12 education: Fostering the resilience of teachers and students. *Mindfulness* 3(4): 291–307.

National Child Traumatic Stress Network. (2005). Promoting culturally competent trauma-informed practices. *NCTSN Culture & Trauma Briefs* 1(1):

National Sleep Foundation, (2020). https://www.thensf.org/ (accessed April 2020).

The New York Times Magazine (2020). https://www.nytimes.com/interactive/2020/09/09/magazine/homeless-students.html (accessed September 2020).

Niwa, M., Jaaro-Peled, H., Tankou, S., Seshadri, S., Hikida, T., Matsumoto, Y., . . . and Sawa, A. (2013). Adolescent stress-induced epigenetic control of dopaminergic neurons via glucocorticoids. *Science* (New York, N.Y.) 339(6117): 335–339. doi:10.1126/science.1226931.

Osher, D. (2018). Trauma and Learning Policy Initiative (TLPI): Trauma-sensitive schools descriptive study. Final report. American Institutes for Research.

Park, S. and Schepp, K.G. (2015). A systematic review of research on children of alcoholics: Their inherent resilience and vulnerability. *Journal of Child and Family Studies* 24(5): 1222–1231.

Pope, D., Brown, M., and Miles, S. (2015). *Overloaded and Underprepared: Strategies for Stronger Schools and Healthy, Successful Kids*. San Francisco, CA: Jossey-Bass.

Pressman, R.M., Sugarman, D.B., Nemon, M.L., Desjarlais, J., Owens, J.A., and Schettini-Evans, A. (2015). Homework and family stress: With consideration of parents' self-confidence, educational level, and cultural background. *The American Journal of Family Therapy* 43(4): 297–313.

Romeo, R.D. (2017). The impact of stress on the structure of the adolescent brain: Implications for adolescent mental health. *Brain Research* 1654: 185–191.

Ryan, S.V., Nathaniel, P., Pendergast, L.L., Saeki, E., Segool, N., and Schwing, S. (2017). Leaving the teaching profession: The role of teacher stress and educational accountability policies on turnover intent. *Teaching and Teacher Education* 66: 1–11.

Sandel, M., Sheward, R., de Cuba, S.E., Coleman, S.M., Frank, D.A., Chilton, M., . . . and Cutts, D. (2018). Unstable housing and caregiver and child health in renter families. *Pediatrics* 141(2): 2017–2199.

Shahid, N.N., Nelson, T., and Cardemil, E.V. (2018). Lift every voice: Exploring the stressors and coping mechanisms of Black college women attending predominantly White institutions. *Journal of Black Psychology* 44(1): 3–24.

Skiba, R.J., Horner, R.H., Chung, C.G., Rausch, M.K., May, S.L., and Tobin, T. (2011). Race is not neutral: A national investigation of African American and Latino disproportionality in school discipline. *School Psychology Review* 40(1): 85–107.

Skoffer, B., and Foldspang, A. (2008). Physical activity and low-back pain in schoolchildren. *European Spine Journal* 17(3): 373–379.

Spear, L.P. (2013). Adolescent neurodevelopment. *Journal of Adolescent Health* 52(2): S7–S13.

U.S. Department of Education. (2016). Non-Regulatory Guidance: Using Evidence to Strengthen Education Investments. http://www2.ed.gov/policy/elsec/leg/essa/guidance useseinvestment.pdf.

Wade Jr., R., Shea, J.A., Rubin, D., and Wood, J. (2014). Adverse childhood experiences of low-income youth. *Pediatrics* 134(1): 13–20.

Walkley, M. and Cox, T.L. (2013). Building trauma-informed schools and communities. *Children & Schools* 35(2): 123–126.

Weir, K. (2016). Is homework a necessary evil? *Monitor on Psychology,* American Psychological Association 47(3): 36.

How We Can Help Students Heal and Do Better in School

Since I've gotten more open to forging deeper relationships, I appreciate teachers and staff more, especially those who show respect and love for me. They help guide me, whether that's learning how to take care of my mental health or talking about the stresses of school.

—Parris Smith, 18,
from "Poverty Made Me Ashamed and Secretive"

We Need More Compassionate Schools (the COVID-19 Pandemic Made That Even Clearer)

Many educators are urging schools to become centers of care that give full attention to the social and emotional needs of children alongside academic instruction. We need to make this shift because we care deeply about our students and want our schools and classrooms to be places where they feel welcomed and supported for their whole selves, not just their academic selves. We know that students are more likely to aspire to academic achievement when they feel safe, secure, and heard, and when they see a connection between their lives and course content.

The relationship between caring and academic performance was underscored on March 11, 2020, and the year that followed. As I was on my way to teach a class that day, a student stopped me and said, "Did you hear? The college is closing after today." That didn't seem possible. But by that evening it was all too real. Schools in several states had already announced plans to close due to the COVID-19 pandemic. Other states would soon follow.

As this information was sinking in, my initial worry wasn't about how to shift my course online. It was about how to maintain the sense of community we had created. The students shared my concern and were anxious that it could suddenly end.

In the first video meeting after the shift to remote learning, I expected to begin as I always did—with an open-ended conversation about how students were doing and then shifting to a class discussion on the assigned readings. This time, we never got to the readings. All we talked about was how they were feeling, the stress they felt, and the personal challenges they faced. Colleagues at the university and teachers in the many school districts I work with had similar stories of needing to connect with our students before returning to academic content (whether they were elementary students or graduate students). We also shared stories of how important it was for us to know how our students were doing so that we could adjust our classes in response to their needs. Several of us also noted that colleagues who tried to plow right ahead with academics quickly learned that they needed to change course.

I soon learned that pandemic impacts varied from student to student. Some were ill themselves and others lost family members to the virus. But most importantly, I learned that the accumulation of simultaneous stressors—including loss, social isolation, unemployment, or working in an essential job, plus the fear of illness—made it increasingly difficult for my students to cope. And I teach adults.

Adolescents were having an even more difficult time. Layla Yagersys, 17, describes how the pandemic exacerbated anxiety that she had already worked hard to control:

> One day last year, during my sophomore year, I was locked in an elevator at school for 30 minutes with about 12 people. It was like being in a cage where I did not know if we were going to get out, and I was worried that we might run out of air.
>
> Claustrophobia had always made it difficult for me to breathe. But no one else seemed to be bothered by it—everyone was laughing, teasing and joking—while I was in a corner, scared, and breathing heavily. Remembering that moment still makes my heart race. The elevator finally started again and we landed on the first floor. Walking out, I was shaking.

I decided I needed to seek help from the school psychologist. She gave me advice like trying to find a distraction in enclosed spaces like the subway, whether it be reading a book or listening to music. She also taught me how to control my breathing, which became an important basis for calming me down and reducing my anxiety levels. My anxiety started to feel more under control. In general I was calmer, going up an elevator was easier, and the breathing exercises were a great help while riding the subway. I was no longer surrounded by constant worries.

But then, the pandemic weakened my grasp on controlling my anxiety.

I knew that worrying too much could worsen my anxiety. But over time, with more countries reporting more cases, my fear increased. When the virus came here, the train became a torture chamber again. With the number of infections rapidly rising, classes were suspended. The last day we had school was also the last day that I went outside for over a month. Not knowing the future became chilling, and being at home locked up with fear caused insomnia, which I had struggled with before. I hardly ate, I had headaches, and my anxiety levels became high again.

I often thought about how a simple phrase like, "I will see you on Monday," in a matter of days became, "Maybe I'll see you in June."

Even for students like Layla, who were healthy and whose family members were relatively safe, the stress of social isolation and uncertainty proved extremely challenging. And then, on top of the pandemic stress, the televised killing of George Floyd by the Minneapolis police and the killing of Breonna Taylor in her bed by police in Louisville, Kentucky, intensified feelings of fragility and anguish, especially for many of our most vulnerable students.

Just as the pandemic exposed anxieties and injustices that had been hidden in plain sight, the widely publicized police killings, and the later anti-Asian attacks, brought to the surface pain and trauma that Black and other vulnerable students were already experiencing. Long before the pandemic, Christina Oxley, 18, was reluctant to join a Black student affinity group at her mostly White school "because I was scared to draw attention to my Blackness." When she entered 9th grade, however, she found supportive peers among the senior class:

> My new friends taught me how to advocate for myself. They taught me how to be unapologetically Black, and more importantly, unapologetically me. I had Black teens to look up to and go to for advice. Between them and the Black girls in my own grade, I had a support system that looked like me.
>
> Feeling empowered by my Black senior friends, I spoke up even more than I had in middle school. I had started growing out my natural hair and I was almost aggressively pro-Black. Freshman year was the first time I said to a White person, "Don't touch my hair," a phrase I would end up repeating countless times.

As she became more comfortable with herself, Christina also became more comfortable speaking out:

> By sophomore year, my nickname might as well have been the Angry Black Woman. By then I was reading Ta-Nehisi Coates and Malcolm X. I followed pro-Black accounts on Instagram and Twitter and found the representation I needed. Influenced by all of this, I finally found words to express my feelings about my Black experience.

But speaking up and speaking out took an emotional toll on Christina, and threatened to take an academic toll as well:

> On top of an intense workload, studying for the SAT, and choreographing pieces for the dance ensemble, I was trying to dismantle the systems that subtly oppress marginalized groups in my school. But it wasn't working. By junior year I'd lost count of all the frustrating conversations I'd had with my peers and the times I'd been called angry or scary. (Not to mention the times I had to correct teachers who called me Stephanie instead of Christina because they couldn't tell the difference between the Black students.)
>
> "Why are they always talking about race? We get it already," my classmates would say, groaning and rolling their eyes. But they obviously didn't get it.
>
> Spending my energy trying to educate people who will never see me as their equal started to affect me in a way I hadn't expected. For the first time ever, I was tired of being an activist.

I walked around feeling defeated. I wanted to be able to go to school without having to think about race. I wanted to be able to change my hairstyle without worrying about being gawked at. I wanted to create a world where bigotry didn't exist, and I wanted to be able to live in it. But I realized that no matter how much effort I put in, or how patient and calm I force myself to be, I can't transform my school into that kind of utopia.

After talking to a few trusted teachers, I realized I was not taking care of myself. Fighting racism 24/7 exhausted me. To preserve my sanity, I had to learn that not every fight is worth my energy, and to let some things go so I'm not angry all the time. I am still trying to figure out how to balance speaking out with putting my mental health first.

Earlier this year, I got a text from my friend Isabel, apologizing for touching my hair in 9th grade. She wrote, "I know it's really, really late, but I've learned so much since, particularly that me being White allows me to get away with crap like that, and I want you to know that I'm really sorry."

Isabel's message reminded me that what I'm doing is necessary and I shouldn't give up. I told her that it's important to acknowledge things like this because that's what progress looks like. It surprised me how much this text meant to me. It's a reminder that change is slow, but not impossible. If racism was easy to eradicate, people would have done it already, so I feel that my goal is to keep moving forward.

Christina is exceptionally self-aware about the traumatic impact of racism. We can't expect every student to be so thoughtful, and we shouldn't place that burden on them. As educators, we need to affirmatively listen and respond to our Christinas. For example, after her story was published, her school administration became more proactive; it began using her story in professional development sessions to build a school culture where all students feel welcomed and safe.

Psychologically Healthy Students Are Better Students

For many of our students, the tragic events of COVID-19 in 2020 simply revealed what they already knew and felt: The historic legacy of systemic racial and economic injustice that undergirds American society compounds the risk of those most vulnerable to trauma, illness, and physical harm.

And, for those who didn't already appreciate the special significance of school as a psychologically safe space, current events underscored that fact. When in-person school shut down, many students didn't just lose a place of learning, they lost a place for safe and supportive socializing in a community of peers and adults. For them, school is a place where they can focus on themselves and their needs. They can think about which of the expectations of their family and home culture they want to honor and which they want to transform or discard as they grow into independent adulthood. It's a place where they receive supportive care from adults during that growth process. Those experiences of community at school help them grow and help them manage the myriad challenges that await them once they're dismissed for the day.

Alesha M., 18, describes how school was a refuge from almost unbearable stressors:

> Growing up, school was a place to escape troubles at home—substance abuse, arguing, and no privacy. I shared a bedroom with my mother, grandmother, and little sister. I often woke up to bickering between my mother and grandfather, who were both intoxicated, in the middle of the night. I got up early every morning and quickly got ready for school, eager to escape the chaos.
>
> I enjoyed learning, especially math. But I felt awkward around other kids and was shy. I didn't know how to react when people tried to be my friend.
>
> My 7th and 8th grade math teacher, Mr. Traynor, made a big impact on my life. He was strict, but he taught me the basics of algebra and respected my intelligence. If I finished my work quickly, he challenged me with harder work. Thanks to him I aced the state math tests during those years.

Alesha's mother lost her job and descended deeper into drinking. Alesha ran away from home, was placed in foster care, and spiraled downward into drug abuse herself. Several years later, however, she was placed with an exceptionally caring foster mom. She writes about the effect of that change:

I went to school more frequently. I began making friends there. I no longer sat by myself in the cafeteria. Now I sat with my friends and occasionally went to the library upstairs, finding new books or playing chess. I had a great relationship with my foster family. I went to therapy at least three times a month, and I finally felt like a normal teenager.

My guidance counselors were all nice and the teachers were helpful as well. If I fell behind, they didn't embarrass me in front of the class. They gave me a chance and didn't make me feel like a foster child with a bad school record. If I was afraid to ask for help, my English and math teachers picked up on it and came over to help me. Because of that, math continued to be one of my favorite subjects.

Alesha experienced several more destabilizing events, including the death of her foster mom. But she persisted, enrolling in a high school equivalency class, and passed the test on her first try—no doubt in part because of the long-term impact of the emotional and academic support provided by her middle school and high school teachers.

While it is important to be knowledgeable and respectful of home cultures, we also must respect the fact that our students are individuals with their own needs and desires. At school, educators and peers can play important roles in helping students feel safe when their families may not be ready to embrace them. Here's an example by an anonymous writer, age 16, from his story *Not a Girl at All*:

I am bisexual and transgender, and I have conservative, religious immigrant parents. At school, most of the teachers and students call me by my chosen name and pronouns, which are he/him. But everyone in my family and at my temple thinks I'm a straight girl and knows me by the name my parents gave me when I was born. It sounds like a stranger's name in my mouth; it doesn't belong to me.

I started asking teachers to call me by my chosen name and pronouns. When I was anxious about doing that, my friends would practically shove me up to the teacher's desk so that I could stutter out the name I wanted to be called.

Though I was starting to express my true identity at school, I still felt a lot of self-hate. I knew my family viewed people like me as freaks of nature. When I told one of my teachers that, he said: "Are you going to live for them, or for yourself?"

> I told him that I felt like I was committing a terrible act of betrayal against my
> parents just by being who I was. My teacher replied that I was walking around as
> if I had a mask on, which was making it impossible to see the good parts of the
> world. He said it wasn't my fault that I felt this way, because someone had put this
> metaphorical mask on my face at a young age and Super Glued it there. He said I
> was no less than anyone else because of the people I loved or the gender I identified
> as. I had never heard that before. I didn't believe him at the time, but I fell in love
> with his words and his promise that one day the mask would be lifted.

In the pandemic, students like this writer lost contact with supportive adults as they
were isolated with parents who didn't fully accept them. It will be a great gift to our
students if the unexpected stress of the pandemic sensitizes teachers to the profound
impact of the routine stress and trauma that many students have always experienced.
And it will be an even greater gift if we can use the insights from our pandemic experience to think creatively about how to address these stresses at school and support our
students' well-being and academic persistence going forward.

This recognition that many students are experiencing stressors that impair their
ability to embrace all we offer leads to an obvious conclusion: We need to broaden our
concept of the purpose of school. Schools have historically played a vital role in helping
students acquire academic knowledge and skills. But the explosion of knowledge about
the impact of stress on the brain, and the ways in which social injustices contribute to
debilitating stress, have made it clear that we must readjust.

Schools as Centers of Healing: The Importance of Trauma-Informed Schools

It's not an overstatement to say that for some students, school has the biggest impact
on helping them recover from chronic stress and trauma. In fact, studies demonstrate
that adolescents can be helped to heal when they are supported by adults and peers
who respond to them with empathy and care, and who model and teach them positive ways to cope with stress.[1] Research also demonstrates that when educators adopt

school-wide systems to support students who have experienced chronic stress and trauma, those students can not only heal emotionally but perform well academically.[2]

This doesn't mean that schools have to become mental health clinics or that teachers become clinicians. Fortunately, taking achievable steps to make schools feel more welcoming, in ways that support the natural caring inclinations we all share, can have profound effects on the young people we live with for six hours a day. These steps include changing *how* we teach and it may mean changing *what* we teach.

To support students who have experienced stress and trauma, we need to intentionally include trauma-informed approaches in our teaching repertoire. Trauma-Informed Care (TIC) is an approach first proposed by mental health practitioners Roger Fallot and Maxine Harris in their book *Using Trauma Theory to Design Service Systems*. It was developed to support mental health practitioners as they became more aware that many clients had suffered sexual or physical abuse that was an unacknowledged contributing factor to their mental illness. To better support their clients, Fallot and Harris proposed that mental health services be designed and delivered in ways that were responsive to the impact of trauma on patients.[3] As mental health professionals and educators have become more aware of the impact that stress and trauma have on youth, they have advocated for trauma-informed approaches in schools.[4]

For example, a study by University of California at San Francisco (UCSF) researchers found that school personnel could mitigate the effects of trauma and chronic stress on students.[5] Through UCSF's Healthy Environments and Response to Trauma in Schools (HEARTS) Program, the university collaborated with schools and school districts to strengthen the capacities of school personnel to support trauma-impacted students by increasing their "knowledge and practice of trauma-informed classroom and school-wide strategies."

In their study of the HEARTS program on four ethnically diverse San Francisco public schools, they found that school personnel reported significant increases in their understanding of trauma and use of trauma-sensitive practices while students showed a decrease in trauma-related symptoms. In addition, 47 students who also received therapy with a HEARTS-trained clinician had especially good outcomes:

- they improved in their adjustment to trauma (their ability to function in daily living);
- they improved their affect regulation (their ability to identify, express, and modulate emotions);
- they improved in their adjustment to intrusions (their thoughts related to the trauma that impact attention and behavior); and
- they improved in their adjustment to attachment (their ability to relate to others and develop healthy relationships).[6]

As any teacher knows, these kinds of improvements in mental health also contribute to improvements in academic performance.

Studies examining TIC find that it includes four essential components typically referred to as Connect, Protect, Respect, and Redirect.[7]

- The *connect* component highlights the importance of social connections and the building of social relationships.
- The *protect* component focuses on promoting physical and psychological safety and trustworthiness.
- The *respect* component emphasizes the importance of engaging in meaningful activities.
- The *redirect* component refers to the encouragement of skill building and competence that promote psychological well-being.[8]

In the following story, S.J. James, 18, writes about adults who failed to connect and protect her when she was vulnerable, and then about adults and settings in which she did find connection, protection, and respect. This allowed her to redirect her energies into meaningful schoolwork and making friends. With support, she also found her voice and advocated for a different school solution than the one proposed for her. Note how the adults responded, and their responses' impact on her emotional health and academic achievement:

> Toward the end of 7th grade I started to get suicidal thoughts and I was self-harming. I felt an overwhelming sadness and I was stressed and anxious.

Many of these feelings were related to my school environment, which I found toxic. The school was mostly Hispanic and the lack of diversity made it hard for me to feel comfortable. I was one of only three Black students.

I was bullied by other kids, and I even felt bullied by many of the teachers. They acted a lot like the kids, choosing favorites while excluding others, and they spoke badly about some students. When they witnessed bullying they turned a blind eye.

I wanted to transfer. Just walking up to the school building every morning gave me anxiety attacks.

In 7th grade I was put in the honors class. I was ahead in my assignments and the material was easy for me, but the stress of staying on top of everything was a lot. Between keeping my grades up, dealing with a group of students that tormented me, and having no support from my teachers, sometimes I felt so overwhelmed I just didn't show up.

I felt tired, but not like I just needed a good night's rest. It was more of a mental tiredness. I decided I would try to talk to my guidance counselor. I wanted and needed help.

But my counselor couldn't make the time to meet with me. When I'd see him in the hall, he'd call out, "I'm just really busy with other students. As soon as I can touch base with you I will." I couldn't blame him; there was only one guidance counselor for each grade.

A few times I waited outside the counselor's office, but he was either with someone else or he was elsewhere, and I had to get to class eventually.

[I was also] self-harming. I had been doing it for at least a year before I finally got a meeting with my guidance counselor. But it wasn't one I had scheduled. I had been in chorus and had my sleeves rolled up after washing my hands. I had forgotten to roll them back down to hide my cuts. Toward the end of the day I got called out of class by the guidance counselor.

When I walked into his office, I got flustered. A student who had often bullied me and a friend of hers were there. I sat down and the girl started talking about how seeing my cuts had upset her. Then the counselor asked me to explain my behavior.

He said it as if I had cut just to upset my classmate. "We don't get it, why would you do this?" the girl asked. I looked to the counselor for help and he gave me a look that said, "Answer the question."

"I started feeling sad last year. It's really a mixture of things." As anxious as I was, I knew it was unprofessional of the guidance counselor to make me talk about my private feelings in front of these girls. I said as little as I could.

After the girls left, the counselor told me he had to call my mom to tell her I was cutting.

"Please don't," I begged.

He told me it was school protocol. If a student mentioned wanting to hurt themselves or others, he had to inform the parent.

The counselor put her on speaker and greeted her in a jokey manner. "Hey!"

He laughed. He beat around the bush for a while until he finally said, "Anyway, it's come to my attention that your daughter has been cutting herself with razor blades."

It felt like my mom took forever to speak. She told me to come home right away, but the guidance counselor told her I couldn't leave until the bell rang. So I went back to class.

When I got off the bus that afternoon, my older brother was waiting for me. He was with his friends acting tough, but when we got home he cried. My mom had told him what had happened.

My mom was quiet at first. She didn't look at me. She just stared at the patterns on the marble kitchen counter.

Then she said, "Why are you doing this to yourself? Why didn't you tell me?" These questions were hard for me to answer. I was afraid that my mom wouldn't understand, and that she would turn out to be another adult I couldn't rely on. So I just stood there.

She called the hospital because the counselor had told her I was suicidal. I was admitted to the hospital and stayed there for one month. Everything was routine and orderly. I didn't have to worry about anything but feeling better. I felt safe and cared for. When you have depression, it gets difficult to take care of yourself.

I also went to school in the hospital. My favorite teachers were Ms. Cohen who taught art, Mr. Fenherty who taught history, and my science teacher who went by Mr. G.

This school was the opposite of my middle school. The teachers, staff, and students were friendly and caring. The hospital provided services that helped students improve their mental health, and I felt understood and heard. I was a straight A student again for the first time in a year. I felt like I might finally be OK.

I even made friends with other patients and staff. Eventually the psychologist decided I was healthy enough to go home. I was feeling the way I hadn't felt in a long time: happy.

After going home, I still attended the school at the hospital. It offered the same mental health support I got when I was an inpatient (someone who stays in the hospital) when I became an outpatient (someone who only comes in for appointments).

So in addition to my classes, I had access to my psychiatrist, nurse, social worker, and psychologist. This was helpful because the adjustment to the outside isn't always smooth. Part of me still needed to be kept an eye on.

Eventually, though, I was expected to return to my old school. Thinking about that riddled me with anxiety. I told my mom about the distress I felt. She spoke to my psychiatrist and they decided it would be best if I stayed at the hospital school until the end of the year. The following year, I'd be starting high school in a new school. I was proud of myself for speaking up, being heard, and getting what I needed.

Still, the adjustment to high school was hard. For example, when I was being bullied, I reported it to the guidance counselor. When it escalated, I reported it again. This time there was a mediation and the threat of suspension if the girls didn't stop. They did.

During my sophomore year, my school hired a social worker. I had sessions with her about once a week. She helped me realize my self-worth and helped me through a lot. But she left the school in June and she has not been replaced. I was devastated at first, but eventually I realized that her lessons would stick with me through my final years of high school.

I had an amazing junior year. I remained optimistic and positive, using a mixture of the skills I learned at the hospital and from the school social worker. Even when bad things happened, like losing some close friends, I was able to tap into my existing support systems and build new friendships.

Even though I was dismissed by certain adults at first, I didn't stop trying to get help. I'm glad I was persistent.

S.J.'s experience is more extreme than many students face, but the lessons from it are applicable in any educational setting: Caring and friendly staff that really listen can make a tremendous difference—in the moment, and in the longer-term trajectory of a student's academic and emotional life.

Why Meaningful Connections Are So Important

Why should we build relationships with students? After all, I remember learning from teachers who I didn't connect with. I remember teachers who I actually didn't even like but who still taught me something. I've also had teachers who I really liked but didn't learn very much from.

So of course students can learn from people they don't connect with and even people they don't like. But it's likely that we will be more engaged and motivated to learn from someone with whom we do feel a meaningful connection. Failing to build connections among ourselves, our content, and our students is like trying to row a boat with only one oar: possible, but not desirable or efficient.

Percy Lujan, 17, describes an approach that a teacher—who was particularly sensitive to the issues facing her students—used to help make content seem relevant to them. Percy attended a school for recent immigrants, where students were thrown together with kids from different countries, cultures, and religions. In their home countries, they might even have been at war. This lesson achieves multiple aims: It's academically sound, it's relevant, and builds connections among students while subtly promoting healing:

> The first year I was in Ms. Sara's class, she taught us about religions. Ours was a school of immigrants, and it's easy to imagine why religion is a sensitive topic. We never talked about it among ourselves.
>
> Ms. Sara was brave enough to bring that topic to light. She put us into groups and had us learn about each other's religions. She gave us books and other research materials so that we could see a more objective view of many beliefs. Then, she made each group give a presentation on one religion.
>
> My group was studying Hinduism, and we were able to learn many details of this religion that non-Hindus might not understand. When I heard the other groups' presentations, I was fascinated by what I heard, and as we learned, we were able to relate more to each other. I remember one day seeing the necklace of a Hindu friend; it was a golden figure of the Hindu god Shiva. "The Destroyer," I said, remembering my research. My friend was impressed with what I knew about his culture, and he was glad to see that other people were learning about his beliefs.

Meaningful Connections Foster Engagement in School and Help Students to Heal

Research within the fields of child and adolescent development demonstrates that children have specific developmental needs that, when adequately addressed, support their positive development.[9] Those developmental needs include the need for meaningful social interaction (where they experience positive social relationships that allow them to explore emerging ideas, views, values, and feelings with peers), and meaningful participation (where they can identify, develop, and use individual talents, skills, and interests in the context of the real world).[10] Using the language of trauma-informed care, this research indicates that all students have a developmental need for meaningful connections to their peers and for meaningful connections to the material they're learning in school.

Of course, unless we're regularly talking with students, reading their reflections, and surveying them about school climate, it's hard to assess their engagement and easy to overestimate it. Talking about stock market investors and their rosy assumptions, Warren Buffett once said that you don't know who's naked until the tide goes out. The remote learning of the 2020–2021 school year exposed the fact that many students are not as intrinsically engaged as we might think. As remote instruction wore on, many teachers I worked with reported that fewer and fewer students were turning on their cameras; others logged in but never seemed to be present; and still others never checked in at all.

Several schools that I work with responded by changing how they measure attendance. They shifted from documenting whether students "showed up" for virtual classes by having their cameras on to simply noting whether students were "present" in class (with cameras on or off), and finally to just recording whether students turned in any schoolwork, regardless of whether they showed up.

Before the pandemic, as long as we had the "high tide" of attendance, we often didn't have to look closely at whether students were actually engaged in learning, or were just showing up because their parents (and state law) gave them no choice. By shifting from measuring student attendance to measuring minimal participation, these schools were tacitly acknowledging that there may be less real student engagement than we wanted to believe.

I also began to notice as the weeks went on that these measures of engagement (or lack of it) were also being interpreted as a sign of students' lack of interest in learning. One frustrated teacher told me, "I've come to accept that my students aren't interested in learning at this time. I totally get it. There are so many things on their mind that are so much bigger than school."

I had a mixed reaction to this assumption. While I appreciated her willingness to adjust her expectations, I was also confused because I've never met a student who didn't want to learn. They may not have been interested in what I was teaching them, or they may not always have been open to the way that I was trying to teach them, but they always were interested in learning something, even when outside stressors made learning difficult. The issue isn't simply that some students aren't interested in learning. Rather, remote teaching exposed the fact that what they're learning might not be as engaging as we thought, and that our teaching methods may not be meeting their need for connection.

Research bears out my experience that all students are interested in learning and that all students have a developmental need to feel connected to others and to feel connected to the material they're being taught. Building these connections is especially important for young people who have suffered trauma—whether it's the collective trauma of a pandemic or police killings, or the intensely personal trauma of being evicted or losing a caregiver. But to build those connections, we must engage them.

Research has typically described student engagement as having three components: behavioral, emotional, and cognitive. The behavioral component is demonstrated by positive conduct, effort, and participation. The emotional or affective component reflects interest, identification, belonging, and positive attitudes about learning. The cognitive component is demonstrated through self-regulation, interest in specific learning goals, and investment in learning.[11]

Furthermore, students demonstrate their cognitive engagement behaviorally and emotionally. If they aren't interested or invested in what they're being taught, they may exert only minimal effort or actively challenge the teacher's authority. They might also have a negative attitude not just about what they're learning at that time, but about school in general. We have a choice about how to get our students to turn on their cameras and to post responses in the chat—or to be "minds on" in an in-person class. We can either spend our energy forcing them to be compliant or we can immerse them in material that piques their interest and inspires an intrinsic investment in learning.

While the pandemic was a special case, it reminded me that even in normal times many students are under severe stress that can make them feel isolated from schoolwork.

It became even clearer to me that helping students feel connected to school means teaching in ways that make them feel valued. Students need to feel like they matter. Even when we are not experiencing social distancing it's easy for students to feel invisible.

Here's how DeAnna Lyles, 16, experienced her large high school. Though she didn't have a camera that she could turn off, she found more traditional ways to disengage:

> Throughout elementary and middle school, I had been a relatively good student. But high school was different . . . everything seemed really impersonal. [My high school] was so big that my daily routine included walking around in a circle, looking for my classes. I felt uncomfortable and unsafe in such a big school with its huge population of students.

> The teachers' attitudes affected how I felt about school, too. Most of them never bothered to learn my first name, which says a lot to me. They also seemed less supportive of students than the teachers in my previous schools.

> After a while, my attitude toward school and the teachers was "Screw them." I felt like I was wasting my time trying to learn if they weren't going to help me, so I started cutting my least favorite classes. A month after my first cutting experience, it had become a part of my regular routine.

Remote learning doesn't cause disengagement, but for many students it intensifies those feelings and gives them new ways to disengage. As one high school student shared with me, "With remote instruction, school feels like I'm watching a TV show and my school makes me feel like the only thing that matters is that I have my TV on and that my eyes are on the screen. I don't really know my teachers and what's worse is that they don't know me."

"Safe" Schools Are Schools Where Students Feel They Can Take Academic and Personal Risks

Safer schools promote engagement and connection. And engagement and connection promote safer schools. The National Center for Safe and Supportive Learning

Environments defines school safety as, "schools and school-related activities where students are safe from violence, bullying, harassment, and substance use."[12] Over the past few decades, school districts across the country have taken many measures to ensure the physical safety of students, including the introduction of security cameras and more safety officers in public schools.

But educators have begun to realize that clumsy efforts to increase student safety can backfire. Studies have demonstrated that metal detectors, school safety officers, security cameras, and other surveillance measures can make some students feel as though their schools are unsafe and make them more fearful.[13]

Konner Stephen observes that the strict security at a school across the street from his own does not make him feel safer. It only reminds him of how Black people can be victims of random violence:

> I go to Scholars Academy, a predominantly White school where there are no police. We have security guards. But right across the street is Channelview High School, which has predominantly Black kids and other kids of color. It is heavily policed, and I have observed fights between cops and students.
>
> I have friends who have spoken to some of the students at Channelview and they talk about how negative the environment is and how they feel like they are in prison. That upsets me.
>
> In a sense, for me, being Black is like being an empath to fellow Black people. I feel their pain when they go through struggles caused because of our race. It's scary hearing about racist incidents because you know that it could have been you if you were at the wrong place at the wrong time.
>
> That's the reaction I had hearing about the conditions at Channelview. It pains me to know that because another school has mostly students of color, some of those kids feel like they are policed and treated like inmates, constantly monitored by security cameras, and having to pass through metal detectors every day.

Ilya Arbit, 16, is a White student and was less attuned to the effect of harsh school security until he was inadvertently subjected to it:

My school dean and a stern male security guard escorted my friend Lenny (not his real name) and me to an empty classroom near the dean's office. They ordered us to put our bags against the wall and stand in the middle of the room, apart from each other. We tried to explain ourselves, but the guard hissed at us and told us not to be "wiseguys."

The dean checked our bags, opening every single pocket and unzipping each zipper, looking through my notebooks and folders and even checking my wallet and cell phone. The guard frisked us and asked us to turn out our pockets so that he could make sure there was nothing inside.

After that, the dean said that we were lucky we didn't have anything we weren't supposed to and that they'd let us go. But they said they'd still call our parents and tell them what we had done.

What we had done was get my bookbag out of Lenny's car, a block from the school, after gym class. We returned to school on time, but behind everyone else from the class. I didn't know this was against the rules. More importantly, I didn't know that it meant I would be treated like a criminal when I re-entered the building.

That was the first time I was frisked and I've got to tell you it wasn't a good feeling. It felt like I was under arrest and they were about to read me my rights.

After what happened to me, I wasn't surprised to learn that some people are questioning the safety measures being used in . . . high schools around the city.

In response to concerns like those of Konner and Ilya, educators have begun to expand how we conceptualize school safety—moving away from measures of surveillance and control to a greater emphasis on the mental and psychological health that contributes to physical and emotional safety.

A challenge for us as educators is that adolescents are self-protective and feel that vulnerability is a risk. They'll tell us they're fine when they know better. They'll tell us they don't need help when they know they do. Thus, we usually see only the tip of the iceberg: the coping strategies that are the symptoms or reactions to the stress. And we often misunderstand those reactions because we don't know what they're coping with. But if we understand how students are interpreting a challenge, by talking with them, for example, we can find ways to help them to feel comfortable with these new risks.

This is precisely why it's so important to foster a sense of psychological safety within our classes. Psychological safety refers to our perceptions of the consequences of taking interpersonal risks in a context such as at work or at school.[14] Research shows that during times of uncertainty and change we feel less safe and our sense of interpersonal risk is heightened.[15]

As psychologist William Kahn notes, psychological safety affects our willingness to express ourselves. So when we focus on promoting psychological safety by being intentional about connecting with our students and helping them to build relationships with their peers, we're building trust and helping to reduce their levels of interpersonal risk. Feeling safer increases the likelihood that they will take the risk to actively participate in class discussions and small group work. Finally, when students feel psychologically safe, they will be more likely to open up to us in the first place, so we'll actually know how they are feeling and can adjust our teaching to fit the circumstances.

Why Respecting Students Is So Important

Throughout my career, I've had the privilege of speaking with many extraordinary teachers who work incredibly hard to create psychologically safe classrooms where their students feel supported and cared for. Two things have become clear through this work: Psychological safety is built on trust, and trust is built on personal connections.

But students' sense of connection extends beyond personal relationships. While relationships are important, the connections that seem to matter even more to students are those that they feel toward the material they're being taught. Focus groups with middle and high school students have shown me that they find it challenging to stay engaged in school when they can't see any connection between the content of their classes and their own lives. When teachers try to draw connections between students' lives and the coursework, it's not just an engagement technique, it is a sign of respect.

It shows that the teacher is paying attention to who they are as people, not just as learners. It makes them feel visible and valued.

When we show our students respect, we're letting them know that we recognize their experiences and abilities, and that we'll draw on them as we work to ensure that they feel connected to the material we're teaching. Asking these three questions can help us design our curricula in ways that make students feel visible and valued: *How does my curriculum relate to my students' lives? What message does it tell them about themselves, their abilities, and their possibilities?* And *What messages does it reinforce in the minds of my students?*

In the following story, 18-year-old Mileyda Evangelista describes her struggle to succeed in math. She notices that her teacher makes time after school to help students, so she's willing to risk asking for help. While the road is rocky, the combination of his sound advice about studying and his clever ways of relating math concepts to things she cares about put her on a path to success.

> Math has always been the hardest subject for me. For years, no matter how many hours I spent in after-school tutoring I still didn't get it. I also didn't understand what I needed math for, so I wasn't motivated to learn it.
>
> My studying consisted of reading my notebook as fast as I could for about half an hour, the day before the test. That didn't work too well.
>
> Finally, in the spring of my junior year, afraid I'd fail the class, I decided to talk to my math teacher. Mr. Guerrero is a dedicated teacher who's always in his classroom after school, helping those of us who are doing badly.
>
> He said he believed I had potential and that all I needed to do was to study for the test correctly. I thought, "He knows I haven't been studying for math."
>
> Mr. Guerrero's comments encouraged me to try to do better in math. We had a test on terminology (the meaning of mathematical words) coming up, so I said, "OK, how do I do it?"
>
> He told me that to learn terminology I should get flip cards and write the word on one side of a card and the word's definition on the other side. After reading the

definition, I could test myself by writing down the word I thought went with it, then flip the card to see if I was right. As I tested myself again and again, I could eliminate the cards with the words I'd already learned.

I realized that was what I had to do to pass the class. But I also thought, "Hell, no! That's way too complicated!" I'd never used flip cards before and it seemed too difficult.

So instead of following his tips, I just did my usual looking over the notebook before the test. Then I failed it. I felt bad for disregarding his advice, like I'd failed myself.

Now I was in real danger of failing the class, so I became more serious about studying. I went to Mr. Guerrero again and asked him how I could study for the problem-solving test that we had coming up, the last big test of the year.

Mr. Guerrero told me that if you're trying to learn a specific type of math problem, like solving for x, that's where the note-taking you're supposed to do in class kicks in.

First, copy as many different examples of the same type of problem as you can. Next, copy the problem on a clean page without the answer. Then try to solve the problem without looking at the answer. This time, I spent about an hour a day, five days a week, studying at home, which I'd never done before. I studied on the subway, too, checking my flip cards. At first, I got most of the problems wrong. It was horrible. Knowing by the middle of the problem that you're wrong is quite frustrating.

Still, I'd stay after school and make Mr. Guerrero give me extra problems and show him the ones I couldn't solve so he could tell me what I was doing wrong.

He made it easier to understand math by talking about it in real-life terms. For example, he explained permutations by saying that it's like going out with three different guys the same day.

If you go out with one first then you can't go out with him again that day—you have to go out with the second guy and then the third. Or you go out with them in a different order, but you can't repeat a date. With combinations, on the other hand, you could go out with one guy twice in a day or even the three of them at the same time—whether you repeat doesn't matter.

After the first week of practicing, I noticed that I was improving. I was and still am quite slow, but I started getting correct answers more often with less practice. I felt increasingly good about myself and about math. Getting the answer wrong was horrible but getting it right—getting it right was heaven!

As the weeks went by, I discovered that math really is all around me all the time and is involved in everything I do. Even one of my favorite activities, shopping, is ruled by math. Do I want to buy a blouse at one store for 25% off or two blouses at 75% off at a different store? It's kind of exciting to go out and notice that I see the world slightly differently than I did before.

The law of gravity was discovered through math, and astronomers use math to discover planets and stars. Even the clothing we wear was measured using mathematical standards. Now I appreciate math as a tool to help us understand nature, not as a torture.

Showing respect, building trust, getting to know our students better, and asking the three above questions of ourselves and our curricula can sometimes make teachers feel like they're straying into the domains of social workers or counselors. But building safe and supportive learning environments is the responsibility of all school staff. Mr. Guerrero is a math teacher, not a social worker. But his "caring," which is expressed in extra tutoring and in paying attention to how he can build a bridge between math and Mileyda's life, helps to reduce her distress.

As teachers, we're held accountable for student learning. Building trust can spark the motivation required to master challenging academic content. Counselors and social workers have important roles to play, but it is in the interests of our students and in our own self-interest as teachers to help create classroom environments that are emotionally conducive to learning.

Here's an example. I was meeting with a teacher who was vexed by a student's response to his assignment on the Columbian Exchange.[16] He asked the students to complete an assignment in which they were to list the positive and negative consequences of the Columbian Exchange—a lesson he had taught for years and was a standard in a state-approved textbook.

After noticing that one student had only completed the "negative consequences" section of the assignment, the teacher reminded him that he had to complete the entire assignment to receive full credit. A few hours before meeting with me, the teacher received an email from the student's parent expressing strong displeasure with the assignment. By coincidence, I had a chance to speak with the student that day and asked about the incident. The response was wonderfully clear: "As a Latinx student, I see nothing positive about the Columbian Exchange and I find it troubling that my teacher would force me to see something positive in something that my family and I view as entirely negative." What the teacher viewed as a lack of compliance was actually a form of protest by the student against an assignment that made him feel invisible and devalued.

This is an example of how the world, and students' understanding of it, often changes faster than our state-approved textbooks and our own understanding. At one time, asking students about the "pros and cons" of slavery, or the subordination of women, may have been "standard" or felt acceptable, just as New York state still approves of asking the "pros" of the conquering, looting, and decimation of native peoples and their cultures in the Americas. But our students' experiences and understanding often outrace what is in their textbooks or what we learned in college. Furthermore, when our students have backgrounds and experiences very different from our own, the gaps can be even wider. It's impossible for our education school courses or our own life experiences to fully prepare us to work with the diverse students we have in our classes nowadays. That's why it is so important to listen closely to them.

Ultimately, as this student made clear, teaching in developmentally and culturally responsive ways means addressing our students' developmental need to feel visible and valued. It also means teaching content that does not further marginalize students because of their race, ethnicity, gender identity, or socio-economic status.

We Help Students Achieve by Helping Them to Strengthen Their Social and Emotional Skills

As we have discussed, achieving our educational mission means broadening our understanding of schools to see them as centers of care that welcome students' "whole selves." And we also must think about providing care in developmentally and culturally responsive ways that make all students feel acknowledged and supported and that help our most traumatized students heal. This means that we should consider the developmental needs of students and draw on that knowledge as we help them to cope. For example, we know from years of research that as adolescents mature, they have a need for greater say in the decisions that impact their lives and greater control in making those decisions (what is typically referred to as "voice and choice").

One important aspect of providing care is helping students build the competencies that enable them to manage and cope with the institutional and external stressors of both school and life. The idea that we need to make schools centers of caring does not mean that, at present, we don't care about our students. Of course, most teachers care deeply about them. But when schools become centers of care, they build on that individual caring to help students strengthen competencies that help them to cope with the stressors they encounter, while also working to reduce or eliminate the systemic conditions that contribute to student stress in the first place.

At the center of a care-based approach to supporting students is an intentional focus on social and emotional development. The Collaborative for Academic, Social, and Emotional Learning (CASEL) has identified five key social and emotional competencies: self-awareness, self-management, relationships, social awareness, and responsible decision-making. CASEL has also shown that these competencies are directly related to school success, and that they can be taught and learned.

As we've gained a more comprehensive understanding of social and emotional development, we've learned that by the end of the preschool years, children who have developed a strong emotional foundation can better manage everyday social interactions. Research studies investigating the impact of social and emotional development on cognition have also found that not managing emotions well can impair thinking.[17]

Conversely, strong social and emotional learning (SEL) skills correlate with many positive emotional, behavioral, and academic outcomes. In its meta-analysis of research examining the impact of school-based interventions to support social and emotional learning on children and adolescents, CASEL found that students who received SEL instruction demonstrated better academic performance on achievement tests, scoring an average of 11 percentile points higher than students who did not receive SEL instruction.[18] They also found that students who received SEL instruction exhibited greater motivation to learn, deeper commitment to school, increased time devoted to schoolwork, and better classroom behavior. Additionally, they found that these students displayed fewer negative behaviors and exhibited less disruptive behavior in class (including reduced noncompliance, aggression, delinquent acts, and disciplinary referrals). The researchers also found that SEL instruction promoted psychological wellness: It was associated with fewer reports of student depression, anxiety, stress, and social withdrawal.

CASEL also found that the most effective SEL programs used a SAFE protocol—lessons were Specific, Active, Focused, and Explicit about the SEL competencies they were designed to strengthen. In short, well-structured intentional SEL instruction helps students acquire a deeper understanding of how to recognize and manage their emotions, and how to maintain positive relationships with others. Programs that help students strengthen SEL competencies, like those designed by Youth Communication, contribute to more caring and supportive schools.

From a developmentally and culturally responsive perspective, a care-based approach to supporting students also includes addressing the systemic conditions within schools that contribute to student stress.[19] This is particularly important for BIPOC students and poor students who, as the ACEs (Adverse Childhood Experiences) studies have demonstrated, typically experience more stressors throughout their youth. For example, BIPOC students experience more racism, racial discrimination, and racial bias both within and outside of school. Thus, a care-based approach in schools also needs to include a specific emphasis on addressing racial equity through a review of school practices and policies to ensure that they do not harm students of color.

Meagan Zullo, 15, has a supportive family, but still suffers from systemic stressors like living in a low-income housing project and the stigma of poverty, and personal stressors, like her stutter. When her parents get her into a better-resourced school, she catches up academically because "If my grades drop, my teachers ask me how they can help. Instead of being ashamed, I tell them what I'm struggling with. I no longer feel 'less than'." Meagan surely received some encouragement from the teachers in her poorly resourced school that contributed to her later success. Nonetheless, her story is both an indictment of systemic inequality and a testament to the power of teachers and schools to make a difference:

> Growing up, I didn't know that I came from a lower class. Once, I even had a birthday party at a Build-a-Bear workshop! My dad was a superintendent at a movie theater, and we often watched movies there and got popcorn for free. My mom was a stay at home mom, and she often helped translate for Spanish speaking parents whose kids went to my school.
>
> I come from a big family. I have four siblings, two nieces, two nephews, and more cousins than I can count. My house is always full of smiles and laughter that make the small space feel bigger. This was a haven to me. But school was a different story.
>
> I went to my neighborhood elementary school, where the computers were old and constantly broken. We had hardly any books in our library. The books that we did have were stained or had pages ripped out. Our play yard consisted of a filthy jungle gym, and our teachers looked overworked because there were over 30 kids in a class. This class size also made it hard for me to understand what was being taught because it was hard to focus.
>
> [Later], my parents enrolled me in a middle school in downtown Brooklyn, hoping I would receive a better education. I quickly realized that I didn't know as much as the other kids. I didn't know my multiplication tables. I couldn't sound out words, because my vocabulary comprehension was so far below grade level. To improve my vocabulary and speech, I listened to other people's conversations and watched

gaming videos on YouTube. Although I wouldn't know the exact definition of the word, I knew what context to use it in.

My classmates sighed loudly whenever it was my turn to read because I had a stutter. They mimicked me when I couldn't pronounce words with the sound "sh." This made me feel self-conscious. I felt embarrassed when my teacher asked a simple multiplication problem and the rest of my class yelled the answer while I just stayed quiet, because I didn't know it.

This school had newer books, smaller classes, and better technology. Each classroom had its own computer cart and tablets that we could use whenever we needed to do research or had an assignment online. My teachers had more patience and time to work with students one-on-one whenever they needed help. They helped me overcome my stutter by giving me practice methods to improve.

I also began to understand through conversations with my parents that our apartment was in a low-income housing project, the food I ate was bought with food stamps, and the clothes I wore were bought on clearance.

This made me feel like I was lower or less than everyone else. But what bothered me the most is when my classmates said, "People from the projects are dirty." Although they lived in my neighborhood, the projects were like a separate world to them. When they found out I actually lived in the brick high-rises, their eyes widened, surprised.

Once, I invited some friends to come over, and their parents told them no because I lived in a "bad part of Brooklyn."

I bounced from friend to friend because I didn't feel like I belonged. I felt that I was less than my friends, so being around them made me feel insecure. In addition to where I lived, I had gotten such a lousy early education. Other kids had the newest pair of Jordans or the latest Apple product. This made me materialistic.

I convinced myself that these luxury items were necessary for a happy life. My friends had printers with colored ink, so their poster board projects were colorful and well decorated. I didn't have a printer, so my posters were mostly black and white because I had to use my teacher's printer. The students with the more colorful posters got the better grades.

Now that I'm in 10th grade and have been in a good school for a while, I have gained more confidence. I still stutter occasionally but I know that my opinion matters. I take my time when solving math problems without feeling bad, and my vocabulary and comprehension are on grade level. Although I make spelling mistakes because I never learned how to sound out words, I still love writing and teachers have let me know I'm good at it. If my grades drop, my teachers ask me how they can help. Instead of being ashamed, I tell them what I'm struggling with. I no longer feel "less than."

Because I was lucky that my parents moved me to a better school, I'm on track for college and I have a group of friends who support me. I've recently learned that there are organizations that help low-income high school students with the college application process and help them find scholarships and grants. They even continue to help them once they're in college.

I know that I have a good future ahead, but I can't help but think about people who are not as lucky as me. There are still schools like my elementary school, and some may even be worse. The students in these schools don't realize that their voices matter and they have a lot to contribute. They are constantly feeling like they are less than everyone, so they become discouraged from trying to improve.

At a good school, you learn more than how to read and do math. You also learn time management, work ethic, and how to communicate well. Activities like oral presentations and Socratic seminars, debates, and overall open discussions help prepare you for college and your future career, because they teach you how important your opinion is and that not everyone is going to agree with you.

Without a good education, low-income children won't be able to get well-paying jobs. This causes an endless cycle of the poor staying poor.

Until the system is fixed, maybe I can encourage kids like me who feel less than. So I want to become a high school ELA teacher. I want to help kids like me learn that they are worthwhile and that their address or test scores doesn't define them. I want to show them by example that they have a chance at a better life. My ELA teachers have always been there for me and have pushed me to have more confidence in not only my writing, but in my everyday life. They saw me as a talented person with potential, not just some kid from the projects.

What Teachers Can Do

1. Teach in trauma-informed ways.

If our goal is to excite students about what they're learning in school, then we have to teach in ways that help them to feel safe, empowered, cared for, and connected to others. This is important for all students, but it is especially important for students of color who may already feel relatively marginalized, voiceless, and powerless in school.

As a teacher, I used to think about engagement in terms of the material I was teaching rather than the student I was teaching. I remember staying up late on Sundays trying to come up with what I thought was an engaging lesson—only to be faced with eye rolls and blank stares on Monday mornings. It was frustrating! Since then I've learned several principles that help me to design lessons that really connect with students.

Address All the Components of Learning: I learned that I could influence the engagement of my students by addressing all three components of learning: the academic or cognitive component (whether my students were interested in the material), the affective component (how my teaching them made them feel), and the behavioral component (what behaviors I expected from them).

Asking these questions can ensure that we address each component:

- Why would a student want to learn this? (Cognitive)
- How does what I'm teaching relate to their lives and their aspirations for the future? (Cognitive)
- How does being in my class make my students feel? (Affective)
- Do my expectations force my students to work against their bodies' needs for movement or rest? (Behavioral)

Support Positive Relationships: When students get along, classroom management is easier. Teachers can nurture those relationships by facilitating small group activities that tie individual success to the success of all members of the group. Activities should allow each student to contribute to the collective effort of the group in their own unique way. One common approach to fostering interdependence is through the use of a method developed by Dr. Elliot Aronson and his students at the University of Texas and the University of California at Santa Cruz referred to as The Jigsaw Classroom.[20] The Jigsaw Classroom (https://www.jigsaw.org/) has a number of research-based tools to help create Jigsaw classrooms in ways that are both developmentally appropriate and culturally responsive.

Help Students De-Stress: Trauma-informed educators also teach in ways that are designed to help students manage stressors and promote their psychological safety. The American Academy of Child and Adolescent Psychiatry provides many helpful strategies in this handy factsheet: (https://www.aacap.org/AACAP/Families_and_Youth/Facts_for_Families/FFF-Guide/Helping-Teenagers-With-Stress-066.aspx) and the American Psychological Association also has helpful resources (https://www.apa.org/topics/children-teens-stress).

Mindfulness techniques are another research-based approach to managing stress.[21,22] These techniques help students learn how to be more aware of their present thoughts, emotions, and bodily sensations without being overly concerned about past events or being overwhelmed by concerns about their future. Mindfulness reduces stress and symptoms associated with depression and anxiety, and increases emotional self-regulation and cognitive flexibility.[23] Mindfulness techniques also provide students with opportunities for quiet self-reflection. It can be rare for many students experiencing stress and trauma to have a quiet moment during their day (something that many of us often take for granted). The infusion of mindfulness techniques into classrooms can create moments of tranquility that allow vulnerable students to relax, regroup, and find their focus.

The Association for Mindfulness in Education (http://www.mindfuleducation.org/) provides many resources to incorporate mindfulness techniques into their instructional practices.

2. Understand the effects of compassion fatigue and adjust your expectations for your students and yourself.

Educators working with students impacted by heightened stress and trauma risk experiencing secondary traumatic stress or what is commonly referred to as compassion fatigue. The National Child Traumatic Stress Network defines *compassion fatigue* as "the emotional duress that results when an individual hears about the first-hand trauma experiences of another."[24] Its research found that compassion fatigue is a common result of working with those suffering from trauma, which includes many of our students and their parents.

One key element in helping your students to heal is recognizing signs of compassion fatigue in yourself. The pandemic was a classic case of the impact of increased stress on students and teachers. Teachers were caring for many more students who felt anxious and alone, including some whose family members became ill or even died. Teachers told me that school shutdowns made them feel more isolated and less effective. It also caused some to feel frustrated, angry, and even depressed. When teachers experience these feelings, they probably are less effective as teachers. They need to adjust their expectations not just for their students, but for themselves.

Use the Four Rs: I recommend that teachers reflect on their teaching using the Four R's: Remove, Reduce, Restructure, and Re-imagine. What are the things that you typically teach that you can simply *remove* from your lessons? What are some areas that you would typically focus on that you can *reduce* in scope? What are some topics that you can *restructure* so that you can help students make better connections between what they're learning in your class and what they're learning in other classes? What have you learned about yourself as a teacher that can help you to *re-imagine* both what you teach and how you teach?

For specific guidance on what to remove and reduce from your curriculum, I recommend using tools such as those developed by Student Achievement Partners through its Achieve the Core initiative (achievethecore.org). For example, its *2020–2021 Support for Instructional Content Prioritization in High School Mathematics* provides specific recommendations for how you can modify your curriculum while still addressing the College and Career Readiness standards.

What Schools Can Do

1. Determine your readiness to become trauma-sensitive.

A recent survey conducted by the Council of School Superintendents about school needs found that "For the third consecutive year, improving mental health services was the most widely cited priority for new funding, chosen by 67% of superintendents as one of their top three priorities—a jump of 11 points from the 56% in 2018."[25]

Furthermore, 2016 data from the National Center for Education Statistics indicates that the need is much greater in schools serving students of color. The percentage of students who attended high-poverty schools was highest for Latinx students (45%), followed by Black students (44%), Asian students (14%), and White students (8%).[26] Students living in poverty, and particularly BIPOC students, are at increased risk of experiencing chronic stress and trauma and are more likely than their White peers to develop post-traumatic stress disorder.

So, the need is clear. But to address the problem we want to make sure that we implement programs that work and that are workable in our setting. That requires carefully assessing the specific needs in the school or district and the readiness to address the needs. Then, an inquiry-based planning process can be used to create and iterate a plan. However, before schools implement interventions that will support students suffering from chronic stress and trauma, they must determine whether they are ready to do so.

In the past few decades, there has been a lot of research, under the rubric of "implementation science," about what it takes to actually implement a successful program in a new setting. Institutional readiness typically requires motivation, willingness, and enthusiasm among school personnel, plus school or district-wide capacity to launch and run the new program. To become a trauma-sensitive school requires stakeholders to reflect on the following questions:[27]

- Do we currently have a sense of urgency and motivation to become a trauma-sensitive school?

- What aspects of our school's culture might support our movement toward becoming a trauma-sensitive school?
- What aspects of our school's culture might pose barriers to becoming a trauma-sensitive school?
- Do we have the fiscal and staffing capacity to set aside time for this effort? If not now, are we prepared to prioritize this work in the near future?
- How aligned will this work be to other initiatives already implemented in our school?
- Do we have anecdotes and/or systemic methods for listening to students?
- Will this new work detract from our current initiatives?
- How committed is our leadership to ensuring that school personnel are appropriately prepared to employ this work with fidelity?

2. Utilize an inquiry-based approach to becoming a trauma-sensitive school.

Assuming a school is ready to implement trauma-sensitive practices, it still needs to determine its goals and how to achieve them and the specific steps the staff will take to achieve the goals. In their book *Helping Traumatized Children Learn: Creating and Advocating for Trauma-Sensitive Schools (Vol. 2)*, Susan Cole and her colleagues at the Trauma and Learning Policy Initiative (a joint venture between Harvard Law School and Massachusetts Advocates for Children) describe a trauma-sensitive school as follows:

> A trauma-sensitive school is one in which all students feel safe, welcomed, and supported, and where addressing trauma's impact on learning on a school-wide basis is at the center of its educational mission. It is a place where an ongoing, inquiry-based process allows for the necessary teamwork, coordination, creativity, and sharing of responsibility for all students, and where continuous learning is for educators as well as students.[28]

Adopting a program or changing a few school-wide policies can be a good start to building a trauma-sensitive school. But Cole and her colleagues suggest that it is also important to shift to a mindset in which school personnel feel personally and collectively accountable for ensuring the physical and psychological safety of all students. That mindset shift is most likely to occur as the result of a multi-step, inquiry-based process.

First, before putting in a new program or practice, it can be helpful to look at what's already working. One of the most common laments that I hear from teachers is that they're asked to enact new practices and respond to new policies in ways that ignore or undervalue the promising practices already in place. To become a trauma-sensitive school, consider the school's current assets. For example, a school team can begin by posing questions such as: "What are we already doing that we would consider to be trauma-sensitive?" Or "Is there a practice or policy that students already find helpful?"

Second, the school should do baseline assessments so that schools can measure growth over time. There are a few reliable and valid measures of school climate that are appropriate for this phase. For example, the National School Climate Center (https://www.schoolclimate.org/), Panorama Education (https://www.panoramaed.com/), and Tripod Education Partners (https://www.tripoded.com/) have developed survey instruments that school districts use to inform decision-making. Used in combination with other data sources like student or teacher focus groups, this quantitative data can help identify the goals of the new program or practice.

Remember the four elements of trauma-informed care: school personnel should help students feel psychologically safe; staff should help students feel connected to their school; students should have opportunities to have a voice in how the school functions; and the school should help students build competence in navigating and managing stress. Any school team that is looking to make the school more trauma-sensitive will undoubtedly find bright spots and good practices that can be encouraged and enlarged. After those have been identified, then staff can begin to look for gaps to fill.

Third, drawing on evidence-based decision-making models, an inquiry-based cycle begins in earnest with an analysis of the specific issues that the school hopes to address by becoming trauma-sensitive.[29]

Fourth, the school then should focus on identifying the root cause of the problems. For example, if stress is the root cause, the team would identify whether the source is institutional, interpersonal, external, or a combination of simultaneous stressors.

Then, the next phase of work would be to design interventions to address stressors. This also includes an analysis of current practices or systems that are working well for students and a look at ways in which the school culture might inadvertently increase the stressor. For example, if the root cause is an institutional stressor like homework, the school should reflect on whether current homework practices or policies exacerbate students' stress. This would include practices such as teachers in many subjects piling on their biggest homework assignments around the same time.

The final phase of the inquiry cycle is to determine whether interventions are effective. During this phase, schools must determine what data will serve as evidence. At times, it may be a change in a predetermined data point such as student attendance or discipline referrals. Student satisfaction surveys also provide important data points.

This is an iterative process, so the data obtained from this phase would then inform a subsequent inquiry cycle.

3. View trauma-sensitive work as a framework for reviewing other school policies and practices, especially school discipline.

The school's trauma-sensitive work should inform its approach to three closely interrelated elements: classroom instruction, management, and discipline. Schools must collectively determine their expectations and norms of practice and develop accountability measures to ensure that trauma-sensitivity is central to the school's practices in each area.

For example, the school will need to determine how the components of trauma-informed care (protect, connect, respect, and redirect) are reflected in policies regarding classroom instruction and management. Questions to consider include:

- How will expectations regarding instructional planning change to ensure that lessons promote collaboration among students and elicit student voice?
- What expectations will the school establish regarding the use of culturally responsive instructional practices?
- What expectations will the school establish to ensure that student voice informs instructional planning?

It is important to look closely at how this work informs the policies and practices regarding student discipline. Discipline is like the canary in the coal mine: When we see discrepancies in how and which students are disciplined it suggests that there are deeper, unnoticed problems in classroom instruction and management. And, as over 30 years of research demonstrates,[30] those students who are subject to the harshest and most frequent discipline are disproportionately Black and Latinx, in part because discipline practices are often ill-suited to looking beyond the immediate problems. Trauma-sensitive schools should treat discipline differently and have different outcomes.

For example, Khyron Lewis, 19, was suspended for kicking a boy during a 7th grade English class in what appeared to be an unprovoked attack. Khyron was suspended. She later wrote about the experience. First, she described an antecedent: A few months earlier, when the class was reading *To Kill a Mockingbird*, Khyron was inspired to exclaim, "I want to be a lawyer someday." The boy next to her erupted in mocking laughter. She wrote, "I felt as if my heart had been placed on a stick for everyone to gawk at."

Several months later, a girl tricked Khyron into handing over her journal during class:

> I watched as Tiara nestled my journal in the crook of her arm. Then my chest clenched as Anthony, one of the loudest boys in our class, approached her. [He hadn't been] the one who'd mocked me, [but] I could feel my stomach churn when he started to approach Tiara. In that moment, I panicked that he was about to trespass on the one thing I tried so hard to protect from other people's judgement: my journal.
>
> He leaned over her shoulder and tried to open my notebook to the first page. Sirens went off inside my mind and body.
>
> Looking back, I can see that what I did next was an extreme reaction, but at the time, all I could think about was the need to keep anyone else from laughing at me. I jumped out of my chair and the world shifted into slow motion. I kicked him in the crotch and he doubled over in pain, screaming, "What the f-ck, you f-cking b-tch!?" I snatched my notebook back and ran out.

I ran into the hallway and hid in the stairwell. I can't remember how they got me to come upstairs to the vice principal's office. I sat in the room clutching my note-book, thinking about how angry my mom, my teachers, and the other students must be. I was barely concerned with how I'd hurt Anthony. I was too busy prepar-ing to defend myself from more perceived attacks—this time, from my mother and the vice principal.

"Khy, what happened during class?" the vice principal asked. "Why did you kick him? I need to know." The towering stacks of old textbooks made me feel small in her office. My mom was sitting next to me. Another chair was stacked with folders.

I kept my eyes down. My feelings of rage, anxiety, and shame were too complicated for me to understand. Forget about explaining my side, even if the vice principal was trying to be understanding.

When I didn't respond, she pressed me further. "What did he do that made you kick him? This incident appears totally unprovoked." I sensed her growing impa-tience. She turned to my mom. "Khy isn't a violent person, but this kind of thing is unacceptable. It's only fair that we suspend her."

I got an in-school suspension for two days, which meant they left me in a room with the school secretary and had me do all my classwork there. I couldn't complete my math work because I didn't understand it. Every time someone came into the office, I felt them looking at me and my shame grew larger.

Anthony didn't deserve to be the target of my anger. But kicking him gave me a strange feeling of power and control. When I went back to class, my peers whis-pered about me. I still didn't have any friends, but at least now nobody tried to mess with me.

After the suspension, I still didn't have any healthy outlets for my feelings. I quietly tried to deal with my social anxiety and low self-esteem. I would have other, more minor emotional outbursts throughout middle school and high school, but this was the only time I had hurt someone else.

What I needed was for someone to listen to me, and for adults to help me manage my anxiety. I had confided in my mom about my issues in elementary school, but by 7th grade, I felt I should be able to handle it on my own. So I kept my struggles inside.

I wish she or my teachers had noticed how isolated I was. After that suspension, I became less likely to turn to grown-ups for help, because I felt even more like a burden than before.

Khyron participated in Youth Communication's summer writing workshop the year that it focused on restorative justice. It was a revelation to her that there was a method for handling transgressions that addressed the needs of both victims and offenders. As she learned:

Accountability is an important part of restorative justice, but it aims to resolve the issues that influenced the offender's actions, not just punish them.

And she began to see how it might have made a difference to her. She wrote:

One method of restorative justice is sitting in a circle with the victim, the offender, and members of the community to see how the incident affected everyone. They discuss how to find a solution. I think this approach would have helped in my case. Although instead of having everyone in class speak about the incident, ideally it would have been me, Anthony, Mr. Meehan and the vice principal.

Anthony would have been given the chance to tell me how I hurt him. I'd have been given the proper space to explain how I was feeling—both to Anthony and to adults who could connect me with help. If I could have shown even a few people that I was in pain too, I think I would have been able to apologize. If you can't acknowledge and begin to process your own pain, it's harder to acknowledge someone else's and understand your role in it.

Since then I've taken the time to reflect on my past mistakes and learned coping skills in therapy. Being suspended didn't help me get to this point. I agree that I needed to be punished for what I did, but punishment should serve as a lesson to encourage growth. Suspension only let my negative emotions boil. I've become the person I am today in spite of getting suspended, not because of it.

If we view problematic student behavior as a response to stressors (which disproportionately impact BIPOC students), then we must also view disciplinary practices as efforts to reduce disproportionality, support students, and teach them skills that help them navigate those stressors while also holding students accountable. Khyron's treatment in this instance, or her school's approach to discipline in general, may or may not have been directly related to her race, but it was definitely related to other stressors in her life—stressors that the adults never learned about because they didn't have a system for unearthing them.

Because of this, I believe that schools should employ a developmentally and culturally responsive approach to discipline. Reflecting on the following questions about disciplinary practices will help schools identify ineffective practices and suggest positive changes.

- Did we do all we could to find out what might be behind the student's actions?
- How will our disciplinary practices need to be modified in ways that are responsive to students who have experienced stress and trauma?
- How frequently do we resort to exclusionary practices that remove students from their classrooms or remove them from school?
- Are there certain characteristics more typical of students we tend to exclude?
- How purposeful are we in helping students feel welcomed after their return?
- How respectful are we to students when meting out discipline?
- Are we using discipline to educate students about inappropriate behavior or are we using it to control student behavior?
- How might soliciting student voice enhance our understanding of the root causes of problematic student behavior?
- What practices promote the psychological safety of our students (such as teaching specific de-escalation strategies, and teaching strategies to promote self-awareness and perspective taking)?

Notes

1. Biglan, Flay, Embry, and Sandler 2012.

2. Jaycox et al. 2009; Phipps and Thorne 2019.

3. Harris and Fallot 2001.

4. Walkley and Cox 2013.

5. Dorado et al. 2016.

6. Ibid., 2016.

7. Bath 2008; Honsinger and Brown 2019.

8. Hummer, Dollard, Robst, and Armstrong 2010.

9. Center for Early Adolescence, University of North Carolina, Charlotte, NC.

10. Ibid.

11. Appleton et al. 2008.

12. https://www.safesupportivelearning.ed.gov/topic-research/safety.

13. National Association of School Psychologists 2013.

14. Edmonsdon and Lei 2014.

15. Ibid.; Frazier et al. 2017.

16. The term commonly used to refer to the transoceanic transfer of plants, animals, culture, human populations, technology, diseases, and ideas between the Americas, the Old World, and West Africa in the fifteenth and sixteenth centuries in the aftermath of Christopher Columbus' voyages that began in 1492.

17. Taylor, Oberle, Durlak, and Weissberg 2017.

18. Durlak, Weissberg, Dymnicki, Taylor, and Schellinger 2011.

19. Simmons 2020.

20. Frey, Fisher, and Everlove 2009.

21. Meiklejohn et al. 2012.

22. Jennings, Frank, Snowberg, Coccia, and Greenberg 2013.

23. Davis and Hayes 2011.

24. https://www.nctsn.org/.

25. The Council of School Superintendents 2019.

26. McFarland et al. 2018.

27. 2018.

28. Cole, Eisner, Gregory, and Ristuccia 2013.

29. Honig and Coburn 2008.

30. Skiba, Horner, Chung, Rausch, May, and Tobin 2011.

References

Appleton, J.J., Christenson, S.L., and Furlong, M.J. (2008). Student engagement with school: Critical conceptual and methodological issues of the construct. *Psychology in the Schools* 45(5): 369–386.

Arao, B. and Clemens, K. (2013). From safe spaces to brave spaces. The art of effective facilitation: Reflections from social justice educators, 135–150. Sterling, VA: Stylus.

Bath, H. (2008). The three pillars of trauma-informed care. *Reclaiming Children and Youth* 17(3): 17–21.

Biglan, A., Flay, B.R., Embry, D.D., and Sandler, I.N. (2012). The critical role of nurturing environments for promoting human well-being. *American Psychologist* 67: 257–271.

Cole, S.F., Eisner, A., Gregory, M., and Ristuccia, J.M. (2013). A vision for a trauma-sensitive school. *Optimizing Learning Outcomes: Proven Brain-centric, Trauma-sensitive Practices* (pp. 166–179). New York, NY: Routledge.

Center for Early Adolescence, University of North Carolina, Charlotte, NC.

The Council of School Superintendents. (2019). *Ninth Annual Survey of New York State School Superintendents on Financial Matters*, November.

Davis, D.M. and Hayes, J.A. (2011). What are the benefits of mindfulness? A practice review of psychotherapy-related research. *Psychotherapy* 48(2): 198.

Dorado, J.S., Martinez, M., McArthur, L.E., and Leibovitz, T. (2016). Healthy Environments and Response to Trauma in Schools (HEARTS): A whole-school, multi-level, prevention and intervention program for creating trauma-informed, safe and supportive schools. *School Mental Health* 8(1): 163–176.

Duckworth, A. (2016). *Grit: The Power of Passion and Perseverance*. New York, NY: Scribner.

Durlak, J.A., Weissberg, R.P., Dymnicki, A.B., Taylor, R.D., and Schellinger, K.B. (2011). The impact of enhancing students' social and emotional learning: A meta-analysis of school-based universal interventions. *Child Development* 82(1): 405–432.

Edmondson, A.C. and Lei, Z. (2014). Psychological safety: The history, renaissance, and future of an interpersonal construct. *Annual Review of Organizational Psychology Organizational Behavior* 1(1): 23–43.

Felitti, V.J., Anda, R.F., Nordenberg, D., Williamson, D.F., Spitz, A.M., Edwards, V., and Marks, J.S. (1998). Relationship of childhood abuse and household dysfunction to many of the leading causes of death in adults: The Adverse Childhood Experiences (ACE) Study. *American Journal of Preventive Medicine* 14(4): 245–258.

Frazier, M.L., Fainshmidt, S., Klinger, R.L., Pezeshkan, A., and Vracheva, V. (2017). Psychological safety: A meta-analytic review and extension. *Personnel Psychology* 70(1): 113–165.

Frey, N., Fisher, D., and Everlove, S. (2009). *Productive Group Work: How to Engage Students, Build Teamwork, and Promote Understanding*. Alexandria, VA: ASCD.

Harris, M. and Fallot, R.D. (2001). Envisioning a trauma-informed service system: A vital paradigm shift. *New Directions for Mental Health Services* (89): 3–22.

Honig, M.I. and Coburn, C. (2008). Evidence-based decision making in school district central offices: Toward a policy and research agenda. *Educational Policy* 22(4): 578–608.

Honsinger, C. and Brown, M.H. (2019). Preparing Trauma-sensitive teachers: Strategies for teacher educators. *Teacher Educators' Journal* 12: 129–152.

Hummer, V.L., Dollard, N., Robst, J., and Armstrong, M.I. (2010). Innovations in implementation of trauma-informed care practices in youth residential treatment: A curriculum for organizational change. *Child Welfare* 89(2): 79.

Jaycox, L.H., Langley, A.K., Stein, B.D., Wong, M., Sharma, P., Scott, M., and Schonlau, M. (2009). Support for students exposed to trauma: A pilot study. *School Mental Health* 1(2): 49–60.

Jennings, P.A., Frank, J.L., Snowberg, K.E., Coccia, M.A., and Greenberg, M.T. (2013). Improving classroom learning environments by Cultivating Awareness and Resilience in Education (CARE): Results of a randomized controlled trial. *School Psychology Quarterly* 28(4): 374.

McFarland, J., Hussar, B., Wang, X., Zhang, J., Wang, K., Rathbun, A., . . . and Mann, F.B. (2018). *The Condition of Education 2018*. NCES 2018-144. National Center for Education Statistics.

Meiklejohn, J., Phillips, C., Freedman, M.L., Griffin, M.L., Biegel, G., Roach, A., . . . and Saltzman, A. (2012). Integrating mindfulness training into K–12 education: Fostering the resilience of teachers and students. *Mindfulness* 3(4): 291–307.

Merrick, M.T., Ford, D.C., Ports, K.A., and Guinn, A.S. (2018). Prevalence of adverse childhood experiences from the 2011–2014 behavioral risk factor surveillance system in 23 states. *JAMA Pediatrics* 172(11): 1038–1044.

National Association of School Psychologists. (2013). *NASP Recommendations for Comprehensive School Safety Policies*, January.

National Center on Safe Supportive Learning Environments. https://www.safesupportive-learning.ed.gov/topic-research/safety (accessed 20 February 2021).

The National Child Traumatic Stress Network. https://www.nctsn.org/ (accessed 3 December 2020).

Phipps, R. and Thorne, S. (2019). Utilizing Trauma-Focused Cognitive Behavioral Therapy as a Framework for Addressing Cultural Trauma in African American Children and Adolescents: A Proposal. *Professional Counselor* 9(1): 35–50.

Reeve, J. (2012). A self-determination theory perspective on student engagement. In *Handbook of Research on Student Engagement*, 149–172). Boston, MA: Springer.

S Yoon, J. (2002). Teacher characteristics as predictors of teacher-student relationships: Stress, negative affect, and self-efficacy. *Social Behavior and Personality: An International Journal* 30(5): 485–493.

Simmons, D. (2020). Confronting Inequity/The Trauma We Don't See. *Educational Leadership, Learning and the Brain* 77(8): 88–89.

Skiba, R.J., Horner, R.H., Chung, C.G., Rausch, M.K., May, S.L., and Tobin, T. (2011). Race is not neutral: A national investigation of African American and Latino disproportionality in school discipline. *School Psychology Review* 40(1): 85–107.

Taylor, R.D., Oberle, E., Durlak, J.A., and Weissberg, R.P. (2017). Promoting positive youth development through school-based social and emotional learning interventions: A meta-analysis of follow-up effects. *Child Development* 88(4): 1156–1171.

Walkley, M. and Cox, T.L. (2013). Building trauma-informed schools and communities. *Children & Schools* 35(2): 123–126.

The Change Process

[At University Heights HS] all the new students had to go to an orientation during the summer where we played a bunch of get-to-know-each-other games. So, by the first day of school we already knew each other. I felt at home there almost right away. I was finally getting a feeling that I belonged [after transferring from another high school].

I always feel respected and cared for by my teachers at University Heights. If I don't, I'll tell them and we'll resolve it. I remember when Marion, one of my teachers, interrupted me when I was talking one time in class. I didn't say anything to her but she could tell that I was upset. She approached me in the hallway and said that she didn't mean to cut me off, but time was running out. I accepted her apology. To tell you the truth, I was shocked that she took the time to apologize to a student.

I didn't know there were other ways of teaching either. In Spanish class, for example, the learning is interactive. My Spanish teacher would write the verbs that we were learning that week on the board. Then we would get up and break into groups of four or five. Each group would have to work together to make sentences with the verbs and the adjectives that we had studied the week before. Then we'd have a contest to see which group made the best sentences. It made you forget you were in class and helped you get to know your peers better.

Now, that I'm about to graduate from University Heights I realize that many things about it have helped to make me a better person. Number one is that I always feel like I'm important there. The teachers care about me and not just the work I do. Knowing that has made a big difference in the amount of effort I put into my work and in my feelings about myself and my future.

—Troy Sean Welcome,
"My School Is Like a Family"

IN THIS chapter, we look at several changes that support developmentally and culturally responsive teaching and schools: building teacher skill and confidence in working with diverse students; using a DCRT lens for professional development and for reviewing curricula and assessment; and using existing strengths and frameworks as we create a more supportive school climate. We look at all of these issues in light of equity.

As we have discussed throughout this book, developmentally and culturally responsive teaching is grounded in the belief that all students have developmental needs and that addressing those needs in culturally responsive ways supports personal and academic growth. When students feel nurtured and valued, they become more motivated. When they can adapt learning to their interests (as Troy and his peers surely did when they built their own Spanish sentences) they find more meaning and purpose in what they are taught. When students can occasionally get out of their seats and move around, even if it is just to form groups, it can help them focus. When students feel that their teachers believe in them and what they can achieve—and see them teaching in ways that match that belief—students are more likely to do the work that leads to achievement. (Troy is a good example. He was on the verge of dropping out. Transferring to a school with a more welcoming climate revived his interest in academic learning. He went on to become a teacher and alternative school principal himself.)

To create school climates where all students feel supported and valued, schools must take explicit steps to disrupt conscious and unconscious systemic barriers—barriers that disproportionately place our most vulnerable students at greater risk of emotional distress and academic failure.

The Change Process: Equity as Our North Star

I've worked with urban, suburban, and rural school districts to help them develop practices and systems to promote equity. Often, the impetus for change is long-standing concerns by BIPOC families and their allies that BIPOC students are not able to take full advantage of the districts' educational opportunities. They are stymied by barriers that cause BIPOC students to feel undervalued and marginalized. In many cases, districts erect these barriers unintentionally; in other cases, they are the legacy of discriminatory policies.

I've found that one of the strongest pieces of evidence for an equity problem is a large gap between how students—especially BIPOC and LGBTQ+ students—experience school and how staff "believe" students experience school. There can be a moment of reckoning when school boards and school district administrators are confronted with information (often student testimonials about painful experiences of bias, racism, exclusion, and invisibility) that forces them to acknowledge concerns they may have been unaware of, minimized, or even ignored. That moment of reckoning is the call to action—that things can't stay the same because districts are not living up to their values of equal education for all. We have seen a classic case of that call to action in E.N.'s story in Chapter 2, where the students' manifesto highlighted racism and called for the school to change how it addressed it.

If we start with equity as our "North Star," then we are more likely to identify and confront the barriers that we must remove to achieve it. Then we need to look at how equity relates to student needs. Developmentally and culturally responsive teaching, by definition, helps to surface those needs. Once we know the needs or gaps, we can identify teaching practices and school policies that will address those needs and close the equity gap.

Equity needs to be front and center because we know that from the moment that BIPOC students begin formal schooling, they are likely to encounter bias.[1] From the curriculum, to discipline practices, to the overall climate and culture within their schools, BIPOC students disproportionately face a series of accumulated systemic barriers that make it harder for them to experience academic success. This reality can make addressing equity in schools seem overwhelming. For those teachers who say, "I can't change the system on my own," I say that you're totally correct. But what you can do is reflect on your place within the system, reflect on ways you may inadvertently be contributing to the barriers to equity, and discover the areas where you can contribute to change. There are more than you may think.

I've found that teachers can help to promote equity by taking specific action in four areas: (1) building the mindsets and confidence to better support students, and BIPOC and LGBTQ+ students in particular; (2) participating in professional development designed to enhance curriculum and assessment to ensure that all students are represented and are valued for their efforts; (3) building a climate that makes all students feel physically and psychologically safe; and (4) making youth voice integral to change. Let's look at each of them.

The Change Process: Teacher Mindsets and the Details of Daily Practice

In my professional development work, teachers often talk about the difficulty of adopting more developmentally and culturally responsive practices. Those struggles typically include the tension between empathy and high expectations, between developing deeper knowledge of students while doing every other part of their job, and being an authentic ally while being aware that your students' experiences are very different from your own. Here's a discussion of how teachers can address those tensions in ways that support DCRT teaching.

How to be empathetic while still holding high expectations: Learning more about our students can build helpful empathy. However, we don't want greater empathy to inadvertently lower our expectations.

I remember telling my high school teachers that I would attend Cornell University. Many expressed concern about the academic challenges I would face, how far away I would be from my family, or how alone I might feel as a Bronx teen going to a school in upstate New York. These teachers meant well, had supported and cared about me, and wanted to protect me. But what I heard through their concern was that they didn't believe I would succeed at Cornell because it was too rigorous.

While my family had challenges as I grew up, they were nowhere near the ones that many teens have shared throughout this book. Yet my teachers' unconscious reactions were to "care" for me by dissuading me from challenging myself.

It's completely understandable that teachers would respond empathetically when they learn of the hardships that some students experience. It's also completely understandable that teachers would adjust their expectations for those same students. But adjusting expectations *for* students differs from adjusting expectations *of* students. When we adjust expectations *of* students, we view those adjustments as responding to a characteristic of the *student* rather than a characteristic of the *condition* affecting the student. For example, rather than making adjustments because our students are experiencing homelessness, we make adjustments because we don't believe that they can succeed at school *because* they're experiencing homelessness.

When we adjust our expectations *for* students, it's a response to a specific event or circumstance. Those adjustments may be temporary or longer-term, but we make them in response to circumstances, not as a reflection of the potential for success we see in students. For a student experiencing homelessness, an adjustment *for* the student might be to allow them extra time to complete a large project because shelters lack workspace for students, or allowing them to write out an assignment because they have limited access to computers. The learning goals of the project and the standards to which you hold the students stay the same. By addressing obstacles caused by the students' circumstances, you allow them to demonstrate their actual abilities.

How to know students in ways that are meaningful but still manageable: Several teachers recently asked for my feedback on a training that focused on the need to have deeper knowledge of their students' cultural backgrounds. One of the teachers summed up their collective reaction by stating, "We're high school teachers with over 125 students apiece. How can we possibly have deep knowledge of the cultural backgrounds of all of our students?"

This dilemma is common and understandable. Many of us lack knowledge of our own heritage let alone that of our students! And as our classrooms become increasingly diverse it simply isn't possible to gain deep knowledge of the cultural backgrounds of every student. But the expectation can still leave teachers feeling inadequate. As one teacher shared, "Since I don't have that deep understanding of who my students are culturally, I'm afraid to teach in a way that's only at the surface of who they are and never gets under the water." There's no completely satisfactory answer to this concern, but here are some strategies.

- **Show curiosity about your students' lives.** Curiosity alone is affirming to students. They don't expect you to know them deeply, but they deeply appreciate interest that is based on something meaningful that you notice about them, like a hairstyle, an interesting food in their lunchbox, or the fact that they missed school for a religious holiday not recognized by your district.

- **Ask questions.** Take time to check in with a few students each week to ask them how they're doing and what it's like for them as a student in your school. Ask a question that shows you're curious and paying attention to who they are and what they care about. Or occasionally use a short writing assignment to ask students to imagine how the content of your course relates to their everyday lives. Asking questions like these will increase your knowledge and empathy in ways that will strengthen your teaching. It also sends a general message that you care. The accumulated bits of insight we learn from these interactions will help you teach in a developmentally and culturally responsive way.

- **Listen.** There's no point in asking questions of students if you don't listen to their responses. Show you are listening by closing your computer and putting away your phone and your papers. You will discover that in most conversations you are not listening for facts as if you are studying for a test. You are making a connection with another human being. Ask clarifying questions to deepen your understanding of the student's life and concerns. And listening isn't only relevant when you've asked a student a direct question. For example, in Chapter 1, Ebony Coleman suggests that teachers could eavesdrop to learn things about student interests and personalities that they can use in lessons. When possible, open up your classroom before and after school as a safe place to gather, quietly socialize, and study. You'll learn a lot by just sharing the same space with your students.

- **Use knowledge of *general* youth development principles to make it easier to see the *individuality* of your students.** Since all students are experiencing the same developmental stages, you can anticipate their behavior and feelings. For example, middle school students are anxious to fit in and highly sensitive to peer approval while high school students are less affiliative and more focused on the future. And, as they move through adolescence, all students struggle to balance the need to individuate with loyalty to family and tradition. But if our understanding stops there, it can make us jaded or lead to unhelpful stereotyping. To go deeper, it may help to think about your students the way a writer thinks about the characters in a good novel. They are all wrestling with the same theme, but what makes a novel interesting is the *unique* way each character responds to the theme. Similarly, your students are all experiencing the same "theme" or developmental stage, so if you know youth development principles, you already have an idea of the general issues they face. That makes it easier to notice *variations* on the theme—the individuality and uniqueness of each student—which enhances your credibility and builds trust.

- **Show concern about the level of stress that school itself causes for students.** One relatively nonintrusive way to get to know students is to ask what is stressing them now at school and how much. What are their educational goals and what obstacles do they have to climb to achieve them? Whom do they turn to for emotional support? These conversations do not have to be deep to be meaningful to students or to help you know them in ways that can contribute to your teaching. You don't need to have answers for them. Just asking without judgment or an ulterior motive and giving the student a chance to talk will deepen your relationship.

- **Understand that different aspects of students' identities can be more important at different times.** Students may be gay, or Black, or recent immigrants. They may be struggling to fit in, or striving to establish independence, eager to lead or eager to join and follow. For example, for Black gay students, their racial identity may be primary at some times while their gay identity may loom larger at other times. And sometimes their identity as a jock, or nerd, or fan of a certain music genre may dominate. And there will always be a developmental identity running alongside those changing demographic identities, such as the lost 9th grader worried about how to gain acceptance in a new school, or the eager and nervous 18-year-old on the cusp of adulthood.

Because student identities are fluid and multidimensional, you need to avoid forming settled judgments. I've seen teachers extract information at the beginning of the school year, but fail to sustain the discussion and curiosity. That can lead to a surface-level and even stereotypical and biased perspective of students. When we view deep knowledge of our students as a *consequence* of being developmentally and culturally responsive, it can motivate us to affirm practices in an intentional and consistent way over time.

How to be authentic: Students are highly sensitive to any gap between what teachers say and what they do. They are also sensitive to teachers who get defensive when they don't know the right answer or action. So, to earn credibility from students we need to acknowledge when we don't know something or are uncomfortable. Showing our vulnerability enhances our credibility and authenticity. It also helps us learn, which enhances and builds our future credibility.

I was recently speaking with several Black high school students in a rural school district to get their perspective on being a student of color in their predominantly White school. One of the things they shared was what happens when a White peer refers to a Black student using the N-word. They said that either teachers addressed it directly and punished the student or they minimized the importance of it and either "told the student to stop clowning around" or "acted like they didn't hear it."

The students offered that one thing that typically didn't happen was a discussion. Their teachers avoided using it as a "teachable moment," an opportunity to discuss the individual harm that the incident caused or the collective harm caused within their classroom. I followed up by asking them why they thought their teachers might choose not to lead such a discussion. Having anticipated my question, one student quickly shared, "I don't think that they agree with the use of the N-word or anything like that. I know that they care about all of us. I just think that they're afraid of having that discussion. I just think it makes them uncomfortable because they don't know what to say."

Later that day, I spoke with a few of these students' teachers. We discussed how they were trying to add more diverse perspectives and inclusive language into a science unit. One of them brought up the topic of race and how he sometimes struggled with knowing what to do when a "racial incident" happened in his classroom.

"As a White teacher I sometimes feel like I'm not authentic. I try to empathize with my Black students, but I'm not Black so how can I possibly understand what it's like for my Black students to be in this school or to live as a Black person in today's society?"

I appreciate the fact that teachers are asking themselves these questions because they stem from their desire to support their students. But this begs another question:

"What does it mean to be authentic?" In my experience, for students, our authenticity rests more on the openness and even the vulnerability we show as we work to better understand them developmentally and culturally than it does on what we already know about their lives or culture.

Authenticity also stems from recognizing commonalities. We can begin by asking: "What experiences do students tend to have in common?" And "What experiences do I have in common with my students?" This is a crucial first step because several studies examining group dynamics emphasize the importance of identifying commonalities in helping to build trust. And building trust is essential. If we want to move from having surface-level knowledge about our students to more deeply understanding them, we need them to take the risk of trusting us and our ability to keep them safe. However, while there are many things we have in common with students, I have observed they respond most positively to shared vulnerabilities. (See the example of the math teacher later in this chapter.)

Finally, authenticity also stems from noticing and respecting differences. In my conversations with many BIPOC middle and high school students who attend predominantly White schools, they often share that they're treated all the same, as though they represent their racial group rather than just themselves. As one student shared, "As soon as the conversation has anything to do with being Latino, all the eyes turn on me and I'm expected to have an opinion. What's worse is that I feel like I'm the voice for everything Latino."

As a teacher, especially if you are a White teacher, you may never have had the annoying experience of having to be the representative for your race or the anxiety of being the only person in a room representing your race. So, yes, you may be different from your students because you don't share the same racial background, but your students who share the same race are also different from each other with different lived experiences, different interests, and different goals. We should not minimize or overlook these differences. So as teachers, we face a difficult balancing act: We want to be aware of meaningful differences among our students and seek to better understand how those differences inform how we navigate our world, while simultaneously seeking to raise our awareness of the similarities that exist among ourselves and our students. (No one said teaching was easy.)

The Change Process: Professional Development

We can use a DCRT lens to strengthen professional development (PD). Broadly speaking, that means asking if PD opportunities are consciously designed to help teachers become better prepared to support the learning needs of BIPOC and LGBTQ+ students and others who may not be heard or see themselves reflected at school. This kind of PD guides teachers to reflect on, question, and, ultimately, change some of their assumptions about their students as well as examining and changing their teaching practice.

Somewhat counterintuitively, studies suggest that we typically change our beliefs *after* we change our practices rather than before.[2] Not surprisingly, these studies also find that teachers change their beliefs about how to teach after they adopt new practices that are successful.[3] We need PD that encourages teachers to try out new approaches that have been successful for their colleagues.

Studies of PD also reveal that what teachers learn in PD—and what they do in response to what they learn—is significantly influenced by their prior knowledge, experiences, and beliefs.[4] Centering a youth voice in professional development can help teachers examine and question their prior knowledge, experiences, and beliefs about who their students are and what they need from us in order to achieve academically. Listening to students can help us become more aware of the gaps in our knowledge and inspire us to adopt new practices.

PD experiences should also explicitly increase awareness of the unique school experiences of BIPOC and LGBTQ+ students. It should prepare teachers to use pedagogical practices that promote positive identity development of BIPOC and LGBTQ+ students, and practices that reduce and eliminate bias in curriculum and assessment. In the next chapter, Tim shows how using teen-written stories like those excerpted in this book can be effective in PD DCRT-based professional development.

Whether it focuses on specific instructional practices or on broader school policies, the most effective PD begins with an attempt to understand problems with current practice. As the stories in this book demonstrate, one of the best ways to identify problems of practice is to talk with students. I recently worked with a middle school math teacher who had participated in a PD training on enhancing student engagement that was facilitated by school colleagues. She said she was concerned and a bit frustrated that she had worked hard to make changes, but that several students remained disengaged.

I talked with the students and learned that a negative experience in their math class the prior year had made them doubt their ability. I also learned that the students, including the most reticent ones, generally appreciated their new teacher's efforts. In response to what she learned, the teacher decided to share her own challenges with math before becoming a math teacher. A few weeks later, she told me that sharing those experiences helped more students feel comfortable enough to participate in class. This is an example of how to draw an educationally meaningful connection between teacher and student experiences.

It was also a telling example of the importance of soliciting student voice to identify a practice issue. The teacher initially believed that the problem of practice (low student engagement) related to her teaching. The professional development training was based on the assumption that student engagement could be enhanced through new techniques. But the problem wasn't a technique; it was students' reduced sense of self-efficacy based on experience of a previous class. If student voice had informed the professional development, the problem would have been pinpointed much more quickly.

The Change Process: Curriculum and Assessment

When we think of a school's curriculum, we often focus on the content that students are taught. Research in the field of curriculum development, however, has identified several different types of curricula, including: the *recommended* curriculum developed by content-area experts; the *written* curriculum developed at the state, district, school, and classroom levels; the *supported* curriculum that includes supplementary materials such as textbooks and multimedia resources; and the *tested* curriculum that includes assessments developed at the state, district, school, and classroom levels.[5] This research also discovered gaps between what is formally taught to students and what students learn. Those gaps are a consequence of a "hidden" curriculum and an "omitted" curriculum that is potent, but mostly invisible. [6]

The term "hidden" curriculum often refers to the things that students learn indirectly that implicitly reinforce their school's culture and climate.[7] In their *Glossary of Education Reform*, the Great Schools Partnership describes the hidden curriculum:

> The hidden-curriculum concept is based on the recognition that students absorb lessons in school that may or may not be part of the formal course of study—for example, how they should interact with peers, teachers, and other adults; how they should perceive different races, groups, or classes of people; or what ideas and behaviors are considered acceptable or unacceptable. The hidden curriculum is described as "hidden" because it is usually unacknowledged or unexamined by students, educators, and the wider community. And because the values and lessons reinforced by the hidden curriculum are often the accepted status quo, it may be assumed that these "hidden" practices and messages don't need to change—even if they are contributing to undesirable behaviors and results.[8]

The hidden curriculum subtly reinforces student mindsets about what aspects of their education they should value and what aspects are less important. For example, if schools place heavy emphasis on standardized tests in math and language arts, no one need tell students that their art or music or history classes carry less weight. Or, if their school does not provide students with the opportunity to identify their preferred pronouns, it may be unintentionally sending messages about how students should treat their gender-nonconforming peers.

The curriculum of omission also directly influences student learning (or lack of learning). Typically referred to as the excluded curriculum, it represents the intentional or unintentional omission of certain perspectives or the failure to address topics at the depth they deserve. Excluding certain topics or marginalizing them signals that lacking knowledge about these topics or only having a surface-level understanding of them is acceptable.[9] Reducing the African American experience to slavery, the heroes of the modern civil rights movement, Barack Obama, and a few novels are classic examples of the curriculum of omission.

Viewing curriculum development through the lens of developmentally and culturally responsive teaching leads us to ask different questions about what we teach, how we teach, and how we assess student learning. At the school level, curriculum planning that is guided by the following questions will help surface hidden and omitted curricula so schools can address them along with the formal curriculum. Individual teachers or school or district curriculum committees can ask these. To avoid blind spots, it is especially important when discussing these questions to include people—including students—who are knowledgeable and experienced with issues facing groups that traditionally lack representation.

- What does my curriculum tell students about themselves and their possibilities?
- Whose voices and perspectives are missing or marginalized, and whose are elevated?
- Where might bias enter into our current approaches to curriculum development?
- What opportunities are there to increase inclusivity and diversity within our curriculum that we are currently missing?
- How does my curriculum demonstrate an understanding of who my students are developmentally?
- How might my current teaching practices constrain my students' ability to fully engage in learning?
- How might my current assessment practices constrain my students' ability to demonstrate their learning?

In addition to asking the preceding questions in rethinking our curriculum, there are many tools that provide more specific guidance on designing culturally responsive lessons. Two popular tools were developed by the Metropolitan Center for Research on Equity and the Transformation of Schools at New York University: the Culturally Responsive Curriculum Scorecard,[10] and the Culturally Responsive-Sustaining STEAM Curriculum Scorecard.[11]

These tools guide teachers and administrators toward ensuring that their entire curriculum—including units of study, books, materials, activities, and assessments—emphasizes inclusivity and provides positive and substantive representation of BIPOC students. The authors view curriculum review as a collaborative process that includes teachers, school administrators, and parents from diverse racial, gender, linguistic, and economic backgrounds. They also focus curriculum review on representation (e.g., which students tend to be represented within the curriculum) and social justice (e.g., opportunities the curriculum provides for cultural responsiveness). This approach helps curriculum review to remain focused on cultural responsiveness rather than simply on diversity (which I've found can unfortunately be reduced to simply *adding* more BIPOC books in the classroom without regard for how those books *represent* the BIPOC students there).

We can also support the developmental needs of students by including culturally responsive formative and summative assessments. Students, teachers, and parents pay close attention to assessments, as they should. Several scholars in the field of culturally responsive teaching have reported that using assessments that reflect the cultural backgrounds of BIPOC students link to increases in their levels of school engagement and academic performance.[12] That is why we have to exercise constant vigilance to root out potential bias in assessments.

Assessment and testing bias can occur in so many ways that it would take a book to address them. Instead, because a major focus of this book is the impact of mindsets on behaviors, I look briefly at the impact of the psychological context in which assessments are administered as a cautionary tale about the need to take test results with a grain of salt.

Over 25 years ago, social psychologist Dr. Claude Steele and his colleague Dr. Joshua Aronson demonstrated that when members of a stigmatized group confront a negative stereotype about their group prior to completing an assessment related to that stereotype, their performance tends to decline.[13] In their classic study of what they termed "stereotype threat," they noted:

> Black and White college students were given a half-hour test using difficult
> items from the verbal Graduate Record Exam (GRE). In the stereotype-threat
> condition, they told students the test diagnosed intellectual ability, thus poten-
> tially eliciting the stereotype that Blacks are less intelligent than Whites. In the
> no-stereotype-threat condition, the researchers told students that the test was
> a problem-solving lab task that said nothing about ability, presumably render-
> ing stereotypes irrelevant. In the stereotype threat condition, Blacks—who were
> matched with Whites in their group by SAT scores—did less well than Whites.

In no stereotype-threat condition—in which the exact same test was described as
a lab task that did not indicate ability—Blacks' performance rose to match that of
equally skilled Whites.[14]

A follow-up study on the impact of stereotype threat on women's math performance revealed similar results: Before a test, when women were told that they tended to perform worse than men, they did. When they were told that the tests revealed no gender difference, they performed as well as the men.[15]

This research demonstrates that test performance is not as objective as advertised in measuring what students have learned or are capable of learning. This means that we must pay close attention to the psychological dimensions of testing and the often unconscious ways in which racial and gender identity may influence performance. Of course, social scientists can't possibly research every way in which bias creeps into curriculum and assessment. That's why we have to keep our eyes and ears open to what our students are experiencing and respond when they report problems, or when we see discrepancies and disparities.

The Change Process: Building a Positive School Climate

School climate is based on patterns of students', parents', and school personnel's experience of school life. It reflects values, interpersonal relationships, teaching and learning practices, and organizational structures. A school's culture is largely determined by the values, shared beliefs, and behavior of all stakeholders within the school community and reflects the school's social norms.[16] While people debate what school climate dimensions are essential to assess, studies suggest four major areas that school climate assessment typically includes: (1) teaching and learning; (2) safety; (3) relationships; and (4) the school environment.[17]

As we have discussed throughout the book, DCRT emphasizes that teaching and learning are most effective when we also recognize students' cultural and developmental needs. Then we need to meet those needs in ways that value students as individuals and acknowledge the importance of their lived experiences. In schools that use developmentally and culturally responsive teaching, safety means more than protection from physical harm. It accounts for students' feelings of psychological safety, including how connected they feel to their teachers and peers, the sense of community that they feel, and the school's discipline policies and practices. Building meaningful relationships, of course, is at the heart of developmentally and culturally responsive teaching. Finally, school climate also relates to the quality of the relationships between the school and the larger community. This often means that school staff know where students spend time outside of school, including after-school programs, libraries, religious institutions, sports facilities, dance studios, and others. And they see adults in those programs as potential allies in supporting students.

Now that we have a pretty good idea of what makes a strong school climate, how do we assess our own school's climate—its strengths and areas that need strengthening? And how will we know if implementing DCRT practices are responsible for improving our schools' climates?

Getting a well-rounded picture of school climate entails gathering qualitative and quantitative data. Gathering qualitative data means creating structured procedures, such as regularly scheduled focus groups with students, teachers, administrators, parents, and other stakeholders. For example, the World Café Protocol can be used to gather information and as an opportunity for both individual and collective reflection.[18] A key feature of this protocol is a series of informal or "café-style" table discussions designed to solicit diverse perspectives on a salient issue. Through this series of discussions, common themes are identified that then form the basis for specific action steps.

Schools should also use quantitative measures to assess school climate. Whether school-constructed or purchased from outside vendors, surveys are helpful tools for gathering feedback from all school stakeholders so that multiple viewpoints on the same topic can be assessed and compared to student experiences.

Surveys developed by the National School Climate Center[19] and Panorama Education[20] align with many components of developmentally and culturally responsive teaching. These surveys can be used to establish baseline data on school climate prior to the implementation of developmentally and culturally responsive practices and then at established periods during the school year to measure change over time.

In my experience, one of the most important catalysts for change to a more developmental and culturally responsive school is seeing the gap between what adults think students are experiencing and what students report as their actual experiences. It can be difficult when students tell us that they do not perceive our work as we do. This is especially true when their critique suggests we are not living up to the goals we have set for ourselves as educators and as a school. But our schools will be better if we know the truth and work for change rather than ignore it.

The Change Process: Making Youth Voice Integral to Change

Finally, in addition to formal qualitative and quantitative data gathering, it is important to center student voice as part of schools' daily life so that youth voices are regularly integrated into the school culture. Advisories, elective periods, and even after-school programs can all provide those spaces. Youth Communication's story-based social and emotional learning programs, which are described in the next chapter, are good catalysts for those conversations. They include well-designed lessons, center the voices of young people of color, and are structured to help young people strengthen the five SEL competencies that CASEL research shows support social and academic growth.

As we work to develop the DCRT mindsets among teachers, it's important for schools to build on existing practices rather than start from scratch. That recognizes the good work already being done in the school and helps to create a psychologically safe climate where teachers feel recognized and valued, and where self-reflection and risk-taking (such as acknowledging bias and implementing new teaching practices) are more likely to occur.

To promote habits of mind that build on existing practices, I recommend that schools align their DRCT practices with instructional planning practices that already exist within the school. For example, instructional practice is linked to instructional planning, so it is important that schools support teachers and help guide their instructional planning. The Danielson Framework for Teaching is widely used to inform both instructional planning and teacher evaluation. The following DCRT guiding questions align with Domain 1 (Planning and Preparation) of that framework.[21]

1A. Demonstrating Knowledge of Content and Pedagogy

1. What are the prerequisite skills that students will need to be successful in this lesson? How did you determine those skills?
2. How did you determine whether all students have attained the skills necessary to ensure the lesson is appropriate for them?
3. How does this lesson connect to the lives of your students? How can they practically apply what they have learned?
4. What connections to other content areas do you intend to develop?
5. How does the lesson move all students from lower- to higher-order thinking?

1B. Demonstrating Knowledge of Students

1. How does your lesson demonstrate your knowledge of your students' interests, strengths, and cultural backgrounds?
2. Have you ensured that all materials used within the lesson contain gender inclusive language?
3. What opportunities for movement will you include in your lesson?
4. What opportunities for interpersonal interactions will you provide to your students?
5. How will you ensure that multilingual learners and students with special needs can fully participate in the lesson (in terms of the comprehensibility and accessibility of the lesson material and their opportunity to participate in class discussions)?

1C. Selecting Instructional Outcomes

1. How will you determine the goals of the lesson?
2. How will you ensure that these goals are appropriate for all of your students at this time?
3. How will you ensure that all students are equitably supported to achieve these goals?

1D. Demonstrating Knowledge of Resources

1. What resources (books, websites, multimedia) do you tend to use most often when you plan instruction?

2. Are those resources representative of the students in your class?
3. How might those resources reinforce bias through the exclusion of certain perspectives?
4. What additional resources may be necessary to include within the lesson to mitigate bias?

1E. Designing Coherent Instruction

1. How will the activities selected promote the cognitive, affective, and behavioral engagement of all students?
2. How will you ensure that the lesson activities are sufficiently differentiated so that all students have the possibility of achieving mastery?
3. Have you included equitable options for how students might demonstrate their knowledge of the material?
4. Have you employed a variety of criteria when grouping students to increase diversity within groups with respect to student ability level, gender, racial, or cultural background?
5. When appropriate, will students have input in the creation of student groups?

1F. Designing Student Assessments

1. Have you included a variety of indicators of growth or achievement within your assessments?
2. How will you differentiate your assessments so that they respond to the needs of multilingual learners and students with special needs?
3. How will you ensure that goals for student growth and achievement are established in collaboration with students?
4. What opportunities have been included within the lesson for students to self-assess and monitor their own progress?

■■■

Throughout this book, we've used youth voice to raise our awareness of their lives both inside and outside of school. Their voice shows that youth are complex and that students often reveal only glimpses of themselves to us. When looking out over a classroom, it can be helpful to imagine that the students are all icebergs. We see the tip of who they are, but there is far more beneath the surface. The stories in this book show some of what is beneath the surface and remind us that we can access it, and when we do we can use that knowledge to improve our schools and their learning.

For example, on the surface, Amya Shaw, whose anecdote opens Chapter 5, was an incorrigible terror, traumatized by her life in the shelter system. Many observers might have assumed that she didn't care about learning or much of anything. But beneath the surface—waiting to be discovered—was the avid reader who wanted to succeed and was crying out for help. Stories like Amya's remind us that all students want to learn, even those experiencing the most challenging circumstances.

Notes

1. Mashburn and Henry 2004.
2. Kagan 1992.
3. Ertmer 2005; Guskey 2002.
4. Darling-Hammond, Hyler, and Gardner 2017.
5. Glatthorn, Carr, and Harris 2001.
6. Ibid.
7. Jackson 1968.
8. https://www.edglossary.org/hidden-curriculum/ (accessed 17 February 2021).
9. Gehrke, Knapp, and Sirotnik 1992.
10. Bryan-Gooden, Hester, and Peoples 2019.
11. Peoples, Islam, and Davis 2021.
12. Ladson-Billings 1995; Slee 2010; Alfaiz, Pease, and Maker 2020; Nortvedt et al. 2020.
13. Steele and Aronson 1995.
14. https://www.apa.org/research/action/ (accessed 13 January 2021).
15. Spencer, Steele, and Quinn 1999.
16. http://www.p12.nysed.gov/dignityact/rgsection1.html.

17. National School Climate Center 2021a.
18. The World Cafe 2021.
19. National School Climate Center 2021b.
20. Panorama Education 2021.
21. Danielson 2007.

References

Alfaiz, F.S., Pease, R., and Maker, C.J. (2020). Culturally responsive assessment of physical science skills and abilities: Development, field testing, implementation, and results. *Journal of Advanced Academics* 31(3): 298–328.

American Psychological Association. (2006). *Stereotype Threat Widens Achievement Gap*. https://www.apa.org/research/action/stereotype (accessed 16 February 2021).

Bryan-Gooden, J., Hester, M., and Peoples L.Q. (2019). *Culturally Responsive Curriculum Scorecard*. New York: Metropolitan Center for Research on Equity and the Transformation of Schools, New York University.

Cook, K.S. and Hardin, R. (2001). *Norms of Cooperativeness and Networks of Trust*. New York: Russell Sage Foundation.

Danielson, C. (2007). *Enhancing Professional Practice: A Framework for Teaching*. Alexandria, VA: ASCD.

Darling-Hammond, L., Hyler, M.E., and Gardner, M. (2017). *Effective Teacher Professional Development*. Washington, DC: Learning Policy Institute.

Drescher, M.A., Korsgaard, M.A., Welpe, I.M., Picot, A., and Wigand, R.T. (2014). The dynamics of shared leadership: Building trust and enhancing performance. *Journal of Applied Psychology* 99(5): 771.

Ertmer, P.A. (2005). Teacher pedagogical beliefs: The final frontier in our quest for technology integration. *Educational Technology Research and Development* 53(4): 25–39.

Gehrke, N.J., Knapp, M.S., and Sirotnik, K.A. (1992). Chapter 2: In search of the school curriculum. *Review of Research in Education* 18(1): 51–110.

Glatthorn, A.A., Carr, J.F., and Harris, D.E. (2001). Planning and organizing for curriculum renewal: Thinking about curriculum. http://www.ascd.org/ publications/curriculum-handbook/398/chapters/Thinking-About-Curriculum.aspx (accessed 18 March 2021).

The Glossary of Education Reform. https://www.edglossary.org/hidden-curriculum/ (accessed 17 February 2021).

Goodwin, A.L. and Oyler, C. (2008). Teacher educators as gatekeepers: Deciding who is ready to teach. In *Handbook of Research on Teacher Education: Enduring Questions in Changing Contexts* (eds. M. Cochran-Smith, S. Feinman-Nemser, and D.J. McIntyre), 468–489. New York: Routledge.

Guskey, T.R. (2002). Professional development and teacher change. *Teachers and Teaching* 8(3): 381–391.

Jackson, P. (1968). *Life in Classrooms*. New York: Holt, Rinehart and Winston.

Jencks, C. (1998). Racial bias in testing. *The Black-White Test Score Gap* 55: 84.

Kagan, D.M. (1992). Implication of research on teacher belief. *Educational Psychologist* 27(1): 65–90.

Knoester, M. and Au, W. (2017). Standardized testing and school segregation: Like tinder for fire? *Race Ethnicity and Education* 20(1): 1–14.

Ladson-Billings, G. (1995). But that's just good teaching! The case for culturally relevant pedagogy. *Theory into Practice* 34(3): 159–165.

Mashburn, A.J. and Henry, G.T. (2004). Assessing school readiness: Validity and bias in preschool and kindergarten teachers' ratings. *Educational Measurement: Issues and Practice* 23(4): 16–30.

National School Climate Center. (2021a). https://www.schoolclimate.org/school-climate (accessed 10 March 2021).

National School Climate Center. (2021b). https://www.schoolclimate.org/services/measuring-school-climate-csci (accessed 21 February 2021).

New York State Department of Education. http://www.p12.nysed.gov/dignityact/rgsection1.html (accessed 15 March 2021).

Nortvedt, G.A., Wiese, E., Brown, M., Burns, D., McNamara, G., O'Hara, J., . . . and Taneri, P.O. (2020). Aiding culturally responsive assessment in schools in a globalising world. *Educational Assessment, Evaluation and Accountability*, 1–23.

Panorama Education. https://www.panoramaed.com/school-climate-survey (accessed 18 February 2021).

Peoples, L.Q., Islam, T., and Davis, T. (2021). The culturally responsive-sustaining STEAM curriculum scorecard. New York: Metropolitan Center for Research on Equity and the Transformation of Schools, New York University.

Spencer, S.J., Steele, C.M., and Quinn, D.M. (1999). Stereotype threat and women's math performance. *Journal of Experimental Social Psychology* 35(1): 4–28. doi.org/10.1006/jesp.1998.1373.

Slee, R. (2010). Political economy, inclusive education and teacher education. *Teacher Education for Inclusion: Changing Paradigms and Innovative Approaches*, 13–22.

Steele, C.M. and Aronson, J. (1995). Stereotype threat and the intellectual test performance of African Americans. *Journal of Personality and Social Psychology* 69(5): 797.

Wang, J., Lin, E., Spalding, E., Klecka, C.L., and Odell, S.J. (2011). Quality teaching and teacher education: A kaleidoscope of notions. *Journal of Teacher Education* 62(4): 331–338.

The World Cafe. http://www.theworldcafe.com/key-concepts-resources/world-cafe-method/ (accessed 21 February 2021).

Reaching DCRT Goals through True, Teen-Written Stories

DEVELOPMENTALLY AND culturally responsive teaching (DCRT) rests on listening to students. It's their development and cultures that we should respond to, after all. But we need to find multiple ways to make youth voice heard in school and in other institutions that serve them—from after-school programs to juvenile justice settings. And we need to give special attention to the voices of BIPOC youth (Black, Indigenous, and People of Color) and LGBTQ+ students, like those who constitute 90% of the writers at Youth Communication.

As you have seen in the Youth Communication stories in this book, reading true stories by teens is one of the best ways to learn about many of the *general* issues and concerns that students often conceal from us, including the impact of poverty, racism, sexism, homophobia, stress, and trauma. The stories also show the many ways that young people use their strengths, creativity, and resilience to overcome those obstacles.

But Youth Communication stories are also very effective tools for learning about the *specific* and ever-changing issues facing *the individual young people in your school or program*. That's because stories are also powerful catalysts for encouraging students to share their own stories and concerns. Furthermore, because Youth Communication stories focus on what the writer did in the face of a dilemma, they surface solutions, not just the problems themselves.

Because the stories reveal the creativity and resilience of the writers, they help educators and administrators to see students in new ways. To use Carol Dweck's term, it

257

helps teachers to have more of a growth mindset about their students; to see them as potential partners in efforts to make schools more equitable. The stories feature social and emotional skills used by youth to manage challenges.

Finally, the Youth Communication lessons and curricula that accompany the stories follow the SAFE protocol (Structured, Active, Focused, and Explicit). The CASEL studies, which are mentioned in Chapter 6, found that teaching this way leads to a host of positive outcomes, including less distress and higher grades among students.

Together, these qualities make the stories and lessons ideal tools to strengthen equity, to build the relationships that support a strong school climate, and to promote academic performance.

How to Use the Stories

There are many ways to use the Youth Communication stories. The most effective is to make them part of a regular program, such as advisory, where the effect of positive relations among students and between students and teachers can build over time. Youth Communication has story-based social and emotional learning programs and professional development for grades 6 to 12. Each program has a carefully sequenced set of 15 to 30 lessons. Each lesson is based on a true story, like the ones in this book, and is designed to help young people strengthen a specific SEL competency. The lessons are fully scripted and easy to use. (See the two boxes for a summary of the CASEL social and emotional learning competencies that the lessons address, and the eight Youth Communication programs.)

You can also use stories as "one-off" readings in English or social studies classes or counseling groups to address a specific issue or learning objective and to increase representation and engagement.

And they can be used as professional development (PD) tools for private reflection, for informal groups of teachers, and in formal PD designed to improve school climate, such as professional learning communities.

To give you a more concrete sense of how stories can be used in a systematic setting, like advisories, we describe the standard lesson format (and some of the reasoning behind it) for the Youth Communication SEL advisory programs. You can see how they elicit youth voice and strengthen the social and emotional skills that support academic and life success. Then we briefly describe ways that individual stories can be used in ELA and other content-area classes.

Finally, we provide information about Youth Communication's PD that shows how stories can be used to strengthen student and educator SEL skills. You can also see how they can be used to build a school culture of listening to the voices of young people—especially those who are least-often heard.

For readers who are interested in where the stories come from, we give a brief peek at the Youth Communication teen writing program.

Using Advisory to Build a Developmentally and Culturally Responsive School

The Youth Communication Lessons: Each lesson in Youth Communication's advisory program has four parts: an opening activity, a story read-aloud, an explore-the-ideas exercise, and a closing circle. Here are the details.

The opening activity activates students' background knowledge of the story topic and sparks interest in the story's theme. It creates a positive, solution-oriented framework. This is often a move-around-the-room activity to stimulate interest and energy and takes less than 10 minutes.

For example, a typical opening activity is an opinion continuum. On one end of the room, the teacher has posted a sign that says "Agree" and on the other end a sign that says "Disagree." The teacher reads a statement (e.g., "I believe I can get better at things when I try") and the students place themselves along the imaginary line between the two signs, depending on how much they agree or disagree with the statement. The teacher then invites students to explain why they are where they are, and to move their position if they change their minds based on what they hear from their peers. Activities like this activate students' interest, prior knowledge, and sense of agency, while also building community and students' social awareness. The focus on "no wrong answers" helps create the community that nurtures youth voice.

Next, the teacher facilitates the whole group as students read aloud and discuss a true story by a peer, which takes 15 to 20 minutes. The teacher stops strategically throughout the text to ask reflective and critical-thinking questions about the writer's experience, thoughts, motivations, and decisions. Questions are included in the lesson, and teachers can add their own.

The questions focus on the actions and motivations of the writer. This allows participants to approach the topic with some level of emotional distance from the action and themes of the story. That gives students the space to think about *the SEL skill* before the distraction of thinking about their own lives. It also allows students who might be facing the same challenges as the writer some emotional distance to explore the issue through the *writer's* experience. We find that as youth talk about "the writer," they often are working through their own relation to the issue.

The questions embedded within the story are specific to the story, of course. But the goal of the discussion and activities is to strengthen social and emotional skills, so we use a set of baseline questions, aligned to the CASEL competencies (see the following box), that inform the specific questions for each story.

Self-awareness

- What is the writer feeling at this point?
- What strengths is the writer displaying? What challenges?
- What are the writer's motivations in what he or she just did?

Self-management

- How does the writer deal with [name of emotion]?
- What strategy does the writer use when he or she is . . . ? How effective is that strategy?
- What are the writer's goals in this situation and what are they doing to achieve those goals?

Social awareness

- If you were this writer, what would you have done?
- What help and resources does the writer use when he or she is . . . ?
- How do [other people, racism/sexism, societal norms] impact the writer's behavior?

Relationship skills
- What strategy does the writer use to handle this conflict? Is it effective?
- What are some other ways the writer could have dealt with this person? Which would you choose?
- How could the writer be an ally to the other person?

Responsible decision-making
- What do you think will be the consequences of the writer's actions?
- What else could the writer have done in response to this problem?
- What factors is the writer considering in their decision-making process?

As students share and respond to these questions, they learn about each other and themselves as the teacher learns more about them—which builds a sense of community among the group. One thing that is different about this discussion is that it is largely student to student, rather than directly responding to the teacher. This kind of sharing and building on each other's ideas puts the students at the center of the conversation. These discussions aren't right-answer conversations per se. They elicit deeper thinking and reflection about the skills, values, choices, and themes in the story.

It can be a challenge to facilitate conversations like this, especially if you are used to directing content-area conversations that are leading to an answer you know in advance. In this case, the students are the experts. The teacher is following their lead while still guiding the conversation to keep it on track. Youth Communication's professional development focuses, in part, on developing these facilitation skills. (See the section at the end of this chapter for more tips on facilitating rich conversations around Youth Communication stories.)

After the shared reading and discussion, we come to the explore-the-ideas activity, where students apply the lessons learned in the story to their own life. The lessons include a wide range of activities: writing a list of their own goals in response to a story about goals; performing role plays to imagine different ways of resolving a conflict in

The Five CASEL Social and Emotional Competencies

In our youth writing program, as well as our professional development work with schools and teachers, we utilize the Collaborative for Academic, Social, and Emotional Learning (CASEL) framework to understand SEL. CASEL has outlined five SEL competencies:

- **Self-awareness** involves recognizing our emotions and how they influence our behavior. As we discover our interests and values, we become better able to accurately assess our strengths and challenges. We all work toward developing a well-grounded sense of self-confidence and hope for the future. Well-developed self-awareness enables us to examine our biases and prejudices, and affirm our own social identities.

- **Self-management** means regulating emotions (such as managing stress), controlling impulses, and persevering through obstacles. Self-management also involves the setting and pursuit of personal, professional, and academic goals. Good self-management enables us to take personal and collective action to, among other things, fight injustice.

- **Social awareness** enables us to look beyond "me" to see other people's perspectives and empathize with them. When we have well-developed social awareness, we appreciate similarities and differences in diverse groups. We also learn to recognize and access resources and supports at work, home, and in the community. Social awareness also includes understanding how organizations and social systems work, including how power is sometimes unfairly distributed in schools and other institutions.

- **Relationship skills** include interpersonal communication skills such as active listening, negotiating conflict constructively, and seeking and offering help. It also includes demonstrating cultural competence in a variety of situations and standing up for the rights of others.

- **Responsible decision-making** means making positive contributions and choices that support the well-being of ourselves and others. Responsible decision-making includes being curious and open-minded as well as understanding the impacts that our decisions and actions have on ourselves, others, and institutions.

the story; writing a reflective journal entry in response to a story about recognizing emotions; or drawing a comic strip that details the process of making an important decision. Whatever the activity, it ties in directly to the skills and themes of the story and as much as possible, it involves the students reflecting on their own SEL skills.

Lastly, the students respond to a short prompt in what we call the closing circle. The prompt is typically a sentence starter that each student finishes as you go around the circle. The prompt is always positive and focused on the skill of the session. For instance, in a session on dealing with stress, the prompt might be: "The next time I feel stressed, to calm down I will. . . ." In a session on solving conflicts, students might finish this sentence: "The most important thing I can do to help resolve a conflict is to. . . ." The stories are such inspiring models that the closing circle is inevitably filled with positive and creative responses.

This activity brings closure to the session. Saying aloud this type of positive statement, students reinforce what they learned. Doing this publicly is a kind of testimonial that also gives everyone in the group a chance to hear what others are thinking. Students are often surprised by the creative and positive commitments that their peers make in the closing circle, which builds on the sense of community. The closing circle also provides immediate assessment. The students' responses give the facilitator a clear sense of what youth are taking away from the session. It is often pleasantly surprising what you learn about the students' insights, goals, and take-aways from just one sentence.

Facilitation is key: To make these lessons work, teachers need to relinquish the role of "expert" and allow their students to talk to one another and drive the conversation. Furthermore, reading the story *together*, as opposed to assigning it for homework or assigning students to read the stories silently at their desk, is key to SEL growth and building community.

We emphasize reading aloud because it is a developmentally appropriate and research-backed strategy that promotes both reading comprehension and connections among peers. It ensures that everyone has access to the text and can engage it regardless of their reading level. This fosters a supportive community experience of the story, which in turn helps group members connect with one another and the text. It also literally makes youth voice heard.

To facilitate a successful read-aloud we use a variety of strategies, including sitting in a circle, when possible, being sensitive to different reading skills, and other skills and routines that we cover in professional development.

Using Teen Stories in English Language Arts instruction (and Beyond)

Though it is slowly changing, the norm in literature taught in secondary schools is still the proverbial texts by "old, White men." While the argument is that these texts persevere because of their universal themes, adolescents aren't so convinced, as any secondary literature teacher can tell you. Another challenge is that many texts by more diverse authors are still written in ways that make them difficult for many teen readers to enter.

A decades-long movement in teaching "young adult literature" written by adults but for adolescent audiences is a step in the right direction. These texts speak to the adolescent experience using adolescent-appropriate language and themes, but they are still written from an adult perspective.

Youth Communication stories are unique in that they are for and by real young people. The stories focus on the complexities of being an adolescent right now. And they are well-written. As such, Youth Communication stories can be important engagement and bridging tools for students. Pairing a story by a teenager about dating for the first time with Shakespeare's *Romeo and Juliet*, and asking students to compare and contrast the texts, can help adolescents understand an older text across time and cultures. Reading Toni Morrison's *The Bluest Eye* along with a young woman's story about dealing with colorism in her family can echo Morrison's themes and engage young people in reading an important, yet linguistically and discursively complex text. (Many Youth Communication stories are available free on our website. See the following "What Teachers Can Do.")

There are many other ways to pair our stories with other texts. The easiest is to begin a unit with reading a Youth Communication story and have students discuss the text and reflect on the themes. The trick, though, is not to do this and then just move on to the "real" text. Instead teachers can keep bringing the teen-written text into the discussion of the canonical text. This helps engage students and reminds them of the relevance of the canonical text. Teachers can ask students to think about how the teen-written text and the adult-written text are similar and different and the meaning of those differences. For example, similarities can help point out the universality of themes; differences can help point out, among other things, how time, place, and culture impact how humans think and interact.

There are many other ways to use the stories in ELA classes. Teachers can use them as independent reading texts, research sources, and the impetus for larger student-centered projects. While school buildings were closed early in the COVID-19 pandemic, several teachers reported giving students the option to read teen-written stories for independent reading. They found that students frequently selected that option over other texts and completed their assignments at a higher rate. (One teacher said, "Youth Communication stories really saved us when school buildings were closed.") Another teacher who implements our stories regularly used one about activism to have students research a cause they were interested in and discover how students could contribute to the cause. Teachers often use our teen-written stories as models for college application essays.

The possibilities don't end at the English language arts classroom door. Social studies teachers can use our stories for enrichment and engagement on countless topics, including racism, immigration, voting, activism, homelessness, and other social issues. Science teachers can use more recent stories about climate change to garner interest in the science of the topic. Art, music, math, and other subject teachers can use stories in which teens write about the importance of those classes as catalysts for conversations that draw connections between their subject matter and students' lives.

Using the Stories in Professional Development

1. Story-based professional development in action.

In my two decades in education—as a teacher of kindergarten through college and as mentor and coach to new teachers—I (Tim) have never seen a tool as versatile and effective as the true, teen-written stories that come out of Youth Communication's writing program. Here is an example of how we use it in our professional development (PD) sessions.

In Desmin Braxton's "Labeled Troublesome: Battling With My Teachers Is Becoming a Big Problem," excerpts of which also appear in Chapter 1, a young man writes about the other side of a common and difficult situation for teachers—when a student fights with teachers nonstop. Here's how it can be used in professional development.

Most teachers will recognize the situation, either because they've witnessed it or they've taken part:

> I spot my math teacher. He does not look happy to see me. He stares at me rudely with his arms folded and his jaw clenched, like I've already done something wrong.
>
> "Hello, Mr. Davis, how you today?"
>
> He continues to stare, so I continue walking through the hall to the auditorium. Before I get there, my social studies teacher from last year stops me.
>
> "Desmin."
>
> "What?"
>
> "Where are you going?"
>
> "To the auditorium, with my class."
>
> "Go there right now."
>
> I start getting mad. It's crazy how he stops me even though he knows where I'm headed, but he walks past the other kids and doesn't say anything. It's like I have on a bright red shirt that says, "Stop me."

"OK, out of all eight people in this hallway you choose me," I reply.

"Yeah, you, because you might hang out in the hallway."

"All right, but you don't seem to see these other kids in the hallway. Tell them to go into the auditorium."

"No, just worry about yourself, not them."

"Aight."

What the second teacher is not privy to, though, is Desmin's interaction with the first teacher, which may have triggered a negative reaction in him. In the narrative part of this story, Desmin described the first teacher he encountered as not looking happy to see him, noting his body language. The second teacher walks right past other students in the hall, saying nothing to them, but stopping Desmin "like [he has] on a bright red shirt that says, 'Stop me.'" He calls the teacher out on this, and the teacher responds that he "might" be the one to hang out in the hallway.

This exchange alone can provide a useful beginning point for teacher reflection. Here are some questions to consider:

- What do teachers' body language and facial expressions communicate to their students?
- What is the impact when students think their teachers aren't happy to see them? How can teachers better communicate their excitement and caring about students?
- We don't know the teachers' side of the interactions that Desmin describes. Perhaps they are having a bad day or are frustrated by the challenges of teaching in a public school. In that case, how can teachers mitigate the effects that their own challenges and emotions have on how students perceive teachers' attitudes about them?

Desmin reflects on the negative cycle he's gotten into. A teacher ticks him off, he reacts by talking back and getting other students off task, and the teacher gets madder. Desmin recognizes the impact the cycle is having on him: "But the arguments with my teachers are cutting into my time for doing my work. It's making me fall behind in class so my grades are dropping. I end up focusing on the teacher and not learning the lesson. Then I'm stuck looking silly, without a clue on how to do the work." In these sentences, Desmin reveals something that is hard for teachers to see in the moment when they are reacting to a student's frequent misbehavior: Even those students who seem not to care want to do well. Teachers can use Desmin's reflection to spark their own:

- When teachers have gotten into negative cycles with students, what can they do to break them?
- How can teachers refocus their attention—and the attention of their students—away from unwanted behaviors and onto their academics?
- What can teachers do when it *seems* like a student doesn't care to remind themselves that the student probably really does care?

Demonstrating a good amount of self-awareness, Desmin writes about what he thinks started him along this path: a 2nd grade teacher.

> I was talking because I like to talk and I hate to be bored. But this day, Mr. Brown reacted by yelling in my face and telling me to shut up. His mouth had an odor. I yelled back at him, "Yo, get out my face!" It was the only thing I could do to defend myself.
>
> Then Mr. Brown grabbed me out of my chair like I was a baby. He gripped my arm so tight that my blood stopped flowing and dragged me to the classroom next door. In that moment I went into such a rage that I was ready to kill him. This teacher had an anger problem, and he gave me one, too.

While Desmin's anger problem is likely not caused by just one incident, this episode highlights how easily and quickly a young person can be turned off by school. A single, traumatic experience with a teacher when he was 7 years old influences Desmin's whole attitude about education. It's doubtful any of his middle school teachers knew about this incident, but its effects linger for Desmin. That teacher broke Desmin's trust and put him on a path to trust few teachers afterward.

Past negative experiences with education and traumatic episodes determine much about how students approach teachers and school. This creates a conundrum for teachers who face the effects of negative relationships and trauma without knowing the cause. Desmin's revelation of this backstory can lead teachers to even more reflection:

- With so much of students' unwanted behavior caused by past or present experiences of trauma unbeknownst to their teachers, what should teachers do when faced with unwanted behavior?
- Teachers' negative emotions and their behavior stemming from those emotions have an immense impact on students. How can teachers develop the self-management skills to deal with uncomfortable emotions without "taking it out" on students?

The preceding review-and-reflection questions represent only the first two-thirds of Desmin's story, but already we can see the possibilities one true teen-written story can have for educators' PD. When Youth Communication staff facilitate PD sessions using stories like Desmin's we bookend the reading and discussion of the story with application activities. For "Labeled Troublesome," a pre-reading activity has teachers think about a student with whom they struggle to communicate and then free-write on a recent, unproductive interaction with that student. After the reading, we put teachers into small groups to brainstorm ways they would revise the interactions they wrote about at the beginning of the session to send positive messages about the student to the student. The session ends with every participant sharing one take-away in a circle setting.

This is difficult work, but the work is also grounded in the world that teachers—and their students—really live in. As a result, it feels more relevant and engaging to teachers, and they are willing to put in the work.

The Writing Program

Stories like Desmin's don't just come in over the transom. Each writer works one-on-one with a full-time, professional editor who is typically a journalist with experience working with youth. Each story goes through 10 or more drafts as the teen goes deeper into the topic and learns the writing skills needed to show readers what happened to them and, more importantly, the resilience and resourcefulness they used to respond. The stories reflect real life, so there is rarely a triumphant ending, and not always even a happy ending.

That's because what is most valuable to readers is not the outcome; it's seeing the writer's persistence in the face of adversity and how the writer applies that persistence in his or her own life. That persistence often takes the form of social and emotional competencies. The editors help the writers to notice and name those competencies so they can use them again in the future, and so readers can have access to them too.

Youth Communication refined this writing process over 40 years of working with teens to write stories that will help their peers manage the challenges they face. As you can see from the stories in this book, the teens represent an astonishing diversity of races, gender identities, sexual orientations, religions, nationalities, and experiences. The writers have gone on to become teachers, principals, counselors, social workers, activists, and positions in many other careers where they have turned their impulse to help others into professions. Many have also become authors; program alumni have published more than 170 books.

What Teachers Can Do

1. Sign up for our weekly story emails and read our youth-written stories.

For your students: Youth Communication's weekly email will provide you with stories that are sure to engage your students. Each week, you will receive a true, teen-written story in your email on a wide range of topics, some of which are sure to interest your students. Because of who our writers are, there is a special focus on stories by BIPOC, LGBTQ+, and other students less likely to see themselves represented in your curriculum.

As a teacher, you will have many ideas about how to use the stories to achieve your learning objectives. If strengthening the social and emotional skills that build community and support academic achievement is your goal, a simple approach is to adapt the previous questions so they reference these skills. They can be used with almost any Youth Communication story.

For you: The act of regularly reading the stories and reflecting privately on their implications for your own interactions with students is invaluable. Of course, not every youth is alike, and YC writers will have different experiences than your students. Reading YC stories regularly, though, will develop and refine your mindsets about your students. You'll read about young people's strengths and resilience, the challenges they face and overcome, and the important topics they are thinking about. Soon, you'll start to see your own students in a new light, and when your best intentions and high expectations are threatened by the stress teachers face, it will be easier for you to keep a positive outlook about the students sitting in your classroom.

You can use questions like these with almost any story for private reflections about your own teaching and students:

- YC writers write their stories so that others can learn from their experiences. What did you learn from the writer's experience?
- How is the writer's experiences similar and/or different from your own experiences as a teen?
- What about the writer's experience was new or surprising to you?
- Does the writer and the writer's experience remind you of any of your students? How so? What did you learn from the writer's story about your own students? How is that going to change your interactions with your students?
- What messages does the story give about students?

For you and your colleagues: In addition to private reflection, it can be especially valuable to talk about the stories with colleagues. Those conversations can provide opportunities to reflect and to be challenged by the students' insights and perspectives. Discussion is a great medium for spurring more reflection than you might do on your own. You and your colleagues can use the baseline questions earlier in this chapter, come up with your own questions, or have an informal conversation about the story.

2. Support restorative justice and trauma-informed practices.

Youth Communication's programs and professional development dovetail nicely with both restorative and trauma-informed practices because they build teachers' understanding of the context in which their students live.

For example, restorative justice approaches focus less on punishment and more on community understanding and atonement. This approach puts the context of behavior in play as well as helps the offender realize the impact they had on their community. When teachers gain experience teaching Youth Communication stories, they develop a deeper sense of how the contexts of students' lives impact their behavior, which makes them more skilled facilitators of restorative justice conversations. When students gain experience participating in story-based lessons and conversations, they build community and strengthen the talking, listening, and analytical skills that make them astute and compassionate participants in restorative justice circles.

Likewise, trauma-informed practices are based on teachers and school staff understanding more about the sources of student behavior and realizing how the psychological impact of trauma affects academic performance and interpersonal behavior. Regular reading of Youth Communication stories increases staff knowledge of how widespread trauma is, especially among their most vulnerable students. Just as importantly, however, the stories show staff how powerful their actions can be in helping young people recover from trauma. And they also show staff that even extremely oppositional young people want to learn to control their behavior, want to do well in school, and have the capacity to change.

What Schools Can Do

1. Make reading and discussing the stories a regular part of your school's professional development.

Any staff trainer can tell you how difficult it is to maintain teachers' attention during PD sessions. In one of our partner schools, I ran a session focused on the reading of a story by a young woman who compared two teachers—one who had communicated negative beliefs about her and the other who communicated positive beliefs. I'd worked with the staff before and experienced them as well-meaning but difficult to engage for all the understandable reasons teachers are unfocused at the end of a long workday. But during this particular session, they stopped looking at their phones or grading papers and were so engrossed with the story that you could have heard a pin drop. In all my years being a teacher myself, as well as working with teachers as a professional developer and mentor, I've never had a group of teachers who were so enthralled with a session.

As we all know, no teacher lives in a vacuum, and while an individual teacher or small groups of teachers reading Youth Communication stories can have an impact on their students, if we want to change a school's culture, we need reflective PD for all the adults in the building. All the teachers (and administrators and counselors and aides) coming together to regularly read our stories can have a profound effect on a school's community.

We recommend limiting the groups to 15 participants. Grade and subject teams usually already exist in schools, but administrators should be sure to mix up the groups so that adults who are unlikely to interact can do so around a teen-written story. This creates a stronger community among teachers and opens them up to the opinions and ideas of adults outside their orbit.

Monthly story reads and discussion sessions, lasting approximately 20 minutes, are effective means of incorporating Youth Communication stories into a larger professional development program, without taking away from valuable and mandated professional development sessions. Reading and discussing stories together can happen more or less frequently, but we do recommend making the activity a consistent part of teachers' continued learning. Reading one story here and there won't *not* help teachers, but if we are to strive for the holistic inclusion of DCRT we have described in the previous chapter, reading many stories regularly over the year can be an important part of changing a school's culture and climate.

Administrators can model honoring the voices of youth by honoring the voices of their staff. Anyone who has ever worked in a school can tell you that how the administration treats its teachers will probably influence how the teachers treat the students. Therefore, allow teachers to select the topics and/or stories that are relevant to them. Youth Communication writers often write about current events, and these can be important opportunities for insight into students. For example, more attention is finally being paid to anti-Asian discrimination as a result of the COVID-19 pandemic. For teachers who are unfamiliar with anti-Asian discrimination, including the model minority myth, several Asian American writers have written powerfully about their experiences with bias and bigotry. As we have discussed at the beginning of this chapter, our writers are often at the vanguard of societal change, and if educators want to be informed about what students are thinking and talking about outside their classrooms, Youth Communication stories are the key.

Their stories remind us how much power schools have to support students' developmental needs in culturally responsive ways. This power moved us to share research, stories, and resources that will help teachers and schools know their students better, recognize how they develop, and understand factors that influence their development. However, we also recognize that building awareness and increasing knowledge isn't enough. What we do with that knowledge and how well we employ skills that reflect our enhanced knowledge is critical. From a developmentally and culturally responsive perspective, the fundamental question is "Now that we know, what will we do?" Now that we've learned about developmental and cultural needs, how do we address those needs? We hope this book will help you to answer those questions.

Youth Communication's Grades 6–12 SEL Programs

#trending is a middle school-level introduction to SEL, covering topics such as family, friendships, peer pressure, stress management, and being healthy.

Between You & Me goes deeper into self-awareness, self-management, social awareness, and relationship skills by reading stories about identity formation, emotional regulation, developing empathy, solving conflicts, and other important middle school topics.

Stay the Course continues the deep-dive into SEL skills by focusing on responsible decision-making. Youth participants read stories by writers who examine their own decision-making processes and offer advice on how to think through consequences of their actions and how to take responsibility for them.

Upgrade is completed at the end of 8th grade or in the summer before youths start high school to help them develop the SEL skills they will need to make the transition to high school, including demonstrating independence and responsibility, goal setting, persisting through failure, and participating in high school academics and extracurricular activities.

In Real Life, like *#trending*, is an introduction to SEL but developmentally aimed at high school students. Topics include dealing with difficult emotions, finding pride in your identity, creating lasting bonds with family and friends, and being an ally to others.

Real Talk, *Real Men*, and *Real As Me* are Youth Communication's gender, gender identity, sexuality, and relationship programs. *Real Talk* is for mixed-gender programs. *Real Men* is for male and male-identifying participants and focuses on developing a positive version of masculinity. *Real As Me* is for female and female-identifying participants, with stories about girls' empowerment. All three are LGBTQ- and nonbinary-inclusive.

All In contains stories and lessons on living in a diverse world and advocating for self and others. Writers in this program tell stories about how they create accurate and affirming identities, how they fight stereotypes, how they learn to communicate across differences, and what it takes to be a reliable ally and advocate.

On My Way is our work-readiness program, covering the SEL skills youth need to succeed in the workplace, including communication skills and setting boundaries.

Level Up focuses on the transition to high school and the SEL skills related to applying to and succeeding at post-secondary institutions.

For more information, contact: training@youthcomm.org.

Acknowledgments

THIS BOOK would not be possible without the contributions of the teen writers at Youth Communication, more than 50 of whom have excerpts from their stories included here. The hope that their stories will have an impact helps sustain the teens through YC's grueling writing process. It is very satisfying to the writers that teachers and administrators will use this book to better serve their students.

Gess LeBlanc would like to thank his wife Pamela LeBlanc and his sons Justin and Jeremy who were instrumental in helping him to complete this book.

He would also like to thank the passionate and dedicated teachers, school leaders, and counselors whom he has had the honor of working with and learning from. They have been instrumental in helping to shape the ideas that are shared throughout this book.

Keith Hefner and Maria Louisa Tucker contributed important developmental editing as the book evolved over several years. Maria Louisa helped clarify the ideas and structure of the book in its early stages, and Keith selected stories, knit them together with the research and Gess's DCRT framework, and provided other developmental editing in the final stages.

For several years, Keith pitched the idea for a book that combined the best in social science research with youth voices to education school professors—with no luck. During that time, however, The W. Clement & Jessie V. Stone Foundation and the Spunk Fund, Inc. saw value in the idea and provided support for work at Youth Communication that kept the idea alive.

Eventually, Keith got an appointment with several staff members at the Hunter College School of Education. As he began his well-rehearsed pitch, one person stopped him. She said that she had used the teens' stories in her counseling work at a residential treatment center and was well aware of their impact. Another Hunter staff member, Kenney Robinson, Director of Career, Professional and Partnership Development, then said that he, too, needed little convincing. In fact, he said that he had been an avid reader of the teens' stories back when he was a high school student. Years later, as a middle school teacher, he used them in instruction.

The meeting quickly moved to who on the Hunter faculty would find this project exciting. We are eternally grateful that Kenney made the match between Dr. Gess LeBlanc and Youth Communication.

About the Authors

GESS LEBLANC, Ph.D., is Associate Professor and former Chair of the Department of Educational Foundations and Counseling Programs in the City University of New York's Hunter College School of Education. He is a co-founder of Hunter College's Urban Center for Assessment, Research, and Evaluation (UCARE).

A developmental psychologist, Dr. LeBlanc's research investigates the impact of developmentally and culturally responsive teaching on school climate. His research has been published in both psychological and educational journals and has garnered awards from the Spencer Foundation and the American Psychological Association.

As an expert in the field of child and adolescent development, he has served as an educational consultant to various urban, suburban, and rural school districts; state agencies; and nonprofit organizations, including the New York State Department of Education; the New York City Department of Education; several suburban and rural school districts in upstate New York; the Schomburg Center for Research in Black Studies; the Boys Club of America; the Harlem Center for Education; Prep for Prep; City Year, Inc.; the Roundabout Theatre Company; and the Arthur Miller Foundation.

In addition to being recognized for his research, Dr. LeBlanc has been honored for his teaching and service to his profession. He is a past recipient of Hunter College's Presidential Award for Excellence in Teaching and the Hunter College School of Education's Harold Ladas Award for Excellence in Teaching. Dr. LeBlanc serves on the Board of Directors of City Year New York, Inc.; the Roundabout Theatre Company; and the

Harlem Center for Education. In recognition of his service, he was awarded the 2013 Distinguished Service Award from the Association for Equality and Excellence in Education, Inc.

Tim Fredrick, Ph.D., is the Senior Director of Education Programs at Youth Communication, where he has worked since August 2018. He is responsible for overseeing the implementation and evaluation of Youth Communication's social and emotional learning (SEL) curricula and professional development for educators.

He began his career teaching in New York City public schools, where he worked with middle and high school students on improving their reading and writing skills as well as their SEL competencies. His expertise is in working with disengaged readers—particularly boys—by pairing them with texts and tasks that reflect their backgrounds and concerns. As part of the Teachers Network Leadership Institute, he conducted a classroom action research study aimed at helping engage adolescent boys in their literacy learning, the report of which was published in *Changing English*. He has also presented his research on language use and student agency at the National Council of Teachers of English, American Educational Research Association, International Conference on Teacher Research, and the American Sociological Association.

In addition to teaching all levels from kindergarten through 12th grade during his career, he has mentored and taught pre-service and new teachers at New York University, City University of New York, and the NYC Department of Education, and has worked with alternative certification programs such as Teach for America and the New York City Teaching Fellows.

At Youth Communication, Dr. Fredrick spearheaded the organization's programmatic response to the COVID-19 pandemic, including converting YC's award-winning SEL curriculum for remote teaching and leading webinars on using YC's true, teen-written stories. Dr. Fredrick has presented Youth Communication's work at conferences sponsored by the Center for the Promotion of Social Emotional Learning (CPSEL); the Collaborative for Academic, Social, and Emotional Learning (CASEL); the National School Climate Center; and other organizations.

Teen Story Index

Source of Teen Stories

All of the writing from teens in this book originally appeared in true stories written by young people in Youth Communication's intensive writing program. Following is an index to where the story excerpts appear in this book and the name of the story from which the excerpt was taken.

Index

A

Abuse: by parents, 70, 114, 149, 154–156; stress and, 154–156, 158; trauma-informed schools and, 195

Academic achievement: assessment of, 74–76; compassionate schools and, 187–191; COVID-19 pandemic and, 190–191; culturally responsive teaching and, 28–29; high expectations and, 25–28; home culture connections and, 23–25; meaningful connections and, 200–201; mental health and, 196–200; physical comfort and, 169; psychological health and, 191–194; recognizing, 106; SEL skills and, 213; stereotypes and, 246–247; stress and, 146, 164–168; student-teacher relationships and, 20

Academic language, 77

Academic risk-taking, 204–207

Accountability systems, 81–83, 226–227

Adolescent development. *See also* Brain development: chronic stress and trauma and, 150–158; complex thinking and, 13–14; culture and, 19–23; experimentation and, 86–89; identity development and, 86–89; peer relationships and, 95–100; sense of purpose and, 104–106; understanding, 11–16

Adults: caring, 10–11, 29, 61–62, 156, 194, 199–200, 210; failure to support students, 196–199; questions to ask students about, 61–62

Adverse Childhood Experiences (ACEs), 158–161, 213–217

African American stereotypes, 44–48

Aggression, 117–118, 153–158. *See also* Negative behavior

285